Black Hawk: The Story of a
World Class Helicopter

Black Hawk: The Story of a World Class Helicopter

Ray D. Leoni
Sikorsky Aircraft, Retired

American Institute of Aeronautics and Astronautics, Inc.
1801 Alexander Bell Drive, Suite 500
Reston, Virginina 20191

Publishers since 1930

American Institute of Aeronautics and Astronautics, Inc., Reston, Virginia

1 2 3 4 5

Library of Congress Cataloging-in-Publication Data on file.

ISBN-13: 978-1-56347-918-2

FOREWORD

When my father Igor Sikorsky came to Paris in 1909 to study aviation, he had a letter of introduction to a great French aviator and pioneer pilot, Captain Ferdinand Ferber. The good captain gave the 20-year old Igor Sikorsky much valuable advice during their first meeting. When that meeting ended, Ferber's last words of wisdom, roughly translated, were as follows: "...*To invent a flying machine is nothing; to build it is little; but to make it fly....Ah, that is everything!*"

I was reminded of those words as I read the story of the design and development of the UTTAS prototypes and their evolution into the Black Hawk series and their many variants. Ray Leoni is highly qualified to tell this story, having served as program engineering manager and then program manager as the prototype helicopters were designed, tested, and modified and as the Black Hawk design matured into the configuration that won the U.S. Army production competition. Going from the first sketches in the late 1960s, through release of the U.S. Army's requirements in early 1972, and finally through development of the prototype utility tactical transport to production standards in 1976 took nearly 10 years.

The Black Hawk family of helicopters has proliferated to the point that they serve in all branches of the U.S. Armed Forces, as well as over 40 foreign services around the world. Thanks to a dedicated design, development, and management team, Black Hawk has become a standard against which other helicopters are measured.

However, to evolve its initial design into the final configuration that flew and performed as planned turned out to be the greatest challenge that the Black Hawk team was to face. Fortunately the challenge "to make it fly" was successfully met.

It seems that, in aviation, some things never change.

Sergei Sikorsky
Sikorsky Aircraft, Retired
May 2003

TABLE OF CONTENTS

PREFACE

The technical difficulties of developing a successful rotorcraft are neither well known nor well appreciated, not even within the aerospace industry. The simple fact is that helicopters are far more complicated than their fixed-wing counterparts for similar missions with similar payloads. One of the beautiful aspects of this book is the interesting detail descriptions and explanations that Ray Leoni has used to help the reader understand the science as well as the art of helicopter design.

The Black Hawk is clearly one of the most successful of the large number of helicopters developed in the United States and around the world. The UH-60 Black Hawk was the first helicopter to be developed completely under U.S. Army management. That development started from a clean sheet of paper and ended up as a highly successful weapon system in operational use by every branch of the U.S. Military. At the same time it has performed missions of mercy bringing safety and relief to people in distress around the world.

Some of the planning that went into the Army's requirement for this helicopter played a very significant role in molding its configuration. The vast majority of the lessons learned that led to these requirements came directly from the Vietnam conflict. The operational requirements having the greatest technical impact on the Black Hawk's size and weight were the U.S. Army's specifications for air transportability, survivability and vulnerability, and, most importantly, its stringent speed and climb and maneuver requirements for high and hot operational environments. This level of detail extended to even specifying the height of the cabin floor above the ground to ease the ingress and egress of combat-equipped troops in a "hot landing zone" environment. The Black Hawk met these requirements by using innovative design approaches combined with the right advanced technologies.

Tools that provided Sikorsky with the technology to design and produce a winning configuration also stemmed from a government program known as independent research and development (IR&D). Examples of IR&D items that had a significant impact on the Black Hawk were the bifilar absorber, canted tail rotor, manufacturing methodology for a titanium main rotor-blade spar to optimize performance and durability, bearingless flex beam tail rotor, and the elastomeric main rotor head.

The diligent work, innovative ideas, and dedication of the Sikorsky team led to the Army achieving its objective of fielding a high-performance and more survivable and durable utility helicopter for its utility tactical air transport missions.

If you want to understand rotorcraft development, this is a must-read book.

Charlie Crawford
U.S. Army, Retired
June 2005

Wesley A. Kuhrt 1917–1988
©Igor I. Sikorsky Historical Archives, Inc.

This book is dedicated to the memory of Wesley A. Kuhrt, who led Sikorsky Aircraft as its president during the formative period of the Black Hawk design and development when the U.S. Army referred to it as the utility tactical transport aircraft system (UTTAS). Wes Kuhrt was appointed president of the Sikorsky Aircraft Division of the United Aircraft Corporation in 1969 to rebuild the division's helicopter technology base and to turn around its declining business base. He came to Sikorsky from the UAC Research Center, where he was director of research for the corporation. His technical leadership proved to be vital in keeping UAC, now the United Technologies Corporation, at the cutting edge of aerospace technology as well as in fields that were new to the corporation. Kuhrt played a key role in creating and leading research programs in gas turbine engines, rocket propulsion, and other technologies of interest to the corporation.

At Sikorsky, the key technologies created under Kuhrt's leadership included the high-performance titanium rotor blade, the low maintenance elastomeric rotor head, and the bearingless composite tail rotor. All proved to be critically important to the success of the Black Hawk helicopter and to all of its derivative models. These new technologies constituted the technical foundation around which the UH-60A Black Hawk was designed in 1972, and they were successfully employed as well in several new Sikorsky helicopters that followed.

Kuhrt's commitment to meeting all U.S. Army requirements during the Black Hawk prototype competition led not only to Sikorsky winning a place in that competition but ultimately to developing the Black Hawk to become a world-class utility transport helicopter. His direction for the company to meet all Army requirements during the early UTTAS design period produced technology and design innovations that made the Black Hawk helicopter unequaled in performance, durability, and survivability. Those attributes, together with built-in structural and performance margins, helped create the largest lineage of models that has ever been achieved by Sikorsky. The company was able to recapture the utility helicopter market with the Black Hawk and its many derivative models. It was further able to develop and successfully market other new helicopters including the S-76 and S-92 series that utilized the technologies developed during Kuhrt's tenure at Sikorsky Aircraft.

ACKNOWLEDGMENTS

Most of the events, decisions, setbacks and victories described in this book took place over a quarter century ago during the 1970 decade. Because of this time span, putting together an accurate and coherent account of the Black Hawk success story could not have been possible without the enthusiastic help of many people who were with the U.S. Army and who were the author's fellow employees at Sikorsky Aircraft during that early period. They were among the heroes who built the foundation for the Black Hawk helicopter during its formative years when it was called the UTTAS program. They helped develop it to become one of the world's most successful utility helicopters, and they created an unmatched succession of derivative models employed worldwide. Their memories, personal diaries, and notes helped to sort out many key issues from winning uphill competitive battles to solving the vexing technical problems encountered during the early flight period of the Black Hawk prototype and finally to help to describe the succession of derivative Black Hawk models. Their many contributions made it possible to document the evolution of this world-class helicopter from the drawing board to record-setting production and mission applications.

The author is especially appreciative of the help provided by the Igor I. Sikorsky Historical Archives in locating photographs, drawings, records, and data relating to the early years of the Black Hawk program. Photographs owned by Sikorsky Aircraft Corporation and the Igor I. Sikorsky Historical Archives, Inc., are used with permission. The helicopter model designations used throughout this book including the S-55, S-56, S-58, S-61, S-64, S-65, S-66, S-67, S-69, S-70, and S-92 are trademarks of Sikorsky Aircraft Corporation.

Special thanks is given to Sergei Sikorsky for preparing the Foreword and to Charles C. Crawford for preparing the Preface. Both gentlemen have had lifelong associations with the helicopter industry and have made important contributions to helicopter design, development, and operation. Charlie Crawford's contributions to U.S. Army aviation deserve special acknowledgment. His outstanding technical leadership throughout the Black Hawk program, from its early UTTAS concept formulation period through the UTTAS prototype development period, through early Black Hawk production and fielding was the cornerstone for this program's enormous success. If there were a U.S. Army father of the Black Hawk helicopter and if he were to be recognized, without question it would have to be Charlie Crawford.

The views, opinions, and projections expressed in this book are solely those of the author.

Chapter 1

BLACK HAWK OVERVIEW

One would suspect that on those occasions when people think about flying machines, helicopters rarely would be the subject of that reflection. This would not be surprising because helicopter flight is not normally the way people travel. But there are special groups of people, bound by a common experience, whose first thought about aircraft would very likely be a vision of the helicopter. It would be reasonable to conclude that those hundreds of thousands of people who have been rescued by helicopters from the ravages of natural disasters would think first of the helicopter and their life-saving experiences. Natural disasters like the recent tsunami in Indonesia, the hurricane Katrina in the United States, and the earthquake in Pakistan add to the long list of such catastrophic events that have occurred since the birth of the helicopter. The vision of an approaching rescue helicopter must be indelibly etched in their minds, and their numbers continue to grow.

Historians estimate that over three million people have been saved by helicopters around the world since the first over-water rescue was performed by the helicopter on 29 November, 1945 [1]. On that date a rescue operation was launched off the Connecticut coast during a raging northeast storm over Long Island Sound. It was launched because there was no other way to rescue two crewmen hopelessly adrift in a barge being blown toward the rocks at Penfield Reef. The helicopter was the Sikorsky R-5 model, and the pilot was Jimmy Viner, nephew of Igor Sikorsky. Viner was chief pilot for the fledgling company that only six years earlier, in September 1939, had demonstrated the first successful helicopter. Viner was possessed with uncommon courage and piloting skill, but most of all he had enormous faith in his uncle's creation.

That successful rescue during the most hazardous weather conditions possible created the vision of the helicopter as an angel for people in distress. Since that first rescue at Penfield Reef, seen in Fig. 1, tens of thousands more have been performed by helicopters around the world making a reality of Igor Sikorsky's dream.

One would expect that the vision of a helicopter would also be forefront in the minds of thousands of military people who are brought by helicopter to and from areas of combat around the world. Added to those would be the thousands more who daily commute by helicopter to offshore oil drilling rigs,

Fig. 1   Two crewmen rescued from a barge blown toward a reef on Long Island Sound. This rescue took place close to Sikorsky's Bridgeport, CT plant using a newly designed rescue hoist, which was quickly installed on learning of the plight of the barge's crew. (©Igor I. Sikorsky Historical Archives, Inc.)

to crew on helicopter medical evacuation missions, to patrol national borders, to fly law enforcement, or to perform the many other missions made possible by the helicopter's unique flight capabilities. Added to those people who might first envision a helicopter would be the hundreds of thousands of professional people who design and build helicopters as well as those who provide training, maintenance support, repair services, and many other vital aspects of the helicopter infrastructure.

If one would venture a guess about which particular helicopter would be named or brought to mind during such reflection, one would have to guess that a Black Hawk would be that vision. Or perhaps, one of its many derivative models in U.S. Navy, U.S. Air Force, or U.S. Coast Guard service. During an earlier time frame, that vision might have been a Huey helicopter when military operations of the UH-1 during the Vietnam conflict were extensively reported.

Ever since their operational introduction in 1978, Black Hawk models have received unprecedented media coverage of their performance both on the battlefield and during their humanitarian missions across the world. Black Hawk images and the people whom they rescued have been captured on television and printed media as they fly difficult missions to help people and to relieve human suffering in ways made possible only by the helicopter.

Black Hawk derivative models from every branch of the U.S. military participated in Katrina rescue operations immediately after the hurricane

Fig. 2   Children safely hoisted from flooded house. (U.S. Army photo)

struck in 2005. Over 35,000 people were brought to safety by helicopters after that hurricane caused incredible destruction in Louisiana. The following photos are typical of so many dramatic Katrina rescue operations.

U.S. Army UH-60L Black Hawk helicopters participated in rescue operations along with Coast Guard Jayhawks, Navy Seahawks, and Air Force Pavehawk models. Figure 2 shows an Army UH-60L bringing up children stranded on a rooftop after Katrina passed.

Figure 3 shows a Coast Guard HH-60J Jayhawk lifting a stranded person held in the arms of a Coast Guard crewman about to be brought into the cabin to safety.

Many U.S. Navy Seahawk models took part in Katrina rescue operations alongside their Army and Air Force counterparts. Shown in Fig. 4 is an SH-60B from squadron HSL-40 based in Mayport.

Fig. 3   Standard operating procedures calls for a trained rescue crewman to descend by the hoist in order to assist the person in distress. (U.S. Navy photo)

Fig. 4   An elderly man hoisted to safety by search and rescue swimmer Tim Hawkins from a U.S. Navy SH-60B Seahawk helicopter from squadron HSL-40 based in Mayport. The man's cane had not been forgotten. (U.S. Navy photo)

U.S. Air Force Pavehawk helicopters from the 38th Rescue Squadron at Moody Air Force Base in Georgia flew many Katrina rescue missions, one of which is shown in Fig. 5.

U.S. military helicopters within range of natural disasters are offered to provide relief assistance if help is requested. The tsunami that struck Indonesia and other countries in January 2005 was one of many such humanitarian missions for which the helicopter excels. Delivering food and medical supplies to survivors where no local airfields exist are natural helicopter missions. Figures 6 and 7 show U.S. Air Force and Navy helicopters delivering emergency food and medical supplies after the 2005 tsunami.

The Army, Navy, and Air Force versions of the Black Hawk family pictured are several of many derivative models that have been developed since this helicopter began its life over 35 years ago. It began when the U.S. Army launched a program to develop a new utility helicopter whose primary mission was to transport troops in the battlefield. The program's prime goal was to transport an 11-man squad of fully equipped troops faster and safer than was possible with the prior generation of helicopters and to be able to do this in the worst weather, temperature, and altitude conditions anywhere. Temperature and altitude conditions in the Middle East established the basic performance requirements for the typical desert operations shown in Fig. 8.

Since the program began, over 3000 Black Hawk and derivative models have been produced. It is likely that an additional similar amount will be produced during its lifespan. They are expected to be in service well into the

Fig. 5   Tech Sargent Lem Torres, crewman aboard an HH-60G Pavehawk, brings a child up to safety. (U.S. Air Force photo)

21st century. Over 40 civil and military organizations around the world are using this helicopter or one of its derivative models tailored to perform their special missions.

Because of its special attributes, especially its flight performance capabilities, the Black Hawk helicopter has achieved status as the world-class utility helicopter of its era. This book is the story of that achievement.

This book describes how Sikorsky Aircraft, not regarded at the time by experts to be a serious contender for potentially the largest U.S. Army helicopter program ever, was able to marshal together the right team, the right strategies, and the right technologies to prevail against its strongest competitors. It is about how near total responsiveness to customer requirements

Fig. 6   U.S. Air Force HH-60G Pavehawk helicopter unloading emergency food supplies after the tsunami in Indonesia. (U.S. Air Force photo)

**Fig. 7   U.S. Navy MH-60S Knighthawk helicopter delivering supplies after the tsunami.
(U.S. Navy photo)**

became a major factor in winning. This story emphasizes how critical it is to demonstrate new technologies at the right scale in order to minimize technical risk. It also highlights the impact of technical unknowns and the glitches caused by inevitable disagreements between theory and reality.

The U.S. Army's Black Hawk program produced an advanced technology helicopter that met its specification requirements. It was developed essentially within the government's authorized budget, and it met the planned schedule to production. There were three critical factors behind this success. First was the Army's avoidance of significant specification changes during the design/ development period. Second was use of advanced but proven technology in

**Fig. 8   U.S. Army UH-60As in Desert Storm operations. (©Igor I. Sikorsky Historical
Archives, Inc.)**

the Black Hawk design. The third key factor was the Army's adoption of a fly-before-buy acquisition strategy for the Black Hawk that pitted two capable helicopter companies against each other for the final production award. During the Black Hawk prototype program, the constant presence of competition produced creative design solutions as well as timely problem solving. It also resulted in bargain-basement pricing. The ever-present shadow of a strong and very competent competitor helped Sikorsky develop the Black Hawk helicopter into a better system during its prototype phase. There is no question that the main beneficiaries have been the U.S. military and especially the U.S. Army because of its procurement strategy together with the Sikorsky Aircraft Corporation by virtue of its perseverance to succeed.

BLACK HAWK'S ORIGIN

How did the Black Hawk program begin, and why was it needed? It probably started in the mountains of Korea during the 1950s, but its capabilities began to take shape and crystallize during the Vietnam conflict in the 1960s. Combat experience with many prior helicopter models and in diverse climate conditions helped the Army shape the specifications around which the UH-60 Black Hawk was designed.

During the war in Korea, the Army pioneered use of piston-engine H-19 utility helicopters, Fig. 9, to dramatically improve battlefield mobility. Troop movement and resupply for the first time were freed from the constraints of terrain that caused slow and often impossible movement of ground vehicles. Unshackled from those same constraints, lives of wounded troops were saved

Fig. 9   U.S. Army H-19 (Sikorsky S-55) from the U.S. Eighth Army delivering C-rations to the 35th Infantry Regiment near Panmunjom, South Korea, in May 1953. Photo from militaryimages.net files. Used with permission.

by the helicopter's ability to rapidly carry them to secure medical units equipped to care for them. Helicopters were replacing trucks as trucks replaced horses in a prior time frame.

Those early successes with helicopters helped establish the modern concept of Army tactical air mobility. General Hamilton Howze in 1962 held a vision that: "Airmobile tactics are revolutionary and military history will never again record a major engagement.... in which vertical rising aircraft do not play a prominent and decisive part.... Army aviators are changing forever the art and science of war on the surface of the earth."

Every U.S. Army military action since that time has validated his prediction through the tactics and equipment used in ground combat. Deployment of ground troops became the domain of the helicopter during the Vietnam conflict leading to its being called the "first helicopter war." During the early period of that war, the operational helicopters available for service were older technology piston engine machines including the UH-34 seen in Fig. 10. They were replaced by the turbine-powered UH-I Huey, seen in Figures 11 and 12, as they became available.

However, the use of helicopters quickly revealed two major weaknesses of models that were neither designed for that mission nor were they powered to operate in that severe environment. Those weaknesses were their inability to carry full payloads during high-temperature and high-altitude conditions and their inability to provide acceptable combat survivability.

The Army's UH-1 Hueys were found unable to consistently transport a full 11-man rifle squad in Southeast Asia because of the region's environmental conditions. That shortcoming seriously compromised the planning and success of air assault missions.

Fig. 10   U.S. Marine Corp UH-34 (Sikorsky S-58) near Cam Lo, Vietnam in August 1966. (U.S. Marine Corps photo)

Fig. 11   In Vietnam, UH-1 Hueys were the primary means to transport troops into battle. Their performance and survivability shortcomings helped the Army define what was needed for the next-generation troop carrier that became the UH-60A Black Hawk. (U.S. Army photo)

As a result, the Army set two bedrock requirements for its next-generation helicopter and also for the next-generation turbine engine to power that helicopter. Those key requirements were the capability to transport a full 11-man squad at conditions of high altitudes and temperatures, specifically 4000 ft and 95°F and the ability to survive in a combat environment. Vietnam combat missions showed that much greater ballistic tolerance to ground fire was needed even in low-intensity environments. In addition, major improvements

Fig. 12   U.S. Army HU-1 powered by a single Lycoming T-53 turbine engine driving a two-blade main rotor was a well-accepted helicopter that spawned many derivative models for the U.S. and foreign governments. It set production records for utility helicopters in its era. (U.S. Army photo)

in crash protection for crew and occupants were essential. The Black Hawk helicopter became the first new U.S. Army aircraft to embody features in its basic design aimed at reducing aircraft vulnerability as well as decreasing the probability of injuries to crew and cabin occupants resulting from aircraft accidents.

In the late 1960s the U.S. Army Combat Developments Command firmed up the specifications for a new troop transport helicopter to replace the UH-1 [2]. At the same time, the Army began development of a new turbine engine that became the highly successful T700-GE-700 engine series produced by the General Electric Company. Both the helicopter and engine were designed to achieve major improvements in performance, survivability, and reliability.

During its early concept formulation period, the Army named this new helicopter "UTTAS" for utility tactical transport aircraft system. The UTTAS acronym stuck throughout the design, development, and Army evaluation phases, but when it entered production its name was changed to Black Hawk following the Army's tradition of using Native American names for its helicopters.

Twenty years of rotorcraft technology development that followed the time frame when the Huey was designed permitted enormous improvements in aircraft capabilities without a significant increase in helicopter size. Figure 13 shows the Black Hawk, which is approximately the same length, and width as the Huey but its height is lower.

The successes of both the UH-60A Black Hawk and the T700 engine were noteworthy achievements from another perspective as well. They were the

Fig. 13   U.S. Army UH-60A Black Hawk seen in Granada in October 1983 is powered by two General Electric T-700 turbine engines driving a four-blade rotor. The Black Hawk is close to the same size of the Huey; however, it has far superior performance and survivability as a result of more modern rotorcraft and propulsion technologies as well as unique design innovations. (U.S. Army photo)

first new helicopter and first new engine to be entirely developed by the U.S. Army starting with their design specifications and proceeding through qualification and production. The former Aviation Systems Command, AVSCOM, achieved a dual success in its first attempt to field a totally new system starting with only the mission need and a blank piece of paper. Its Flight Standards Office provided technical management for both the engine and helicopter under the dynamic leadership of Charles C. Crawford assisted by Vernon Edwards for the T700 engine and by Robert Wolfe for the UTTAS helicopter. Both programs met their scheduled milestones right up to first production deliveries. The first production UH-60A Black Hawk was delivered to the Army six years and nine months from the date when the Army issued its request for proposal for the UTTAS prototypes. Several months later the 101st Airborne Division (Air Assault) at Fort Campbell became the first operational unit to receive UH-60A Black Hawk helicopters.

The Army's procurement plan for UTTAS was based on the "fly-before-buy" evaluation process. At its core, the Army's strategy was to apply competitive pressure every step of the way in a program that had very demanding performance and cost goals. It did this very effectively by funding the development of two competing prototype helicopters, pitting them against each other in a grueling eight-month evaluation and then selecting the one for production that offered the best value and least risk to the Army. The goal of the competing contractors, who were the Bell Helicopter Company, Boeing Vertol Company, and Sikorsky Aircraft, was to win a sole source production award estimated at the time to total over 1000 aircraft by the time the procurement filled the Army's operational requirements. The incentives to win could not have been greater for the three competitors who fought to capture this critical program. Winning a place in the prototype program was absolutely essential for having an opportunity to win the ultimate production award. For Sikorsky Aircraft, with its very depressed state of production business at the time, winning was felt to be a matter of survival.

UTTAS PROGRAM LAUNCHED

The Army formally started the UTTAS program in January 1972 with the release of a request for proposal (RFP) to the helicopter industry for what was called the basic engineering development (BED) phase. At that early stage, most industry observers felt that Bell would hold the lead position because it was the supplier of the incumbent Huey helicopter of which many thousands had been built. Second position favored Boeing Vertol because it was producing CH-47 Chinook transport helicopters for the Army. Although Boeing Vertol focused on the tandem rotor configuration, their interest in single rotor machines was well publicized as was their interest in "rigid rotor" technology. Sikorsky on the other hand had not built helicopters for the Army during the prior 15 years, and it had recently lost two major Army competitions for new helicopters. The first was a gunship called the advanced aerial fire support system (AAFSS) awarded to Lockheed in 1965, and the second and even more traumatic loss was the heavy lift helicopter (HLH) awarded to Boeing Vertol in 1970, only six months before the UTTAS RFP was issued. Chapter 2 describes how the losses of both major programs added to the urgency of winning the UTTAS program and how those losses helped shape Sikorsky's key strategies to win.

With the company's history of recent failures to win new Army helicopter programs and the commanding position of its competitors in producing Army helicopters, few industry observers expected Sikorsky to win or even to bid on the UTTAS program. Indeed, even within the Army there was skepticism. The Army contracting office at AVSCOM, headed by Maurice D. Schneider, began to form three teams to negotiate the proposals expected from the three companies on its bid list. But no experienced person in that office asked to be assigned to the team tasked to manage the Sikorsky proposal. That appeared to Army personnel like a dead-end assignment, and the team remained unstaffed until Sikorsky's proposal arrived. At that point an Army pilot, Captain Arthur J. O'Leary, Jr., just back from flying Huey Cobras in Vietnam and as a junior member of the contracts staff, was assigned to manage negotiations for the Sikorsky proposal. That turned out to be a fortunate assignment for both Capt. O'Leary and for the Army.

Although there was early debate even within the company on the wisdom of making a substantial effort to bid UTTAS, management gradually became optimistic for several reasons. In 1971, new Sikorsky research and development initiatives in rotor-blade and rotor-head technologies, sponsored in part by the Navy and quite apart from the UTTAS program, began to show very encouraging flight-test results on a test Marine Corps CH-53D helicopter. Flight data demonstrated that major new aerodynamic and material technologies were ready to be incorporated in UTTAS without incurring significant risk. At the same time, design studies indicated that this new main rotor technology plus an entirely new concept for tail rotor design would help create a UTTAS configuration capable of meeting all critical Army requirements. In mid-1971, only five months before the Army released its RFP, the decision was made by Sikorsky to bid on the UTTAS program. That decision set off the most determined and focused effort ever made by Sikorsky to put together a winning proposal. During that process, it received enthusiastic support from United Aircraft Corporation, since renamed United Technologies Corporation, and particularly from its new corporate CEO, Harry J. Gray.

In addition to an increasingly strong technical rational for bidding, Sikorsky's declining production business trend, then in its 15th year, provided the most compelling reason to bid and to win. The company's future was viewed to be dependent on first winning a place in the UTTAS prototype program and then winning the production award to reestablish Sikorsky Aircraft as an Army helicopter supplier and industry leader. Chapter 2 describes the company's helicopter production history and explains the reasons for its decline and depressed state of production at the time when the decision was made to compete for the UTTAS program. It also describes the strategies, corporate participation, and people assigned to generate one of the best helicopter designs that the company and the government ever created.

WINNING AGAINST LONG ODDS

In August 1972, seven months after proposals were submitted to the Army, industry observers were surprised to learn that Bell had not been chosen to build the Huey's successor. They were surprised to learn that Sikorsky, along with Boeing Vertol, had each been awarded contracts to build UTTAS prototypes. These were designated as the Sikorsky YUH-60A and Boeing Vertol YUH-61A. The critical competition for the production award would only be between these two companies. Now, however, the final winner would be selected 52 months later on the merits of actual flight aircraft rather than on the promises of paper proposals. A new helicopter industry order could be a possible outcome.

If there were a single reason why Sikorsky was awarded one of the two UTTAS development contracts, it would have to be because of the company's nearly total responsiveness to the Army's specifications. In Sikorsky's UTTAS design, only five minor deviations to the specification were proposed, and all were accepted by the Army. A second reason would be the degree to which Sikorsky demonstrated its new technologies in large-scale flight testing. Every new technology proposed for UTTAS including its titanium main rotor blades, elastomeric rotor head, bearingless composite tail rotor, and canted tail rotor were test flown on helicopters all larger than UTTAS. That strategy avoided the potential risks of adverse scale effects if smaller scale demonstrations were conducted.

The Army was satisfied with Sikorsky's efforts to contain risk, and its feeling likely was influenced by the termination of the Lockheed YAH-56A AAFSS program only two years earlier. That program was terminated because of unproven rotor technology resulting, in part, from attempting to apply new technology to a new helicopter very much larger than the size that had been successfully flight demonstrated.

Chapter 3 describes how the Sikorsky UTTAS design evolved to its final configuration, as the Army's requirements gradually became known while the RFP was being drafted. The key Army requirements that shaped the Sikorsky design are reviewed, with emphasis on those relating to flight performance and air transport. Those requirements had the most pronounced impact on the UTTAS design especially the requirement to squeeze a UTTAS into an Air Force C-130 transport aircraft. That was felt to be the most onerous of the Army's requirements, but in the end it was met. However, the compact design of Sikorsky's UTTAS configuration to meet this requirement seriously compromised key aircraft's attributes and came back to bite the program during the flight development phase. Chapter 3 also presents the Army's Source Selection and Evaluation Board assessment of Sikorsky's UTTAS capabilities against Army requirements, which became the cornerstone of a winning proposal. Chapters 4 and 5 describe the new rotor technologies and new survivability design innovations that were the foundations of Sikorsky's design for the Black Hawk.

EARLY SETBACKS

First flight of Sikorsky's YUH-60A, Fig. 14, took place 26 months after contract, which was two months ahead of the contract date and six weeks ahead of Boeing Vertol's first flight of its YUH-61A. Preliminary results of limited flying "in the yard" were most encouraging, and with this significant accomplishment morale of the Sikorsky team could not have been higher. But it was short lived.

Several days after first flight, when the prototype was cleared to proceed beyond flight field boundaries, reports from the flight crew could not have been more discouraging. Sikorsky test pilots reported encountering severe vibrations much in excess of predicted levels. They also found that flight at higher speeds required much more engine power than was predicted. Attempting to reach predicted maximum speed was like "flying into a brick wall."

But that was not all of the bad news. The pilots also reported that landing was difficult because very high nose-up fuselage attitudes, especially during "quick-stop" deceleration maneuvers, impaired their view of the flight field directly ahead. Several flights later, another serious problem emerged: the presence of excessive tail shake felt in the cockpit during certain flight regimes.

Overcoming those setbacks would set Sikorsky's work agenda and focus for the next year and a half, and it would need the support of the entire company to design and build all of the new hardware finally installed on the three proto-types. The impact on expenditures would be significant. It soon became clear that much more than normal design "tweaking" would be needed to correct these problems. Major redesign would likely be required with no guarantee of success especially because the causes were not yet understood. That early flight-test period was absolutely the lowest morale point of the UTTAS team and indeed of the company as well as the Army UTTAS project office. The good news was that there was still time to recover. Scheduled delivery of the prototypes for Army evaluation was still 15 months away.

The time available to correct the prototype's problems was used productively, and every month brought more optimistic feelings. One by one, the problems

Fig. 14 Most distinguishable external features at the time of first flight of SN 21650 were the low position main rotor and large-area vertical and horizontal stabilizers. (© Igor I. Sikorsky Historical Archives, Inc.)

found during flight testing were gradually understood, and solutions began to be demonstrated. All of the 15 months scheduled for flight development were needed to build new hardware, qualify it for safe flight, and experiment with design changes to achieve acceptable results. All major problems were corrected, and all three prototypes were reconfigured to a new standard that finally met the Army's specification.

Fig. 15 Visible design improvements to the YUH-60A include the raised rotor, fly-by-wire stabilator, vertical tail area reduction, and main rotor aft pylon flow separator. This became the basic UH-60A Black Hawk configuration. (©Igor I. Sikorsky Historical Archives, Inc.)

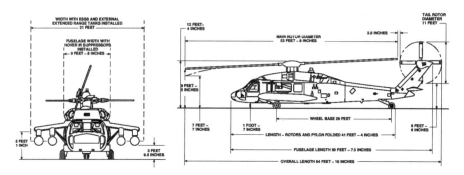

Fig. 16   Black Hawk dimensioned general arrangement.

Although these early setbacks were severe and unexpected, they were not caused by any of the new technologies incorporated into Sikorsky's design. Instead they were related to certain geometric features of the prototype explained in Chapter 7. The lengthy experimental investigation to find solutions and to modify the aircraft is chronicled in that chapter. Those modifications transformed the prototype YUH-60A UTTAS into the production UH-60A Black Hawk.

The significant external changes can be seen in the following pictures of the same YUH-60A prototype before and after the many changes were made during the 15-month flight development program. Figure 14 shows the YUH-60A as it was configured at the time of first flight in October 1974, and Figure 15 shows its configuration when the prototypes were delivered to the Army in March 1976 for the start of the fly-off evaluation against the Boeing Vertol YUH-61A. At that point in time the Sikorsky UTTAS was essentially identical in its physical configuration to the Sikorsky production Black Hawk whose general arrangement is shown in Figure 16.

FINAL SELECTION

In March 1976, the Army accepted the six UTTAS prototypes, three YUH-61As from Boeing Vertol and three YHU-60As from Sikorsky, to start the government competitive testing (GCT). That head-to-head testing took eight months and covered operational, performance, and climatic testing at seven U.S. military bases while accumulating over 700 flight hours on the prototypes from each company.

Army flight crews measured aircraft performance in the same severe climate conditions expected to be encountered during combat operations. During all testing, every component failure, maintenance action, and mission abort were recorded. When the Army's competitive evaluation was completed, there was little that was not known about the two competing prototypes in terms of compliance to the Army's design specification. The only major requirement whose compliance was not planned for obvious reasons was the requirement for crash survivability. But as events occurred, compliance with even that requirement was partially demonstrated.

The crash landing of one of the three Sikorsky prototypes, serial number 21650, with 14 soldiers and crewmen aboard could have ended Sikorsky's drive to win. It occurred during night operational testing in a heavily wooded area of Fort Campbell, Kentucky. Part way into this simulated mission, the Army flight crew elected to make an emergency landing because of one-per-revolution vibration within the helicopter that was steadily growing worse. But because of darkness and mist, the pilots mistook the visible tops of a dense pine forest to be a corn field suitable for a safe landing. To the crew's shock, they landed their YUH-60A right into a forest of mature trees.

As it tried to land, the helicopter's rotor blades chopped down over 40 pine trees, and its rotor continued to sever the same trees many times as the helicopter descended and finally came to rest on the ground. Fortunately there was no major airframe damage, fuel leakage, nor post crash fire. The only injury was a minor bruise when a soldier jumped out of the cabin in the dead of night and ran into the stump of a freshly chopped-down tree.

Instead of being the catastrophe that it could have been, that crash landing turned out to highlight the value of the Army's crashworthiness requirements and the consequent structural robustness of the YUH-60A prototype. Only two days after the crash landing, with the site cleared of tree stumps and with only the rotor blades replaced, Army pilots flew the Sikorsky prototype out of the woods and back to base to resume competitive testing. The Army's reaction to this crash and its cause are described in Chapter 8.

By the end of 1976, after eight months of testing, the Army was ready to make its final selection that would shape its operational capabilities as well as the destinies of two companies for decades to come. On 23 December 1976, 52 months after winning the UTTAS prototype contract, Sikorsky was notified that it had won the production program.

The Army stated that its decision was based heavily on the maturity of the YUH-60A design, which it felt represented low production risk. The Army further noted the extent to which its specification was met by this aircraft. Chapter 9 discusses how the Army rated the Sikorsky design and the rationale for its selection.

That award was the beginning of a new era in Army air mobility, and it brought about a major turnaround in Sikorsky's prospects for the future.

Throughout the last quarter of the 20th century, Black Hawk models maintained leadership in rotorcraft technology, which helped secure a large share of the world utility helicopter market. During the beginning of the 21st century, a new generation of technologies became available for insertion into this helicopter to improve its mission capabilities and its compatibility with the digital battlefield of the future. Chapter 10 concludes with a description of the new U.S. Army/Sikorsky UH-60M model and the benefits that proven new technologies bring to the UH-60 series. The "M" model will create its own lineage of derivative models that will take advantage of further technology insertion. Black Hawk variant models will continue to be the workhorse for Army Aviation well into this century, and the Black Hawk's operational deployment could extend to over 50 years.

Chapter 2

A MATTER OF SURVIVAL

When the Army launched the UTTAS program in 1972, industry experts ranked Sikorsky as a long shot and unlikely to be one of the two planned winners. Many in fact did not believe that the company would even bid on the program. In spite of that assessment, Sikorsky regarded this major competition as a challenge that had to succeed. The Army's large production program offered a way, however remote, to reverse a long period of declining helicopter production as well as an opportunity to again become an Army supplier.

This chapter discusses the company's decline in production output and the internal changes that were made to reverse what looked like a going-out-of-business trend. Significant changes were made in top management to invigorate development of new helicopter technologies as well as to improve customer relationships. New management brought about substantial increases in both internal and government sponsored research and development projects. It also brought about organization changes to focus more on understanding and responding to customer requirements. These changes together with innovative design concepts helped Sikorsky earn a place in the UTTAS flyoff competition. Its critical win in 1972 of the UTTAS prototype program was followed by the Black Hawk production win in 1976 that totally changed Sikorsky's business outlook. It set the stage for the company's third major business cycle.

Figure 17 shows the company's first two major cycles. The first cycle ended in 1950, and the second cycle ended when Sikorsky delivered its first production UH-60A Black Hawk helicopter in 1978.

Why did the company's business decline so drastically during the years preceding its UTTAS win? It declined because its two major models, the S-55 and S-58, were becoming obsolete as the transformation from piston to turbine engines was taking place. Adding to this problem was a major structural change in the marketplace together with a loss of focus on customer needs, particularly those of the Army. Following dramatic increases in helicopter output starting in 1950, the company's deliveries began a sharp drop-off in 1957. That drop-off continued for 15 years bringing the company to a precarious position.

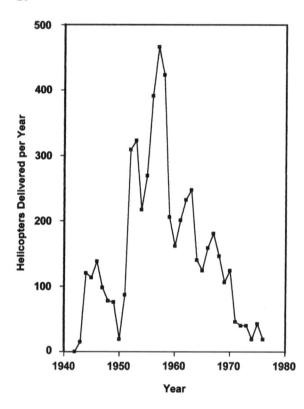

Fig. 17 The 15-year drop-off in helicopter output from 1957 to 1972 added urgency to the decision to bid on the Army's UTTAS program. Sikorsky unit output continued to decline until the turnaround began with winning the UH-60A production program in December of 1976. Chapter 10 describes the extent of the company's recovery.

Sales forecasts were not optimistic because Sikorsky was no longer an Army supplier during the period when the Army had become the dominant helicopter operator within the U.S. military organization and indeed in the world.

In the years just before the UTTAS competition, Sikorsky had lost two highly sought after Army development contracts. Taken together, the company's reduced helicopter sales and its loss of new Army helicopter development programs raised the concern about its survival as an independent producer. It also raised the question of whether or not to make the investment needed to bid on the UTTAS program. That bid clearly would entail a steep uphill battle against two well-respected and entrenched Army helicopter suppliers, the Bell Helicopter Company and the Boeing Vertol Company.

Prior to that long decline, Sikorsky experienced an enormous upsurge in production starting in 1950. The large upswing in delivery quantities shown in Fig. 17 was driven by two new models that not only permitted Sikorsky to enter the utility market for the first time in its history but to capture a major share of that market. Both models, the S-55 and S-58 helicopters, shown in Figs. 18 and 19, featured unusually large cabins along with large center-of-gravity ranges that permitted nearly unrestricted placement of passengers and cargo. They were just what the market needed as land- and ship-based utility helicopter operations began to expand around the world.

Fig. 18   U.S. Army H-19 (Sikorsky S-55) first flew in November 1949 only seven months after contract. Nearly 1300 were built for U.S. military plus several hundred under foreign license. Key innovations included a large cabin with the engine placed in the nose, offset hinge rotor, and hydraulically boosted flight controls. (©Igor I. Sikorsky Historical Archives, Inc.)

The enormous worldwide success of these two models can be largely attributed to their incorporation of the right combination of innovative design and advanced helicopter technologies. Many years later this "right" combination of design and technologies was a major factor for Sikorsky's success in the UTTAS and Black Hawk programs.

Fig. 19   U.S. Army H-34 (Sikorsky S-58) first flew in March 1954. Over 1800 were built for U.S. military services and commercial operators plus over 500 built under foreign license. It was larger than the S-55 model and had more new features including automatic stability equipment for precision hover flight. Versions of the S-58 model became antisubmarine warfare helicopters for the Navy and troop carriers for the Army and Marine Corps in Korea. (©Igor I. Sikorsky Historical Archives, Inc.)

Before creating the new S-55 configuration with its piston engine in the nose, the company's earlier models during the WWII period were all small observation helicopters. They essentially had no cabins, and their piston engines were placed in the fuselage directly underneath the main rotor. That engine placement permitted simple transmission designs and good structural load paths; however, it effectively eliminated usable cabins. Because of that serious deficiency, Sikorsky was unable to enter the utility markets that began to open up right after WWII where large cabins were required. Its failure to enter the utility market was largely responsible for the first decline noted in Fig. 17.

That changed quickly soon after the S-55 model was designed in 1949. It gained dominance in the new utility market paving the way for the S-58 helicopter that was even more successful.

Special versions of both models were placed in service by the U.S. Navy, Air Force, and Army, which helped Sikorsky set new production records. In addition, hundreds of S-55 and S-58 models were built under license by French, British, and Italian helicopter companies. Licensed production placed Sikorsky-designed helicopters in every corner of the world, and other manufacturers adopted this successful new configuration. However, production licenses had the inevitable effect of technology transfer and eventual creation of independent helicopter designers and producers as well as competitors in the world market. On the positive side, widespread production and worldwide usage helped convert the helicopter from the oddity that it was only a decade earlier to an essential means of transportation for the military.

During the mid-1950s, the market forces and design innovations that propelled Sikorsky to a leadership position began to change dramatically. During the latter half of that period, Sikorsky faced an abrupt downturn in helicopter requirements as the war in Korea began winding down. Military requirements for Sikorsky transport helicopters tapered off, and sales of the company's record-setting S-58 models were coming to an end. But besides a shrinking military demand for helicopters, there were two other reasons for the downturn that caused it to persist long after that war and well into the 1970s. The first reason was growing obsolescence of Sikorsky's product line, and the second reason was a major change in U.S. military helicopter usage that occurred at a time when Sikorsky was poorly positioned to react.

Sikorsky's helicopters of the 1950s were based on the rotorcraft and propulsion technologies of that era with the result that emerging new technologies set the stage for their obsolescence. Newly designed helicopters introduced by Sikorsky's competitors for the Army during the 1960s took full advantage of technology advancements, principally replacement of piston engines by lighter and more powerful gas turbine engines. During the Vietnam conflict, Bell's turbine-powered UH-1 series became the Army's troop assault helicopter replacing Sikorsky's piston-powered H-19 and H-34

Fig. 20   U.S. Navy SH-3 (Sikorsky S-61) designed for antisubmarine warfare achieved first flight in March 1959. They were used by USAF (CH-3C), Coast Guard (HH-3F), USMC (VH-3D) and by commercial operators. A total of 791 were built by Sikorsky plus several hundred under foreign license. (©Igor I. Sikorsky Historical Archives, Inc.)

models. In that same period Boeing Vertol's turbine-powered CH-47 Chinook replaced Sikorsky's piston-powered H-37 as the Army's medium transport helicopter.

As its Army business shrank to near zero, Sikorsky was actively developing and producing rescue and antisubmarine warfare helicopters for the U.S. Navy and troop transports for the Marine Corps. In that period the Navy's NAVAIR became the leader in rotorcraft design and qualification replacing the Air Force who had managed the development of earlier Army helicopters. During the 1950s, the Navy funded design and development of the new turbine-powered SH-3 (Sikorsky S-61), Fig. 20, for anti-submarine warfare and the CH-53A/D (Sikorsky S-65), Fig. 21, for U.S. Marine Corps (USMC) medium transport. Both models were widely used by the Navy and Marine Corps during the 1960s and 1970s, and versions were also put in service by the Air Force and by commercial and military operators worldwide.

The CH-53E, Fig. 22, was a larger version of the CH-53D developed to provide the Marine Corps with a heavy lift capability. Rotor diameter was increased from 72 to 79 ft by use of titanium blade extenders, a seventh main rotor blade was added along with a third T-64 engine.

Production of these models at very low rates could not reverse the long-term decline in deliveries, but they did allow Sikorsky to hold its technical team together to rebuild its technology base and respond to new customer requirements. Company employment did not decline as dramatically as did unit deliveries because the product line was shifting to larger and heavier helicopters although far fewer were produced.

Fig. 21   USMC CH-53A designed as a troop/cargo medium-lift transport (Sikorsky S-65). They first flew in December 1965. A total of 412 units were built, including CH-53A and D versions. (©Igor I. Sikorsky Historical Archives, Inc.)

A major change in helicopter market composition took place during the 1960 decade when the Army emerged as the dominant helicopter operator as a result of changes in operational doctrine. In 1961 the Army created the Tactical Mobility Requirements Board to examine how it could better accomplish its mission and General Hamilton H. Howze was assigned as its chairman. A year later the Howze Board released its report citing the need for development of airmobile theory and doctrine. General Howze proposed establishment of several air-assault divisions equipped with helicopters for transport, reconnaissance and fire support [3]. His proposal was adopted by the Army and creation of the 1st Cavalry Division (Airmobile) was its first

Fig. 22   USMC CH-53E Heavy Transport developed from the CH-53D first flew as the YCH-53E prototype in March 1974. First production CH-53E flew in December 1980 and entered service with the USMC in mid-1981. (©Igor I. Sikorsky Historical Archives, Inc.)

implementation. The board's recommendations revolutionized mobile warfare concepts based on use of organic aviation [4].

That concept established the helicopter as the Army's primary troop carrier in place of trucks. The airmobile doctrine proved to be most applicable in the difficult terrains of Korea and Southeast Asia where it was first applied. This new war fighting doctrine in effect established the Army as the U.S. military's largest helicopter operator bringing with it the need for surveillance, armed attack and heavy transport helicopters to support its troop assault helicopters.

By 1966 nearly 4000 helicopters were deployed in Vietnam. They included observation helicopters, utility transports, gunship attack helicopters, and medium-transport helicopters. Reflecting the company's decline within the Army was the fact that almost none of these helicopters were made by Sikorsky Aircraft. The company's future clearly was dependent on earning a new place in the Army's helicopter production base. The road to that achievement was much longer and much more uphill than envisioned at the time. It would take another 10 years of research and development work to acquire and demonstrate the new technologies needed to win. During that long drought, Sikorsky submitted major proposal efforts for new Army helicopters. They were supported by large investments in full-scale flight aircraft demonstrations but were unable to win Army contracts. Finally in the 1970s, Sikorsky started a major turnaround when it won participation in the UTTAS program and then when it was awarded the Black Hawk production award by the Army. The key long-and short-term strategies that helped realize this goal are reviewed in this chapter.

LONG ROAD AHEAD

The Army's dramatic dominance in helicopter tactical employment and later in research and development was clearly a new direction that would have major impact on the U.S. helicopter industry. Sikorsky's President Lee S. Johnson, seen in Fig. 23, recognized the long-term impact of this change, and he began the process of responding to Army performance and operational needs. More aggressive research and development programs were initiated as well as a more focused and determined pursuit of Army helicopter programs.

Achieving that goal would require a long and focused effort. Along the way there were two major losses sustained by Sikorsky for new Army helicopter programs that nearly caused senior management to change its focus.

Those two very disappointing losses were for the Army's armed attack gunship called AAFSS for advanced aerial fire support system, which was awarded to Lockheed in 1965, Fig. 24, and for the Army's new heavy-lift helicopter, the HLH, which was awarded to Boeing Vertol in 1970. Both of these new helicopter starts were very actively sought after by Sikorsky.

Fig. 23 Lee S. Johnson, Sikorsky president, with Igor Sikorsky in front of the S-64 flying crane that was one of the many creations of Mr. Sikorsky. His demonstration of that heavy-lift concept made the company's loss of the HLH competition that much harder on company morale. (©Igor I. Sikorsky Historical Archives, Inc.)

Loss of the AAFSS competition was particularly disappointing because of the major effort that Sikorsky invested in demonstrating its capability to achieve the high speeds required by the Army. Moreover, in order to minimize risk, the company demonstrated its high-speed capability at an aircraft size and gross weight almost equal to the AAFSS. Sikorsky flew its S-61F research

Fig. 24 U.S. Army YAH-56A Cheyenne built by Lockheed achieved first flight on September 1967. Maximum take-off weight was 22,000 lb. Pusher propeller used for forward flight and conventional tail rotor for yaw control. Main rotor was of the rigid, bearingless type with a large stabilizer bar. (U.S. Army photo)

Fig. 25   Sikorsky S-61F high-speed research compound helicopter featured a reduced drag SH-3 airframe and propulsion system with retractable landing gear, small wings, and two P&W J-60 jet engines. First flight was May 1965. It achieved 210 kn in the compound mode. (©Igor I. Sikorsky Historical Archives, Inc.)

compound helicopter, shown in Fig. 25, close to the 200 kn required by the Army specifications and at a weight of 20,000 lb, about equal to what the AAFSS was expected to weigh.

Sikorsky had extensive experience in designing and building helicopters in the AAFSS size and weight class but less experience in integrating weapons and fire control systems. Lockheed, who was Sikorsky's prime competitor, was new to helicopter engineering, and its experience was limited to its XH-51A helicopter, Fig. 26.

The XH-51A weighed in the neighborhood of 4000 lb, which was approximately one-fifth of the projected AAFSS weight. The XH-51A did successfully demonstrate the high control power of the rigid rotor concept that

Fig. 26   Lockheed XH-51A high-speed research helicopter first flew in 1962. In 1964 it flew as a compound helicopter and achieved an unofficial speed record of 263 kn in 1967.

Lockheed was proposing for the AAFSS. In the full compound version, the XH-51A set an unofficial speed record of 263 kn. Lockheed's demonstrator was flown and enthusiastically reviewed by military pilots. Its unique rotor system appeared by some observers to represent the technology of the future, which in retrospect appears to have been a good forecast, but, at the time, that rotor concept seemed to be too far ahead of supporting analytic and materials technologies.

After reviewing a first round of proposals from industry, the Army selected only Sikorsky and Lockheed to submit final proposals to design and build 10 AAFSS prototype helicopters. Sikorsky's proposal for its S-66 design, shown in Fig. 27, was approximately $66 million, and Lockheed's proposal was approximately $106 million.

After a second intensive review of AAFSS proposals, the Army selected Lockheed to build its advanced gunship. Losing this award came as a severe blow to the people at Sikorsky. Not only did it lose after making substantial investments in both the S-61F compound helicopter and in the Roto-Prop propulsion concept to demonstrate speed capability in large scale, but it lost to a company that was new to the helicopter industry.

However, that loss did cause the company to react to the Army's assessment of its strengths and weaknesses. As a result, major changes were made to Sikorsky's program management structure for future programs. In its award debriefing, the Army ranked Sikorsky higher on basic helicopter technology, but it ranked Lockheed higher on both weapons systems integration and much higher on program management. That latter category of program management turned out to be 25% of the total score behind the Army's award criteria.

Fig. 27 Sikorsky S-66 compound helicopter was proposed for the AAFSS competition. It used a single tail rotor/propeller that pivoted 90 deg for combinations of lateral and propulsive thrust. The "Roto-Prop" was flight demonstrated on an S-61 in 1965, and it was the first to demonstrate full conversion of a tail rotor to a propeller. The S-66 main rotor was a conventional fully articulated design. (©Igor I. Sikorsky Historical Archives, Inc.)

The prototype contract was awarded in 1965, and the Lockheed YAH-56A Cheyenne began its flight development program in September 1967. By 1968, 10 prototypes were delivered, but after years of development and experimentation the AH-56A program was cancelled by the Army at the end of 1969. It is fair to conclude that the technical risks associated with the rigid rotor operating at high speeds were not fully understood or appreciated during the AAFSS proposal phase. As a result, Lockheed did not have sufficient time to satisfactorily solve the basic helicopter problems associated with its unproven rigid rotor during the development phase. Because of accidents and delays, the Army considered that the risks of committing the AH-56A to production were too great, and the program was terminated. The perceived strengths that led to Lockheed's win appeared to be unrelated to the reason that it finally lost, which was an inability to scale up new technology and demonstrate an acceptable helicopter platform in time.

Following the AAFSS cancellation, the Army began a search for alternative armed attack helicopters. That search led to a fly-off competition between Hughes and Bell for the AAH similar to the competition between Sikorsky and Boeing Vertol for the UTTAS. The AAH competition was won by the Hughes YAH-64A over the Bell YAH-63A. The Hughes AH-64 Apache became the preeminent attack helicopter in the United States as well as in international inventories.

Soon after the AAFSS program was terminated, and before the Army launched its new search for a new gunship, Sikorsky began work on a high-speed attack-type helicopter again designed around S-61 dynamic components. That company-funded program produced the S-67 Blackhawk shown in Fig. 28, which went on to set a new world speed record. In spite of its outstanding performance and proven dynamic components, the S-67 was not able to find a customer. This only prototype was lost in a tragic accident at the Farnborough air show in 1974.

As a result of the AAFSS loss, Sikorsky senior management, under the direction of John A. McKenna, began to introduce program management concepts into the company as well as to shape a more customer-focused marketing organization. At that time, managers of functional departments were accustomed to having near total control of program activities pertaining to their departments. They had to be won over to the new program management culture if the best interests of the programs were to be served. Some had to be rolled over, but eventually the new culture began to take hold.

A second organizational deficiency of that period was in the way that the company's marketing department was structured. It was organized by product line rather than by major customer. This inhibited full understanding of customer needs, and it did not present the same marketing person to the customer for all of the customer's requirements so that communications and insight into the customers' real needs suffered. That structural weakness was

Fig. 28   Sikorsky S-67 Blackhawk with a low-drag fuselage designed around S-61 engines and drive systems set a world speed record for pure helicopters, with no auxiliary propulsion, of 217 mph in 1970. Its name Blackhawk had no relation to the UH-60 Black Hawk, but it was an excellent omen for the future. (©Igor I. Sikorsky Historical Archives, Inc.)

corrected by McKenna, who was placed in charge of Sikorsky marketing following the loss of AAFSS. He did so by realigning the department into five groups to concentrate on Army, Navy, Air Force, Coast Guard, and commercial customers.

One of the most important benefits of this realignment was the ability to focus on the operational and technology needs of each customer. That encouraged the commitment of internal R&D funds to support needed technology improvements and further helped the company receive R&D contracts. During the years of declining production described earlier, Sikorsky made excellent progress in winning R&D contracts from both the Army and Navy. In fact, in the years just preceding Sikorsky's UTTAS win, it had more Army-sponsored research and development contracts than the rest of the helicopter industry combined. However the company still had no Army production work.

The advanced rotor-head and rotor-blade technology used in UTTAS design was acquired during that period. Its funding was shared between Sikorsky and the Navy for application to the CH-53A Marine Corps transport. However that technology was perfectly applicable to UTTAS in view of the Army's demanding performance and durability requirements. As the start of the Army's UTTAS program drew near, Sikorsky was becoming well positioned with the right technologies to support that program. That was one of the most important benefits of the long-term strategies put in place during the earlier decade. The company's technology base, demonstrated at larger than full UTTAS scale, was one of the most important reasons that Sikorsky was able to create a winning design.

STRATEGIES TO WIN UTTAS

When the Army released its request for proposal for UTTAS, it was viewed to be the "only new helicopter game in town." All major U.S. helicopter manufacturers were expected to aggressively pursue that program. The UTTAS was an especially attractive new development because it had a large production requirement with over 1100 units planned for the Army alone. In addition, its utility configuration made it potentially adoptable to many other missions both in the United States and abroad. But to participate in that program meant that two competitive battles would have to be won and both would be hard fought.

The ultimate winner had to first win one of the two planned UTTAS prototype development efforts, emerge successfully from a head-to-head fly-off evaluation, and then win the sole-source Black Hawk production program. For Sikorsky, the battles promised to be decidedly uphill; however, the option of not participating was an unacceptable alternative in view of the clear need to turn around its production decline.

Sikorsky's only business with the Army at the time of UTTAS was production of spare parts for its out-of-production models and research and development work. As a result, the challenge to win UTTAS was especially daunting because Sikorsky was not a significant part of the Army's industrial base. Nor was it participating in the Army's only other new helicopter development program.

Just six months before the UTTAS RFP was released, Sikorsky was notified that it had lost the Army's HLH competition to Boeing Vertol. The company had high expectations of winning not only because it had a proven configuration with relatively low risk but also because its CH-54A flying crane performed very well during the Vietnam conflict. Losing the HLH competition was devastating to the entire company. The morale of its workforce reflected that setback just at the time the UTTAS program was emerging. It was another negative consideration that led some senior managers within the company to advocate no bidding the UTTAS program to avoid wasting another several million dollars on proposal activities as they saw happen with the HLH proposal.

The thought of Sikorsky not bidding on the UTTAS program was not confined to the company, but it was also in the minds of Army personnel especially since Sikorsky's recent loss of the HLH competition. Many people within the AVSCOM management staff felt that the UTTAS competition would end up just between Bell and Boeing Vertol. As a result, senior AVSCOM personnel in the contract office and other disciplines lined up to garner assignments on the Bell and Boeing Vertol teams within the Army. No one looked forward to an assignment on the team to manage the Sikorsky UTTAS program because a Sikorsky program might never materialize.

However within the company and corporation, logic overruled emotion, and the reality of Sikorsky's tenuous production base coupled with the enormous importance of being an Army supplier argued otherwise. If the advocates for not submitting a bid for UTTAS had been able to crystal ball the future, they would have seen a near empty factory four years later.

The downward slide continued, and by 1976, when the UTTAS production contract was awarded, Sikorsky's factory was operating at only 22% of capacity, and its final assembly line was devoid of new production helicopters for the first time. The following year was the worst in company history in terms of helicopter production. After 35 years of continuous helicopter deliveries, there were no Sikorsky helicopters scheduled for delivery to any branch of the U.S. government during the year 1977. Clearly, winning a place in the UTTAS competition was essential; it was indeed a matter of survival.

NEW MANAGEMENT AND NEW FOCUS

Sikorsky's performance during the 1960s decade strongly indicated that new leadership was needed to rebuild the company's technology base and to restore a relationship of trust with its customers based on responsiveness to their needs. At that period in its long history, Sikorsky needed a renewed focus on both technology development and design innovation. This situation was similar in many respects to what Sikorsky faced 20 years earlier when it found itself unable to scale its successful small R-4 and S-51 type models up to the sizes representative of utility-type helicopters. It was new technology plus design innovation that pulled Sikorsky out of its doldrums following WWII and paved the way for it to capture the utility market with its new S-55 and S-58 models and dominate it for many years. Sikorsky had to repeat that spectacular turnaround as the 1970s decade was about to start.

As the 1960s were ending and Sikorsky's fundamental problems were becoming apparent, United Aircraft Corporation (UAC) made changes in Sikorsky senior management to better confront the company's new challenges. In 1967, it appointed Wesley A. Kuhrt, to whom this book is dedicated, to the position of Sikorsky executive vice president. One year later Kuhrt became president and remained in that position until after Sikorsky was awarded one of the two UTTAS prototype contracts, and the company began to focus on winning the production award.

Kuhrt was the right executive to lead Sikorsky at that critical period. His accomplishments and credentials in developing advanced technology combined with his ability to relate to people and his unquestioned integrity made him the ideal choice. He came to Sikorsky from the UAC Research Center, where he had been director of research for the corporation [5]. At Sikorsky, Kuhrt led the application of advanced material and aerodynamics technologies to the design of helicopter rotor systems. That effort began two years before the Army began to award UTTAS development contracts. He was able to obtain corporate as well as U.S. Navy funding for developing what was referred to at that time as the improved rotor blade (IRB) to be flight demonstrated in a USMC CH-53D medium-transport helicopter.

Chapter 4 discusses why this new rotor-blade technology was arguably the most important technical factor in winning the UTTAS program. Better blade structural materials, cambered airfoils, optimized twist distribution, and blade tip shaping were decisive factors in achieving performance superior to competition. But advanced rotor-blade technology alone would not have been sufficient to win. The other important technology advancements and design innovations discussed in Chapters 4 and 5 all contributed to the Army's high technical ranking of Sikorsky's UTTAS proposal.

As the UTTAS program drew closer to contract award, a number of Sikorsky's advanced technology projects began to show promise. As they did, they became candidates for inclusion in the UTTAS design. Flight demonstrations of experimental rotor systems on company-owned and on borrowed U.S. military models were confirming predicted benefits in flight speed, structural characteristics, and in other critical attributes. At the same time, design innovations and attractive configurations for the UTTAS helicopter appeared on the drawing boards. Enthusiasm within the company began to rise while a plan to win began to evolve.

During this critical period, the company was strongly supported by senior management from United Aircraft Corporation, later renamed United Technologies. That support was especially strong from its chief executive officer, Harry J. Gray, who took a keen interest in the UTTAS program. The corporation's research labs enthusiastically provided both advanced technologies and technical experts to enhance Sikorsky's position. The fact that the lab's former director was now Sikorsky president provided great motivation to the lab's participation. Winning UTTAS became a corporate mandate and a shared objective. All that were needed included the right design, the right technologies, and the right team. These were hardly trivial issues, but all were possible, and all were in the cards. But the cards were face down at the time.

RIGHT TECHNOLOGIES AND THE RIGHT DESIGN

Concept formulation studies, performed by industry several years before the UTTAS contracts were awarded, helped the Army establish performance, survivability, air transport, and other requirements that could be met by industry with a certain amount of stretch. These studies helped the Army create prime item-development specifications for both the UTTAS air vehicle and for the engine that were achievable with reasonable stretch. Although for industry, these studies helped to define the UTTAS configuration broadly as well as to give direction where rotorcraft technologies needed to be improved.

It seemed clear from the parametric studies conducted during the concept formulation phase that a conventional helicopter configuration of the single main rotor with antitorque tail rotor arrangement would best meet the Army's emerging requirements. However, at the time when the Army's requirements were being defined, Sikorsky briefly considered changing to its then emerging coaxial rotor advancing blade concept (ABC). The reason behind this consideration was a feeling that perhaps the only way Sikorsky could win a part of the prototype program was to propose a dramatic speed increase substantially above the Army's stated requirement. The ABC configuration offered this potential, but it was a new concept not yet proven but close to achieving first flight under an Army/NASA/Sikorsky-funded program. This unique high-speed helicopter was the S-69 (XH-59A), pictured in Fig. 29, which ultimately reached a speed of 262 kn.

The company felt that high speed might be a potentially defining capability because of the Army's value of flight speed for the troop assault mission. The way that the Army chose to define its speed requirement, which was a band of performance from 145 to 175 kn rather that a point requirement, suggested that achievement of the minimum value would be essential, but flight speed above the bottom of the band would be rewarded. However, the Army also inferred that pushing or exceeding the high end of the speed band would not be a wise tradeoff if doing so compromised achievement of other important requirements.

Preliminary design studies showed that, although capable of higher speeds, the ABC was not well suited to many Army requirements. In particular the layout of its cabin was compromised by the swashplate controls for the upper rotor. The controls for the upper rotor had to be located below the main gearbox, thus seriously infringing on cabin volume.

Fig. 29   U.S. Army/NASA XH-59 ABC research aircraft first flew July 1973 as a pure helicopter and later as a compound helicopter, pictured above, with two J-60 engines for auxiliary propulsion. (©Igor I. Sikorsky Historical Archives, Inc.)

Further, Sikorsky considered that the technical risk of this concept, given its immaturity at that time, could not be justified. At that point Kuhrt directed that all UTTAS design efforts focus on a conventional single rotor configuration designed around emerging new rotor technologies.

As the company considered many novel design approaches, an assessment was made as to how Sikorsky's competition would likely configure their designs. It was felt that Bell would probably not make a significant departure from its successful UH-1 Huey configuration and would likely rely on its well-developed technology of two-bladed rotors. On the other hand, Boeing Vertol, whose helicopter experience was basically with the tandem rotor configuration, was thought to likely offer a single rotor design. Because it had no significant experience with the single rotor configuration, it was expected that Boeing Vertol would promote the incorporation of new concepts in an attempt to achieve competitive advantage.

Boeing Vertol was expected to capitalize on its publicized involvement with the Messerschmitt-Bolkow-Blohm (MBB) BO-105 helicopter program. That German helicopter featured a fiberglass hingeless main rotor system, which strongly suggested that Boeing Vertol would adopt that technology in its UTTAS proposal. Thus in 1971, Sikorsky believed that its competition would likely be between a two-bladed Bell candidate and a multibladed hingeless rotor Boeing Vertol candidate, each with its own unique strengths and weaknesses.

Sikorsky concentrated its efforts on designing a helicopter around several new home-grown technologies that were just entering the flight-test evaluation phase. These included the new titanium-spar rotor blade with cambered airfoil, highly optimized twist distribution and swept tips. Also being flight tested was an all-new elastomeric main rotor head and a newly invented bearingless tail rotor. In addition, Sikorsky's design featured a canted tail rotor as well as new approaches to achieve high levels of ballistic tolerance and crashworthiness.

All of these technologies and design innovations, described in Chapters 4 and 5, were well matched to the Army's requirements, especially in performance, maneuverability, reliability, and survivability. Sikorsky believed that it could offer a UTTAS design that would be totally responsive to Army requirements while containing technical risk as a result of the many full-scale demonstrations already in process as part of the company's research and development program.

Sikorsky management then set up an internal design competition to stimulate new and novel design solutions for UTTAS and to determine the extent to which the company could comply with Army requirements. This internal competition consisted of two teams each led by a senior advanced design engineer and staffed with experienced specialists dedicated to each team. Lewis Knapp, who was the assistant chief of advanced design activities and who helped create many prior Sikorsky helicopter designs, was chosen to lead one team. The author, who was chief of advanced concepts, was selected to lead the other team. Both teams were located well apart and not in communication with each other. They each received the same set of specifications, including direction to use two T700-GE-700 engines that were expected to be specified in the Army's RFP. The teams had two months to develop their best design.

The team leaders each presented their design solutions for UTTAS to Wes Kuhrt and his senior managers on the same day, 12 August, 1971, which was five months before the Army released its RFP. Senior management selected the design of the team led by the author, as they felt that its features offered the better chance of winning. Both teams benefited by having excellent team members. In particular, an experienced designer and renowned aviation artist, Andrew Whyte on the author's team, helped create the pleasing shape of the Black Hawk in spite of the dimensional constraints imposed by the Army's air transport requirement. His application of "golden rectangle" proportions to cockpit shaping became apparent.

RIGHT TEAM

Several months before the Army released the UTTAS RFP, Sikorsky began to put the people in place to generate its proposal. Two important assignments were made by Kuhrt. First was the assignment of John A. McKenna, who was Sikorsky executive vice president to the full-time position of UTTAS proposal manager. McKenna was tasked to direct all of the activities of the several hundred people assigned to the proposal team and to win the contract. Kuhrt considered that winning UTTAS was the company's single most important challenge and consequently put his best man in charge with the support of Harry Gray, CEO of United Aircraft Corporation.

Most of Sikorsky's internal department managers followed this example. They selected their best people to staff the proposal effort, and as a result a very competent team was put together. Space was created for the co-located proposal team in an open basement area of Sikorsky's Stratford, CT facility, which was guarded to control access.

With the proposal leadership in place, Kuhrt appointed Ken Horsey as vice president and UTTAS program manager to lead the team that

John A. McKenna

would be responsible for all contract work when the company won the UTTAS development contract. That same team prepared the UTTAS proposal and would be responsible to meet the commitments made in that proposal.

Each manager assigned to Sikorsky's UTTAS program team had a direct counterpart in the Army UTTAS program office led at that time by Brigadier General Leo Turner. They were as follows: James E. Campion, cost/schedule manager;

Kenneth E. Horsey

Sam White, systems engineering manager; Ted R. Yazdzik, quality control manager; Joseph M. Konner, configuration manager; Ray D. Leoni, program engineering manager; Anthony L. DeLallo, production manager; William E. Dever, procurement manager; Thomas R. Griffith, logistics support manager; and Charles P. Martin, contract manager.

Both McKenna and Kuhrt were convinced that the personal involvement of Sikorsky department managers was essential to create a winning proposal. Involvement of the "bench," as Harry Jensen, Sikorsky vice president of engineering at the time, referred to functional management, was vital to success. Putting his top engineers on the UTTAS proposal effort reflected Jensen's commitment. Most other organizational departments followed his example of giving local control of the program to people assigned to the program. That change also reflected a cultural shift toward stronger program management. However, responsibility for their work always remained with functional managers.

The Sikorsky UTTAS design was guided by two objectives fundamental to the company's win plan. First was to propose a UTTAS design that was totally responsive to the Army's specification. To reinforce this strategy, Kuhrt directed that each potential deviation to the Army's specification sought by the designers would need the approval of both McKenna and himself.

The mandate of complete responsiveness to the RFP was strengthened by the frequent personal participation of United Aircraft Corporation's senior management led by CEO Harry J. Gray. During Sikorsky's proposal preparation activity in the first quarter of 1972, Gray brought a high-level review team from the corporate office to Sikorsky nearly every Saturday morning to review progress. This process had a profound effect on stimulating creativity to solve difficult specification requirements. No engineer wanted to take the life-threatening position of suggesting a deviation to a difficult Army requirement.

This review process was so successful that only five minor deviations were taken in Sikorsky's proposal, and the Army accepted all five. It could be argued that the emphasis on preparing a responsive proposal is simply good management practice which it clearly is. However in the case of this UTTAS proposal, the persistent reinforcement of this directive at the highest corporate levels made it seem to be an imperative that became ingrained in the designers' thought process as well as life-preservation instinct.

It was no coincidence that the presence of corporate management greatly improved Saturday attendance by the proposal team. On many Saturday mornings, at about nine o'clock, the team would hear the corporate S-58T helicopter carrying the group from UAC headquarters in Hartford to Stratford, Connecticut preparing to land on the company's flight field. The humorous response to the helicopter's arrival was always "well, the we're-here-to-help gang is back in town!"

In spite of the humor, there was great appreciation for the enthusiasm and interest shown by corporate leaders. Seeing and talking to corporate executives, most of whom were never previously seen in real life, were regarded as something special to the proposal team. Their presence clearly confirmed corporate commitment to winning. They impressed the Sikorsky team by not only being informed about the Army's specification and the importance of responsiveness but by even wearing suits and ties on Saturday mornings.

The second key objective to winning was to convince the Army that technical risk was low for all of the technology advancements and unique features of Sikorsky's UTTAS design. Sikorsky invested in full-scale flight demonstrations of every key technology feature incorporated in its UTTAS design to prove that risk was contained. Many flight demonstrations were conducted to prove performance claims of the advanced rotor blades, swept blade tips, elastomeric rotor head, bearingless tail rotor, canted tail rotor, and other advancements that became signature trademarks of Sikorsky's UTTAS design.

The most important aspect of these flight demonstrations was that they were conducted on helicopters that were equal to or larger than the proposed UTTAS design, thereby greatly reducing the possibility of adverse scale effects. The technical data acquired through these flight demonstrations proved to be invaluable in convincing the Army that Sikorsky's UTTAS design could achieve its performance and agility requirements with a high probability of success.

In summary, the road to Sikorsky's UTTAS award was at times not clearly marked. But in the end, the objective and the strategies became focused, and they were continuously reinforced by company and corporate management and fully accepted by the team.

Chapter 3

DESIGNING A WINNER

Sikorsky's UTTAS design began to take shape in mid-1971 using sketchy information about what the Army planned to specify for performance and for many other key attributes that would ultimately shape the configuration. Early designs alternatives, including the coaxial rotor ABC mentioned in Chapter 2, were evaluated along with various arrangements for engines, landing gear, cabin design, fuel system location and many other design options. Finally as the RFP release date drew near, work began to focus on the UTTAS configuration selected from the internal design competition described earlier. The aircraft design and technologies selected were refined in many ways until the Army's RFP was received in January 1972 soon after which the configuration was in effect nailed down. This chapter describes how the design features and innovations evolved during the period leading up to the final proposal submission to the Army in March 1972. Chapter 7 describes the second UTTAS design evolution that started right after flight operations began and ended 17 months later as the final Black Hawk configuration.

The initial design solution selected on 12 August, 1971 following an internal company design competition is shown in Fig. 30. Later, two major changes were made when the Army's plans and requirements were released. The first was a change to a front drive engine from the rear drive shown in these figures following Army guidance, which it planned to develop only a front drive version of the T700-GE-700 engine rather than both drive options as was initially contemplated.

The second major change was to relocate the main rotor plane from the conventional high position to a significantly lower position because of very strict air transport requirements. The prototype YUH-60A was initially built and flown with its rotor located close to the fuselage; however, its rotor was raised early in the test program when severe vibration problems surfaced.

This early design had two cabin doors on each side that rolled up and were stored in the cabin overhead similar to garage doors providing quick ingress/egress for troops as well as more options for weapons mounts. This unique approach to cargo door design was also impacted by the air transport requirement, where height limitation of the C-130 cargo compartment forced

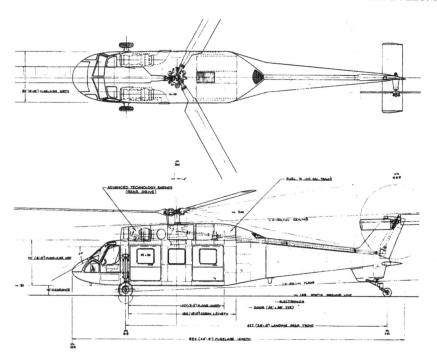

Fig. 30   Three-blade, 50-ft 10-in. diameter elastomeric rotor was the baseline design, but both the rotor diameter and its solidity had to increase when the final performance and maneuverability requirements became known. At this early stage of the UTTAS design, gross weight was estimated to be 14,735 lbs with an empty weight of 9,570 lbs.

a limited UTTAS cabin height that did not permit adequate overhead space in which to accommodate the opened doors.

The initial selection of a three-blade main and two-blade tail rotor was influenced by the Army's design-to-cost target expressed in 1972 dollars. That target was $600,000 excluding government furnished equipment, for the average unit cost of 1107 aircraft based on expected learning curves. When the Army's RFP was received, flight performance and maneuverability were found to be far more demanding than expected. The driving requirements were vertical rate-of-climb performance in hot and high ambient conditions and vertical load factor capability at those same conditions.

To achieve the new performance requirement, the main rotor diameter was increased from 50 ft 10 in. in the August version to 52 ft while the number of blades was increased to four. More importantly, it was found that much improved aerodynamic and structural features for both the main and tail rotors would be needed because Sikorsky designers found that it was not possible to close in on a design solution that would meet Army requirements using state-of-the-art rotor technologies of that era.

The search for the right aerodynamic and structural design parameters for both the main and tail rotors was a major aspect following receipt of the RFP. This effort proved to be especially critical to Sikorsky's winning design. Chapter 4 is devoted to a discussion of the features and rationale for the main and tail rotors that are the foundation of Black Hawk's success. The features finally designed into the UTTAS rotors resulted in the highest rotor efficiencies ever achieved by Sikorsky. They as well resulted in the highest level of structural integrity ever achieved as confirmed by over 20 million blade flight hours since the first UH-60A Black Hawk was delivered to the Army in 1978.

The early design of Fig. 30 was gradually transformed into the UTTAS configuration shown in Fig. 31. The rotor designs were upgraded and increased in size to meet all performance requirements. In addition, the engines were relocated aft of the main rotor because the Army indicated that it planned to develop only a front drive version of the T700 engine. As a result, the two fuel cells were relocated behind the cabin aft bulkhead. This revised aircraft configuration became the baseline for the Sikorsky YUH-60A UTTAS. Many design compromises were made to achieve the Army's requirements

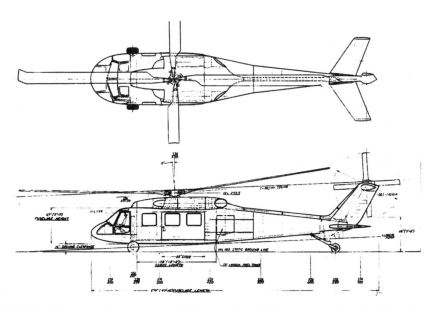

Fig. 31 This general arrangement of November 1971 became the basis of Sikorsky's design submitted in its UTTAS proposal. The 52-ft main rotor now incorporated all of the improved rotor-blade features described in Chapter 4 including swept tips. The tail rotor was the cross-beam bearingless concept canted upward 20 deg, and the engine/ drive system arrangement was finalized using front drive engines. The low rotor position reflects the requirements for air transport in a C-130 without removal of dynamic components.

regarding air transportability. Those requirements rapidly became serious design drivers in terms of rotor size and location as well as airframe configuration. The total effect of the air transport requirements on the UTTAS design was far more substantial than initially expected.

One of Sikorsky's key win strategies was to create a design that would be completely responsive to all requirements spelled out in the Army's prime item development specification (PIDS) [6]. It was understood that the Army intended to select two winners from the proposals expected to be submitted by Bell, Boeing Vertol, and Sikorsky. In effect, the Army had only to select one loser from these three companies, and Sikorsky was determined not to give the Army any reason to reject the company's proposed design.

Sikorsky president Wesley Kuhrt had directed that every proposed deviation to the PIDS must first be approved by the proposal manager and then by himself if necessary. This directive was so effective that when the Sikorsky UTTAS proposal was submitted in March 1972, only five minor deviations were taken to the Army's specification. These deviations had to do with the main rotor's acoustic signature in specific octave bands but not in the overall perceived noise levels and in placement of certain cockpit switches and circuit breaker panels. All five deviations were accepted by the Army's technical evaluators.

UTTAS DESIGN REQUIREMENTS

Of the hundreds of RFP specification requirements, the following four categories had the greatest impact on the size, shape, weight and cost of the UTTAS design: 1) rate-of-climb and maneuver load factor at hot and high conditions, 2) air transport in a C-130 cargo aircraft, 3) cabin provisions for an eleven-man squad plus crew chief/gunner, and 4) survivability during combat and crash conditions. Although flight performance, maneuverability, and cabin provisions were obvious drivers, it later became apparent that the need to air transport UTTAS in U.S. Air Force fixed-wing cargo transports would play a far more dominant role in both aircraft configuration and size than was expected. That requirement was dominant because the specified elapsed times and man-hours to prepare and load UTTAS into the cargo transports were so low that any significant disassembly of UTTAS was effectively prohibited. This meant that other than folding of the rotor blades the rotor and drive systems had to remain intact on the aircraft during air transport unlike air transport of prior-generation helicopters where partial disassembly was common.

Of the three transports specified to carry UTTAS, the C-130 was especially difficult because of its limited cargo compartment height and length dimensions. Although air transport was viewed by designers as the most onerous constraint on the UTTAS configuration, it did force the achievement of a highly efficient lift system in order to minimize rotor diameter so as to be able to squeeze into the C-130. That high lift efficiency provided a positive and lasting effect on the design in terms of performance. However it can be argued that without the C-130 requirements, the Black Hawk helicopter would have ended up with a larger, more versatile cabin. But as a result, it would then have become a larger, heavier, and more expensive helicopter. Although the Army's air transport requirements were fully met in the proposed UTTAS design, its low rotor position (because of the 9 ft C-130 cabin height) turned out to create a major aircraft vibration problem that was discovered during early flight testing. This vibration problem was a potential showstopper for the YUH-60A program, but it was finally solved as discussed in Chapter 7.

The Army's most critical performance and maneuverability requirements were as follows. All had to be achieved at an altitude of 4000 f and ambient temperature of 95°F.

1) Carry 11 fully equipped troops (2640 lb), a crew chief, and two-man flight crew.

2) Operate for 2.3 hour endurance with 20-min fuel reserve.

3) Achieve a vertical climb rate within the band of 450 to 550 ft per minute.

4) Use no more than 95% of engine intermediate rated power.

5) Achieve a cruise speed within the band of 145 to 175 kn.

6) Achieve a yaw rate of 15 deg per second while flying 35 kn sideways.

7) Achieve a pull-up load factor of $1.75g$ within 1 s and hold for 3 s.

8) Achieve a push over load factor of $0.25g$ within 1 s and hold for 2 s.

These were the requirements that basically sized the diameters and blade areas of the main and tail rotors as well as influencing selection of rotor blade aerodynamic parameters including blade twist, airfoil, and tip geometry. The normal parametric process of optimizing rotor design for best weight and performance could not be fully applied because rotor diameter was limited by the C-130's cabin size. Additionally, the Army specified that performance calculations could only use 95% rather than 100% of available intermediate rated power. The 5% margin was intended to allow for engine wear and consequent power degradation in service. At the time of the UTTAS proposal, the intermediate rated power of each engine was 1150 hp at 4000 ft 95°F.

These constraints on rotor size and engine power very strongly indicated the need to achieve the highest possible efficiencies of rotors, transmissions, engine inlets, and exhausts, as well as of electrical and hydraulic power systems. In essence, the UTTAS design challenge was to extract the greatest lift from the smallest diameter main rotor at a given engine power and, at the same time, constrain aircraft weight to be as low as possible. As a result, Sikorsky's focus on efficiency produced the highest rotor lifting efficiency ever achieved to that time in its history. The term used to express rotor efficiency is figure of merit. A figure of merit of 0.75 was achieved for both UTTAS main and tail rotors. That was approximately five points better than prior generation rotor systems. The rotor blade aerodynamic and structural features responsible for that achievement are described in Chapter 4.

In addition to better rotor efficiency, the total aircraft's lift efficiency was helped by use of a tail rotor canted upward 20 deg, as well as by a main transmission design needing only three stages of reduction, thereby reducing power losses. Other less dramatic design innovations in secondary power systems further contributed to higher overall efficiency. The bottom line was that an extra margin of vertical climb rate and cruise speed performance was designed into Sikorsky's UTTAS in spite of the power and size constraints. That focus on improving overall rotor efficiency and reducing power losses has benefited all Black Hawk derivatives and represents the positive legacy of a very difficult air transport requirement whether or not that capability is used.

Other Army requirements, such as service ceiling and single engine performance, generally fell out of meeting the preceding critical list and they ended up better than required. The one exception was the Army's single engine takeoff requirement. That requirement was to hover, in ground effect, with one engine inoperative 5 ft above the ground measured to the bottom of the tires. The Army specified that the payload of 11 troops could be off loaded to permit takeoff, but full fuel still had to be carried. The purpose of this requirement was to be certain that UTTAS would be able to take off and return to base in the event that one of its engines was disabled. Rather than increase rotor size to meet the letter of the requirement, Sikorsky proposed that the 5 ft be reduced to 2 ft in order to take advantage of a stronger ground effect cushion or, alternatively, to offload some fuel to lighten the aircraft. The suggestion to use less than full fuel for calculating in-ground-effect hover altitude was accepted by the Army in consideration of the fact that some fuel must have been consumed while flying to the point in the mission where an engine had become disabled.

The pull-up and push-over flight path was referred to by the Army as the UTTAS maneuver intended to minimize exposure to ground fire when avoiding obstacles during low-level flight. Figure 32 illustrates the profile achievable with both the specified ($0.25g$) and the actual ($0.0g$) load factors compared with the ideal profile.

The Army's survivability requirements for crashworthiness and ballistic tolerance also had major effects on Sikorsky's UTTAS design and are described in Chapter 5. These special requirements, invoked by the Army for the first time in the UTTAS specification, affected such design considerations as landing-gear arrangement, spacing of engines and aircrew, and location of fuel cells. However, the starting point in developing the overall configuration was the troop assault mission itself. Requirements for that primary mission

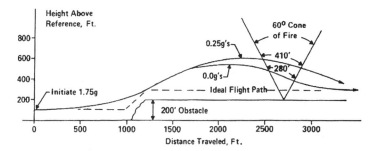

Fig. 32 Dotted line represents the ideal flight path that clears the 200-ft obstacle with the least exposure to potential enemy ground fire. The Army's UTTAS maneuver required a 1.75-*g* pull-up ahead of the obstacle followed by a 0.25-*g* load factor to quickly get back to a low altitude. During flight testing, the UTTAS prototype was able to demonstrate a 0-*g* load factor achieving the contour shown, which reduced exposure to ground fire by almost a third of the distance within the cone of fire.

established cabin design features such as personnel space, cabin door sizing to meet the specified ingress/egress times, provisions for adequate fields of fire for defensive weapons, emergency escape provisions, space for six litters, and other equipment/access requirements. Cabin structural height and width had to be defined early given the influence of the C-130's cargo compartment size on design of the UTTAS transmission, rotor, and landing gear.

Cabin Design

Seat location and rapid access by the 11-man rifle squad and three-man crew was the critical consideration for cabin design. The troop seats contained special energy-absorbing features plus they were wider, at 22 in., than prior troop seats. The design focused on optimizing cabin size, cargo door location and size, gunner window placements, arrangement of troop seats, and provisions for accommodating 4 to 6 liters. The Army's dimensional requirements were that cabin internal height could be no less than 54 in., width at the floor to be at least 82 in., and at least 92 in. at seat level. Cabin length was to be no less than 108 in. and static ground clearance under the cabin a minimum of at least 16 in. Figure 33 shows cabin dimensions.

The cabin seating layout and sliding door sizing finally settled on the arrangement in Fig. 34 for the basic 11-man rifle squad plus the crew chief/ gunner. A full-scale mock-up was built to support the design effort and to confirm that the specified troop ingress and egress times of less than 5 s could be met. The mock-up also helped to refine the gunners' window configuration to verify that the gunners had sufficient freedom of movement to achieve the specified firing angles. Battle-equipped National Guard troops participated in developing the cabin configuration and verifying ingress/egress timing, while

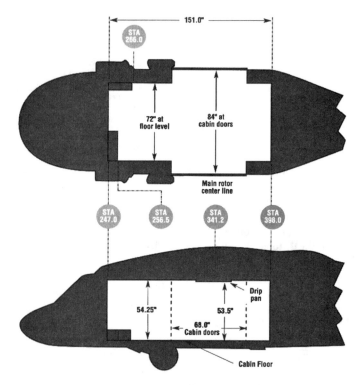

Fig. 33   Minimum internal cabin height of 54 in. was one of the most difficult dimensions to meet because of the C-130's cargo compartment height.

Army soldiers experienced in operating helicopter window-mounted M-60 machine guns helped verify gun deployment procedures and firing angles.

During the initial production, cabin-seating arrangements were further optimized to include high-density troop transport, medical evacuation, and rescue provisions.

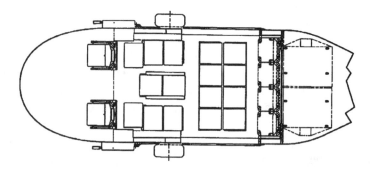

Fig. 34   Higher density seating to transport as many as 20 troops in crash survivable seats.

As speculated earlier, the Black Hawk cabin likely would have been made somewhat larger were it not for the air transport requirements. It was well appreciated that performance margins would easily have allowed a larger complement of troops. However a larger cabin would have degraded performance as a result of corresponding increase in airframe weight and drag. As it was designed, the UH-60 can be categorized as a volume-limited helicopter rather than a performance limited helicopter. All prior Sikorsky models, and indeed most worldwide helicopters, tend to be performance-limited in that utilization of cabin volume is strongly dependent on ambient temperature and/or altitude conditions. As a result, helicopters in general must reduce payload or useful load when operated at higher temperatures and/or altitudes. The Black Hawk helicopter, on the other hand, can transport its full payload under all or most extreme ambient conditions. Indeed, the Army's requirement to transport its full infantry squad under all ambient conditions was among the primary reasons that it developed the Black Hawk.

LANDING-GEAR DESIGN

The Army specified a wheeled-type landing gear for UTTAS, as opposed to the UH-1 skid-type landing gear, but arrangement of the landing gear was left to the bidders. Selection of gear type was a major decision that had to be made early because the landing gear has important structural and operational implications. Sikorsky selected a tail wheel arrangement with the main landing gear forward of the center of gravity and the tail wheel located as far aft as possible. This choice was based largely on crashworthiness considerations as well as its experience with the earlier H-34 (S-58) models seen in Fig. 35.

Fig. 35 Service experience with the Army H-34 led to the tail landing gear arrangement for the Sikorsky YUH-60A. The Boeing Vertol YUH-61A was designed around a nose-wheel arrangement. (©Igor I. Sikorsky Historical Archives, Inc.)

Sikorsky designers were convinced that the tail-wheel configuration was ideally suited to the Army's typical operations in unprepared, sloped, and rough terrain as well as being best from a safety consideration. The tail wheel provides greater safety than a nose-wheel arrangement because it protects the tail rotor and empennage during nose-up landings and particularly during the higher flare angles characteristic of single-engine and autorotational landings, especially in downhill landing situations. In addition, the likelihood of skidding during hard braking is reduced because the resulting nose-down moment loads increase the loads on the main wheels, which contain the braking system. Further, the tail wheel keeps the tail rotor well above the ground making it safer for taxiing over rough, uneven terrain. Crashworthiness of the tail-wheel arrangement is better because the hazard of a nose wheel penetrating into the cockpit is eliminated, as is the possibility of the main landing gear penetrating into the fuel tank area of the fuselage.

The benefits of the UTTAS tail-wheel configuration were inadvertently but dramatically demonstrated during early flight testing at Sikorsky's Stratford Connecticut flight field when a very hard and extreme nose-up landing was made. During autorotation envelope expansion testing to explore maximum flare angle conditions, Sikorsky test pilots experienced a severe wind shear during one of the landing touchdowns. Analysis of the films taken during this event showed that the aircraft was descending at a sink rate speed of 2600 ft/min (43 ft/s) with a forward speed of 70 kn. Because of the wind gusts, the descent rate did not decrease in the flare just prior to ground contact, with the result being that the tail wheel hit the ground at a speed well in excess of the design limit speed of 15 ft/s. The attitude of the aircraft was 29 deg nose up as shown in Fig. 36, which is a frame from the movie of this landing. This movie also shows that the main rotor-blade tips were never closer than 6 ft from the tailcone and were in no danger of striking any part of the airframe, Fig. 37.

The aircraft damage was found to be minor and limited to a blown tail-wheel tire, crushed tail-wheel rim, and buckled stabilator trailing edge. There was no damage to the airframe or tail-wheel strut, and the aircraft was back in flight status the next day. The same impact conditions on helicopters with nose-wheel or skid-type landing-gear arrangements would likely result in extensive aircraft damage and possibly occupant injuries. The Army's long operational experience with the UH-60 series has confirmed the benefits of its tail-wheel design.

AIR TRANSPORT DESIGN

Long-range transporting of helicopters by fixed-wing cargo aircraft had always been a labor-intensive and time-consuming process because of the extent of disassembly required, often including removal of rotors and transmissions. The Army wanted a much faster response time for long-distance

Fig. 36 Benefits of a tail wheel were convincingly proven during a very hard landing of a YUH-60A at an extreme nose-up impact attitude caused by wind shear. The photo shown in this figure is a frame of the landing sequence caught on film. (©Igor I. Sikorsky Historical Archives, Inc.)

deployment for its new helicopters and therefore specified very low elapsed time and man-hours to prepare and load UTTAS into Air Force cargo transports. The time specification was set so low as to effectively preclude any significant disassembly of the helicopter. The design challenge was to find the best ways to fold all rotor blades and tail stabilizers and to retract main

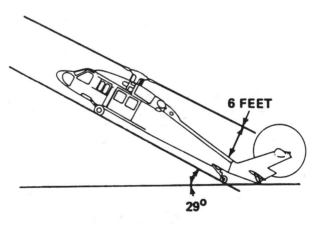

Fig. 37 At the ground impact speed of 43 ft/s, the main blade-tip clearance to the airframe was approximately 6 ft during the near crash landing.

and tail landing gear into a package able to fit in restricted cargo holds of fixed-wing transports of that era.

The C-130 and C-141 were especially challenging because of their limited cabin height of 9 ft minus a 6-in. desired clearance allowance. For the C-130, cabin length from the cockpit bulkhead back to the edge of the loading ramp added to the challenge of making the UTTAS fuselage short enough to fit. The design had to be as compact as possible, which had both the positive and negative ramifications described next.

The Army's air transport requirements were stated in elapsed time and man-hours: 1) preparation for loading elapsed time and man-hours; 1.5 h and 5.0 man-hours; 2) loading and unloading elapsed times, 30 min; 3) preparation for flight elapsed time and man-hours, 2.0 h and 5.0 man-hours; and 4) one UTTAS in the C-130, two in the C-141, and six in the C-5A.

Figure 38 shows a line drawing of UTTAS prototypes inside the cargo compartments of the C-130, C-141, and C-5A, which were the Air Force transports specified by the Army in 1972.

UTTAS was designed to permit manual folding of the main rotor blades and indexing of the tail-rotor blades. Its tail pylon structure and stabilizer were foldable, plus the landing gear was able to be kneeled incrementally as the folded UTTAS was being hauled up or down the C-130's loading ramp.

Although the Army's demanding vertical climb performance argued for a large diameter rotor, Sikorsky pursued two approaches to achieve the required performance with a rotor that would be smaller than that suggested by parametric studies based on prior helicopters. The first was to use new aerodynamic technologies to significantly increase rotor efficiency, whereas the second

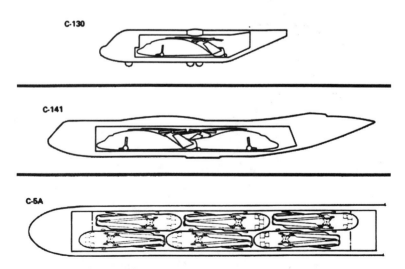

Fig. 38   One, two, and six UTTAS aircraft fit into the C-130, C-141, and C-5A.

approach was to modify the traditional helicopter configuration by use of an upward canted tail rotor. The canted tail rotor helped reduce the main rotor diameter because the lift component of tail rotor thrust reduced the lift required from the main rotor permitting it to be smaller. As explained in Chapter 4, the additional lift produced by canting the tail rotor is actually generated at less power than would be required by the main rotor if it had to produce the same lift increment. This beneficial effect further contributed to higher lift efficiency.

However, the most important benefit of the tail rotor's lift component was to be able to place the center of lift slightly aft of the main rotor, which then allowed the aircraft center of gravity to also be moved aft. This permitted the cockpit nose and cabin to be located several inches further aft thereby shortening the fuselage. Shortening the nose and folding the tail pylon just made UTTAS small enough to fit inside the C-130's cabin. As a result, no compromises to performance were made, and in fact performance was improved because of reduced airframe vertical drag combined with the high lift efficiency of the tail-rotor lift component.

With the length problem solved, squeezing UTTAS within the C-130's cabin height limit proved to be an even greater challenge than its cabin length limitation. Because removing the rotor and main gearbox was not an option, the rotor had to be located as close as physically possible to the fuselage. That was the origin of the "low rotor" configuration that later proved to be an unacceptable design solution.

The low rotor was found to be responsible for creating major vibration problems whose solutions included raising the rotor by 15 in. The initial close proximity of the rotor to the fuselage was intuitively contrary to past practice. This was especially so because the Army's maneuver and agility requirements would suggest increased rather than reduced rotor-blade separation from the fuselage to assure ample blade-tip-to-tailcone clearance during aggressive maneuvering.

The concern over adequacy of blade-tip clearances with the low rotor location prompted selection of a main rotor hinge offset of 15 in. (4.75% of rotor radius) so as to provide sufficient rotor control power without attendant high blade flap motions. Nonetheless, the concern about blade clearance was always in the minds of the designers and especially the UTTAS pilots until the main rotor height was later increased to a position that seemed intuitively correct and, more importantly, to a position that worked. Figure 39 shows one of the flight-test prototypes in a folded configuration ready to be loaded.

ENGINE SELECTION

The Army was convinced that the UTTAS would need not only twin engines but it would need new engines designed around the lessons learned during the Vietnam conflict. New design innovations and technologies would

Fig. 39   YUH-60A prototype with the low rotor and its blades, tail pylon, and stabilizers folded and landing gear kneeled ready for loading aboard the C-130 cargo transport aircraft. (©Igor I. Sikorsky Historical Archives, Inc.)

be needed for the engine as well as for the airframe to meet the challenges of future battlefields. The Army's concept formulation studies conducted by industry during the 1960 decade showed that the UTTAS airframe would need two engines in the 1500-hp category to achieve the Army's stringent performance requirements. Further, the engines would need to be designed to operate efficiently in hot and high ambient conditions, to be highly survivable in the battlefield and to be easily maintained in the field with a standard Army tool kit. In addition, the new engine would be required to operate in sand and dust as well as in conditions of natural icing.

The Army conducted an industry competition during the mid-1960s aimed at awarding two contracts to design and demonstrate engines meeting the UTTAS performance and operational requirements. From that competition, the Army selected General Electric and Pratt and Whitney to build demonstration engines. Both engines were similarly configured with axial low-pressure and centrifugal high-pressure compressors, a cooled axial gas generator turbine and a free turbine with front output shaft.

Following a thorough engine demonstration and evaluation program, the Army selected the General Electric entry that was designated as the T700-GE-700. This engine incorporated many novel features including an integral inlet particle separator for operation in dusty environments, a self-cooled accessory gearbox and bearing lubrication system, and an electronic control unit to manage engine performance. It featured many improvements to reduce field maintenance and to improve access to line replaceable engine modules.

The T700 team, led by Bill Crawford of General Electric, developed this engine to become the world standard in the 1500 to 2500 SHP class. Its outstanding performance and reliability clearly helped the Black Hawk and its derivatives achieve similar status in the class of utility helicopters. The main sections and key components of the T700 engine are illustrated in Fig. 40.

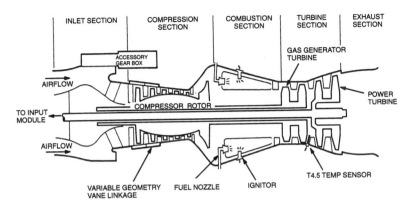

Fig. 40   Airflow and power delivery paths of the T700-GE-700 engine are shown along with the major engine internal components.

PROPULSION SYSTEM DESIGN

With the new T700 engine specified by the Army in its UTTAS request for proposal, the aircraft design challenge was to integrate the engine and all elements of the propulsion system with maximum attention to survivability, maintenance, and with minimum power losses. At Sikorsky, this task fell to a young propulsion engineer, Ken Rosen, who led his team in designing the total propulsion installation including engine inlets and exhausts, engine control system, and the UTTAS fuel system with its crashworthy tanks. His team was also responsible for developing the engine exhaust infrared suppression system, initially designed to reduce IR signature during cruise flight but later redesigned to achieve low IR levels during hover flight conditions. Rosen also led the development of the rotor deicing system that was successfully demonstrated during the Army's flight testing in artificial and natural icing conditions described in Chapter 8.

The engine inlet incorporated many new design features notably in its aerodynamic design and anti-ice system. Specifically, the inlet was designed to produce an installation loss of about 1% with a subsequent power loss of about 2%, coupled with a temperature rise of less than 0.5 F. These challenging values were achieved by transitioning the inlet surface from a kidney shape, which was necessary to physically avoid the gearbox input module and shafting, to the annulus of the engine inlet particle separator (IPS) front frame. The resulting high value of aerodynamic pressure recovery was accomplished by using a gradual cross-sectional area transition that resulted in a continuously accelerating flow to minimize local separation. Additionally, the inlet was separated from the surface of the airframe by about 2 in. through the use of a boat-tail-type lip surface. This was done to avoid swallowing the boundary-layer flow or ice shed from the side surface of the airframe. The inlet was successfully tested using a 1/5-scale-powered model to evaluate inlet pressure drop and distortion.

The inlet anti-ice system posed many design challenges. Notably, the Army preferred to avoid use of electrothermal heating elements, which were then judged to be unreliable. As a result, emphasis was placed on providing inlet ice protection purely by engine bleed air. However, what made this goal more difficult was that GE had used much of this air to anti-ice the considerable surface area of the IPS. This design challenge was made worse by the minimal thermal energy available during a low-power descent when little bled air pressure and mass flow are available. Figure 41 shows the general shape of the inlet assembly as well as the major engine external components.

To solve this problem, a very extensive thermal and supercooled droplet impingement analysis was conducted. The design was required to maintain a minimum metal surface temperature of 40°F down to a 22°F ambient temperature while in an icing condition with a liquid water content of 1.0 g/m^3. The resulting design was a very carefully tailored convective heat exchanger that utilized an inner wall that was separated from the outside inlet surface by a series of local standoff rivets. These rivets produced a heat-exchanger gap, which varied in height to address local heat-transfer flux requirements. The system also incorporated localized impingement heat transfer on the boat-tail lip just described and film heat transfer locally as the bleed air exited from the heat exchanger through locally controlled slots. These slots controlled flow distribution, and total mass flow was choked through the use of control orifices located at the inlet anti-ice control valve.

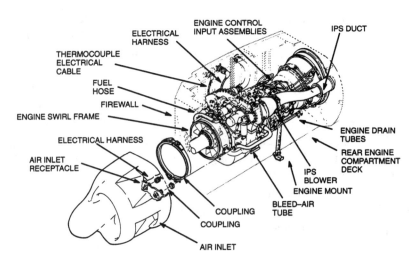

Fig. 41 Kidney-shaped, electrically de-iced engine air inlet was designed with an axis of symmetry such that the left and right side inlets are the same. The IPS components noted in this figure refer to the inlet particle separator system that greatly reduces the amount of sand and dust ingested by the engine.

Although difficult to build, compensation for nonuniform sheet metal shapes in the inlet was provided by a heat-exchanger wall that was designed to be flexible using both composite and rubber materials. The heat-exchanger gap was controlled by the local stand-off rivets, and it remained unchanged because of the internal pressure difference between the inlet bleed air supply manifold and the convective gap. This design was successfully tested in the NASA Glenn Icing Research Tunnel prior to first flight and later during in-flight icing tests. The inlet design has remained unchanged through the production history of the Black Hawk and its derivative models described in this book.

The UTTAS fuel system also proved to be a design challenge because of the aircraft's operational and survivability requirements. The goal was to develop a suction fuel system capable of operating with just about any fuel including the Army's JP-4, which gives off a significant amount of volatile fuel vapor during hot day operation. The gas vapor given off by the fuel at lower pressures and high temperatures tends to cause cavitation in fuel pumps which had to be avoided.

The suction fuel system design incorporated break-away fittings with two crashworthy fuel cells and was designed to operate at less than atmospheric pressure in the supply fuel lines. Sikorsky had pioneered the use of suction systems on the CH-53 helicopter that incorporated a highly successful engine-mounted suction pump. However the company who manufactured the CH-53 pumps declined to participate in the UTTAS program. The result was the use of a marginal engine-provided fuel pump and aircraft fuel system. During the flight development period, fuel pump cavitation occurred in certain flight and ambient conditions. Cavitation was traced to the collection of vapor bubbles in fuel line segments that were essentially horizontal in slope. Repositioning certain lines helped but did not ensure a total solution. Later in the UTTAS program, fuel boost pumps were installed in the tanks, which eliminated any possibility of cavitation and engine shutdown.

DRIVE SYSTEM DESIGN

The integration of the T700 engines with the main and tail-rotor systems proposed for UTTAS was as shown in Fig. 42. The wide separations of engines and the redundant drives for the hydraulic and electrical power systems were a special ballistic survivability consideration. As noted in Chapter 5, UTTAS was the first helicopter to be designed from scratch with battlefield survivability as a requirement as important as flight performance. This resulted in spacing the T700 engines 5 ft apart along with the installation of redundant hydraulic pumps and electrical generators. The objective was to prevent a single ballistic hit from disabling both engines and secondary power systems.

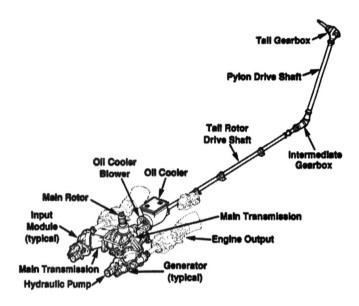

Fig. 42 UTTAS drive system provided wide separation of engines and secondary power systems as well as the ability to interchange left- and right-hand gearbox modules. Both accessory drive modules are interchangeable as well.

All components and installation features were chosen with the intent of minimizing power losses. Keeping power losses at low levels is a normal design objective; however, for the UTTAS design this was especially critical because of the air transport requirement.

Past practice suggested that the overall reduction ratio of the UTTAS main gearbox of approximately 75:1 would require four stages of gearing to achieve this speed reduction ratio. Using new design approaches, John Carlin and his transmission design team were able to create this reduction ratio using just the three gearing stages shown in Fig. 43. That produced not only a lighter gearbox but reduced power losses by approximately 1/2%.

The first-stage gear reduction sets were designed as field replaceable modules with an axis of symmetry chosen to permit either module to be installed on the left or right sides. Both interchangeable modules contain internal oil supply and drain back provisions so as to permit operation in either position where they would be installed upside down. Figure 44 shows the single main module, the two bevel input modules, and the two accessory modules, which are also interchangeable.

The Army's survivability requirement included the capability for the drive system to operate without lubricating oil for at least 30 min. And it required that this capability be demonstrated in a bench test lasting 60 min. The Army specified that the gearboxes operate successfully for 60 min after draining all of the oil in order to provide confidence that the 30-min safe-flight

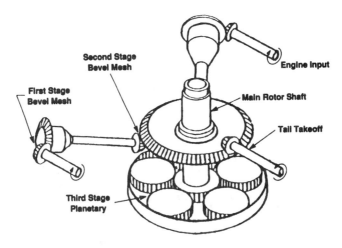

Fig. 43   Two spiral bevel gear stages plus a single five-pinion planetary stage provide the required rotational speed reduction from the T700 engines to the main rotor.

requirement could be met. Unique proprietary design innovations were used to meet this requirement including special materials, bearing internal clearances, and oil dams around critical components. The 60-min test was successfully passed on the first attempt.

The major components attached to the Black Hawk main transmission module are shown in Fig. 45.

The dual generators and hydraulic pumps shown in Fig. 45 were augmented by a third level of redundancy for increased safety and battlefield survival. Installation of a turbine-powered auxiliary power unit (APU) used

Fig. 44   First assembled UTTAS main gearbox is shown without the hydraulic pumps and generators that mount on the pads facing forward. The wide separation of accessories and engine inputs is evident. (©Igor I. Sikorsky Historical Archives, Inc.)

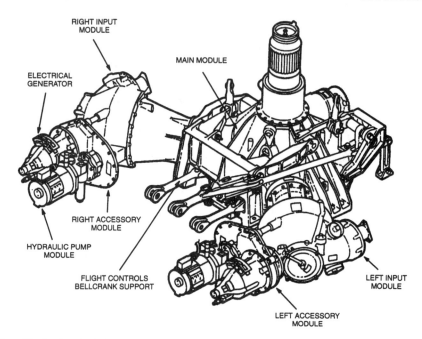

Fig. 45 Both the left- and right-side accessory modules drive identical electrical generators and hydraulic pumps. The left- and right-side input and accessory modules are interchangeable.

for pneumatic starting of the T700 engines provided the opportunity to have another source of electric and hydraulic power when needed.

The APU shown in Fig. 46 drives a generator that can power the aircraft electrical system which also operates an electrically driven hydraulic pump identical to the two pumps shown in Fig. 45. This pump is referred to as the "third chance hydraulic system." It is brought on line automatically in the event that either the primary or secondary hydraulic systems lose pressure. It further permits complete checkout of the aircraft hydraulic and flight control systems prior to starting the main engines.

Sikorsky's proposed UTTAS design featured use of newly developed grease for lubricating the tail and intermediate gearboxes. The motivation for using grease was to reduce the likelihood of losing all lubricant as a result of battlefield damage of the housings. Field maintenance would also benefit. Both gearboxes were intended to be sealed-for-life units such that periodic checks of lubricant levels would no longer be needed.

This proposed grease, MIL-G-83363 (USAF), was formulated specifically for helicopter gearboxes and was successfully bench tested by Sikorsky in S-61 tail and intermediate gearboxes. However during the initial phase of the UTTAS test program, an overtemperature situation occurred in the intermediate gearbox during operation of the ground test vehicle. Detection of this

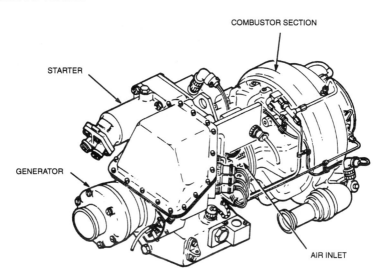

Fig. 46   Auxiliary power unit is started by a hydraulic motor powered by a cabin-mounted hand pump with ignition provided by a small battery. When running, the APU supplies air at high pressure to start the main engines either individually or simultaneously as desired by the pilots.

overtemp was delayed from reaching the gearbox heat sensor because of the insulation provided by the grease itself. In addition, several unexplained instances of gear hardness loss were experienced during bench development testing using this grease. As a result of this experience, the decision was made to quickly change back to traditional oil lubrication.

The application of grease lubrication for gearboxes in that time period is example of a new technology that showed initial promise but that still suffered from unknown unknowns in this case caused either by the grease or by the design of the gearboxes. Fortunately, this significant unknown surfaced during ground testing that was corrected prior to the prototype's first flight.

ARMY EVALUATION OF SIKORSKY'S UTTAS PROPOSAL

Evaluation of industry proposals by the Army took from March through August of 1972 during which hundreds of requests for data and clarifications were asked of the three bidders. These requests were referred to as errors, omissions, and deficiencies or EODs as the Army called them. The EOD process, together with frequent negotiation and meetings at the Army's request, also helped to refine the UTTAS design.

Many design changes were made during the Army evaluation period that improved the proposed design. Chief among them was Sikorsky's increase in main rotor diameter by four inches to 52 ft. 4 in. as a result of aircraft gross weight increases caused by an accumulation of these changes. Later, during Army performance testing at its AEFA facility, the rotor diameter was increased by another 4 in. to its final 52 ft 8 in. to enhance the aircraft's performance capabilities. Both diameter increases were made to preserve performance margins that later proved to be of significant competitive importance. Its larger rotor diameter helped provide the YUH-60A with lifting capability greater than that of its competitor as measured by Army testing.

Sikorsky's UTTAS configuration as it was proposed to the Army on 27 March, 1972 is illustrated in Fig. 47.

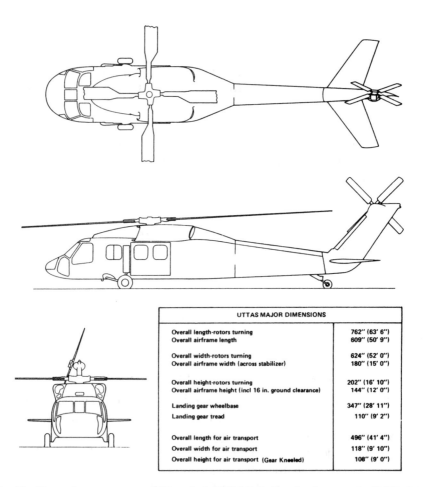

UTTAS MAJOR DIMENSIONS	
Overall length-rotors turning	762" (63' 6")
Overall airframe length	609" (50' 9")
Overall width-rotors turning	624" (52' 0")
Overall airframe width (across stabilizer)	180" (15' 0")
Overall height-rotors turning	202" (16' 10")
Overall airframe height (incl 16 in. ground clearance)	144" (12' 0")
Landing gear wheelbase	347" (28' 11")
Landing gear tread	110" (9' 2")
Overall length for air transport	496" (41' 4")
Overall width for air transport	118" (9' 10")
Overall height for air transport (Gear Kneeled)	108" (9' 0")

Fig. 47   General arrangement of Sikorsky's UTTAS design that became the YUH-60A. U.S. Design Patent 232,168 was awarded to Ray D. Leoni, Woodbridge, CT, and assigned to United Aircraft Corporation. Filed 30 June 1972; patented 23 July, 1974.

SIKORSKY AIRCRAFT
DIVISION OF
UNITED AIRCRAFT CORPORATION
STRATFORD, CONN.

OFFICE OF
DIVISION PRESIDENT

March 27, 1972

I have full confidence in the ability of the Sikorsky UTTAS team to meet this U. S. Army challenge. Never before in our history have we entered a competition better prepared. We thoroughly understand the requirement, we have the technology, and we have the experience. Our UTTAS team is handpicked to respond to Army requirements. I selected Ken Horsey as Vice President, UTTAS Program Manager because of his proven record directing the CH-54A, CH-54B, and S-67 Blackhawk programs. These aircraft currently hold the world's altitude and speed records.

Day by day throughout long months of analysis of Army requirements, preliminary design response, maturing design, and systems coordination, I have personally participated in the Sikorsky UTTAS effort. Now, in the final stages of proposal preparation, I am gratified to observe that our program plans and our final aircraft system design are worthy of Army sponsorship and the Sikorsky tradition of excellence. Our experts in the areas of maintainability, reliability, availability, and logistics have done their jobs well. Full attention has been paid to the vital areas of safety, human factors, and survivability. Above all, we have a design that can be produced in the quantities projected by the Army in confidence that each aircraft will meet all expectations and do so at lowest possible procurement and operational costs. '

Sikorsky Aircraft is proud of its record of no price overruns ever on U. S. Army aircraft programs. We intend to continue that success on the UTTAS program.

Very truly yours,

UNITED AIRCRAFT CORPORATION

Wesley A. Kuhrt

Wesley A. Kuhrt
Division President
SIKORSKY AIRCRAFT DIVISION

Fig. 48   Letter of commitment from Sikorsky Aircraft to the Army Source Selection and Evaluation Board.

The UTTAS proposal for the basic engineering development (BED) phase was delivered to AVSCOM with letters expressing company and corporate commitment to program success, Figs. 48 and 49.

The statement of work for the UTTAS proposal included a wide range of ground and flight-test activities deemed necessary by the Army to ensure flight safety during the course of the prototype aircraft development and government evaluation activities. The total test program was defined in the Airworthiness Qualification Specification. This specification required military qualification for major rotor, propulsion, and transmission systems. However,

Office of the Chairman

United
Aircraft

March 27, 1972

UTTAS Program
Source Selection Evaluation Board
Gentlemen:

We take pride in the Sikorsky Aircraft response to U. S. Army Request for Proposal DAAJ01-72-R-0254(P-40). In the Sikorsky UTTAS, we are submitting the finest design that the Division has ever created. It was configured from the start to meet all Army performance and operational needs.

With the help of the United Aircraft Corporation Scientific Advisory Committee consultants, we have regularly reviewed Sikorsky's work on UTTAS. The program has also been first on the agenda of our monthly Operating Committee meetings and, recently, of our daily United Aircraft Corporation Operating and Policy Committee meetings. We have funded design, fabrication, ground test, and flight test programs to demonstrate technology advancements applicable to our candidate UTTAS design.

We have directed the application of all necessary resources and talents to support the Army's recognized requirement for an advanced utility tactical transport aircraft system, and we have committed ample corporate resources and skills to support Sikorsky Aircraft in meeting these requirements.

The full corporate commitment to UTTAS success that we have made to date will continue throughout our participation in the program.

Very truly yours,

UNITED AIRCRAFT CORPORATION

W. P. Gwinn   H. J. Gray
Chairman   President

Fig. 49   Letter from United Aircraft Corporation, Office of the Chairman, pledging corporate commitment to the UTTAS program.

full qualification of all systems and components was planned by the Army to be deferred to a later phase called the maturity phase, but it would be performed only by the contractor selected for the production award.

The Airworthiness Qualification Specification (AQS) defined the flight-test assignments, instrumentation, and estimated flight hours for each of the three flying prototypes. It also defined the test plans of the two nonflying prototypes, which were the ground test vehicle (GTV) and the static test article (STA). Negotiation of the contents and schedule of the AQS was as intense as it was for the PIDS. This focus on the AQS emphasized the Army's contention that contractor test data would be a vital part of its final selection process and additive to Army data from its government competitive test (GCT) program. The final negotiated AQS and PIDS contained respectively 575 and 437 pages, which became part of the BED phase contract.

After several months of negotiations at AVSCOM, contracts were awarded to Sikorsky and Boeing Vertol in August 1972 for design and development of prototypes designated as the YUH-60A and YUH-61A, respectively. Sikorsky's contract value was $61.9 million [7] and Boeing Vertol's was approximately $91 million (1972 dollars), and the contracts were of the "cost-plus-incentive-fee" type. The Bell proposal, with a two-blade rotor, was said to be close to $150 million. This large difference in contract value led to the conclusion that Sikorsky "*left $30 million on the table*." That observation had some merit as the company's pricing strategy, like its technical strategy, was to provide the Army with no reasons to select Sikorsky as the one loser in this competition.

This $30-million difference created a potential problem for the Army contracting officer because the statements of work and contract deliverables were essentially the same for both contractors. Some attempts were made to encourage Sikorsky to raise its offer in order to achieve comparable pricing for comparable work. However Sikorsky felt comfortable with its pricing and made no upward revisions. The Army did create an internal reserve of approximately $30 million to cover possible development problems. That was a prudent decision in light of the unexpected technical issues that surfaced after first flight and described in Chapter 7.

During the Army's contract award debriefing to Sikorsky on 11 September, 1972, the Army presented its assessed values for the company's proposal. Table 1 compares the Army's RFP requirements with the Army's assessment of Sikorsky's proposed UTTAS design. This chart shows the extent to which Sikorsky's UTTAS design met the Army's requirements in the most critical attribute categories.

At the conclusion of the debriefing to explain why the company was selected to develop one of the two UTTAS prototypes, Brigadier General Turner, UTTAS project manager, stated that Sikorsky came close to becoming a sole source supplier for the prototype program. The Army, however, wanted a competitive program and was convinced that such a program would achieve best value even at its higher cost as compared with a single source development effort.

Best value was indeed ultimately achieved as the intense pressures of that competition forced the development of a far better aircraft than likely would have resulted from a noncompetitive procurement. The competitive pressure during the entire 52-month UTTAS design/development program produced creative and timely solutions as well as encouraging company investments in major supporting R&D areas. The single largest investment in the UTTAS

**Table 1 Comparison of the Army's key technical requirements
with the assessment made by the Army's Source Selection and
Evaluation Board of Sikorsky's UTTAS proposal**

Technical evaluation	Army requirement	Army assessment of Sikorsky's proposal
Performance 4000 ft-95 deg		
Vertical rate of climb	450 to 550 ft/min	550 ft/min
Cruise speed	145 to 175 knots	148 knots
Cruise speed/doors open	80 knots	Over 80 knots
Single engine speed	100 knots	126 knots
Single engine ceiling	5000 ft	7100 ft
Single eng IGE hover wheel ht[a]	5 ft	2 ft
Maneuverability 4000 ft-95 deg		
Pull-up load factor	1.75 g/s	1.75 g/s
Push-over load factor	0.25 g/s	0 g/s
Yaw rate	3 deg/s	3 deg/s
Reliability		
Dyn comp. time between repair	1500 hours	1722 hours
System time between failure	4.0 hours	4.17 hours
Sorties aborted per 1000	26	18
Maintainability (MMH/FH)		
Total system corrective maint.	6.7 man-hours	4.08 man-hours
On aircraft corrective maint.	0.5 man-hours	0.305 man-hours
Scheduled maintenance	1.0 man-hours	0.89 man-hours
Air transport		
Prep for loading-elapsed time	1.5 hours	0.90 hours
Prep for loading	5.0 man-hours	2.1 man-hours
Loading time	30 minutes	22 minutes
Unloading time	30 minutes	22 minutes
Prep for flight-elapsed time	2.0 hours	1.0 hours
Prep for flight	5.0 man-hours	2.76 man-hours

[a]The only area falling short was the wheel height during hover in ground effect with a single engine and with full fuel but no payload.

program was the construction of a fourth company-owned prototype essentially identical to the Army-funded prototypes. Its purpose was to help develop technical improvements that could be applied to the UTTAS program. Both Sikorsky and Boeing Vertol elected to fund construction of their own fully instrumented flying UTTAS prototypes for R&D as well as for marketing demonstration purposes. Sikorsky's company-owned prototype is shown in Fig. 144.

Clearly, the Army's additional expenditures to create a competitive UTTAS program and to buy on the basis of actual aircraft performance was money well spent by the government.

Chapter 4

THE RIGHT ROTORS

The Army's rigorous performance, reliability, and survivability requirements set for UTTAS could not have been met by state-of-the-art technologies typical of operational helicopters of the 1970s era. It was not possible to close in on a design solution for this new helicopter by parametrically scaling existing operational helicopters. Because the Army needed a substantial improvement in operational capabilities, its technical community encouraged a clean sheet of paper for the configuration as well as a new look into the rotorcraft technologies that UTTAS would need. Creative design approaches and new technologies were clearly expected of the bidders, and a degree of risk would inevitably be incurred. As a result, the depth of substantiating data and assessment of technical risk became critical evaluation factors for both the prototype and production proposals.

When taken together, the Army's UTTAS requirements strongly indicated that the main and tail rotors would need the benefits of new technologies more so than any other system. This was not unexpected as rotors have always been the heart and soul of the helicopter. Rotor systems provide the forces and moments to achieve performance and maneuverability, but they also are the dominant causes of vibration, noise, and maintenance. As a result, helicopters are remembered by the unique characteristics of their rotors especially vibration, maneuvering agility, noise, and maintenance burden.

There was no question that Sikorsky's then-current rotor technologies, characterized by all-aluminum blades, symmetrical airfoils, and oil-lubricated articulated rotor heads, would miss the mark for UTTAS by wide margins. The UTTAS helicopter would need significantly advanced blade and rotor head designs to meet its specification requirements. So it was necessary to look at new blade aerodynamic design parameters, new blade structural design and materials, and new rotor head concepts from full articulation to hingeless rigid rotors.

The challenge would be in achieving the right balance between technical risk and technical benefits and then in convincing the Army that the scale was well balanced. Over 30 years of Black Hawk service experience, during which more than five million flight hours have been accumulated, has proven that in fact the right balance was achieved.

None of the new rotor technologies or design approaches incorporated into UTTAS and retained for the Black Hawk needed any fundamental modification, and none became problem areas during the long service of all H-60 models. They performed as planned, and all were incorporated in succeeding Sikorsky models until replaced by newer technologies a quarter-century later. This chapter discusses those rotor innovations most responsible for the Black Hawk's success. Specifically, they were the titanium main rotor blade, elastomeric rotor head, the crossbeam tail rotor, and the canted tail rotor.

TITANIUM/COMPOSITE MAIN ROTOR BLADE

The UTTAS rotor-blade's aerodynamic features were largely responsible for the aircraft's performance, whereas the rotor-blade's structural features provided high reliability and combat survivability. The blade's unique twist distribution, cambered airfoil, and swept tip, combined with the structural properties of its titanium spar, produced a rotor blade well matched to the Army's priorities. Its aerodynamic efficiency, structural integrity, and ballistic tolerance were unmatched by any prior Sikorsky blades and probably unmatched by blades of any other helicopter manufacturer in that era. This rotor's efficiency, expressed as its figure of merit (FM), of 0.75 was the highest known efficiency ever achieved in an operational helicopter. From a structural perspective, its blades have demonstrated unlimited fatigue life, absolute corrosion resistance, and excellent tolerance to 23-mm ballistic damage. These attributes continue to be of world-class standards.

ROTOR BLADE AERODYNAMIC DESIGN

A primary UTTAS design objective was to increase aircraft lift efficiency to as high a value as possible not only because of the Army's tough performance requirements, but also because of the airframe compactness needed for air transport. This led to a search for the right blade aerodynamic features that would increase efficiency 5 to 10% above rotors in production at the time so as to achieve the smallest rotor possible. In addition, the canted tail rotor innovation was also incorporated to further reduce main rotor size and weight.

The search for the right blade was influenced by the blade designer's dilemma succinctly summarized [8] by Sikorsky engineers, Pete Arcidiacono and Bob Zincone:

> The helicopter rotor presents a major challenge to the designer. This is due primarily to the wide variety of conditions under which the rotor blades must operate. These conditions range from the "simple" pure hover operation to the unsteady transonic flow operations of the advancing blade and the unsteady stalled flow operation of the retreating blade in forward flight. Achieving a proper balance between the generally

conflicting design requirements associated with these operating conditions will be a determining factor in the success of a given blade design ..... The extent to which hover efficiency improvements can be made compatible with high speed and maneuver requirements depends greatly on the ability of the designer to develop materials and an aeroelastic configuration which will keep the forward flight characteristics of the rotor under control.

When the UTTAS program began in the early 1970s, Sikorsky was starting to develop what could be called "second generation" main rotor aerodynamics. Earlier rotor blades typically used symmetrical airfoils, principally NACA 0012, to keep pitching moments low so as to hold control loads and spar torsional deflection to low levels. Earlier blades had a negative twist of from six to eight degrees to improve hover performance, but twist was limited by blade structural constraints imposed by forward flight loads. Because the twist was created by yielding the aluminum spars in torsion after they were machined, its distribution was linear along the span. Production rotor blades at that time were constructed of extruded aluminum spars with bonded aluminum pockets to complete the airfoil shape aft of the spar and with no special tip cap design. Hover efficiencies of those earlier generation rotors were in the range of an FM of 0.65 to 0.70. That rotor-blade technology was used for essentially all Sikorsky production helicopters until the advent of titanium spars, new airfoils, and swept blade tips.

Sikorsky's first fielding of a production rotor with an appreciably higher FM was in the late 1960s for the Army CH-54B Heavy Lift "Flying Crane" helicopter. This model was the first to embody both a nonlinear twist as well as a high twist compared with contemporary blades. The CH-54B's blades had an equivalent linear twist of minus 14 deg compared to minus 6 deg for the CH-53 blades. Because of this twist increase, the CH-54B rotor achieved a maximum FM of 0.73, considerably better than the CH-53's FM of 0.69 that had a lower twist. However the CH-54B was limited in flight speed to only 110 kn because its high twist significantly increased vibratory stresses in its aluminum spar. But because the CH-54B mission was to carry large external loads, the speed compromise was acceptable to the Army. In the case of UTTAS, high twist was essential for vertical performance, but the speed compromise was not acceptable because the Army required cruise speeds in the 150-kn range. This led to selection of titanium for the UTTAS spar primarily because of its much superior strain allowable and corrosion resistance properties compared with aluminum.

Although the CH-54B rotor developed a maximum FM of 0.73, it did so with six blades. When the CH-54B blades were tested on a special four-blade rotor head, to simulate the UTTAS rotor, its FM dropped to 0.71, other factors being the same. That value was far below the target set for UTTAS. The surprising reduction in FM was caused either by the less uniform wake generated by fewer blades or by the greater circumferential distance between each tip of a four-blade rotor compared with a six-blade rotor. The increased distance between tips placed the blade tips in a different position in the tip vortex generated by the preceding blade. Bridging the gap between this lower FM of 0.71 and the 0.75 goal set for the UTTAS rotor was a major challenge that was ultimately overcome by good engineering work.

A Sikorsky aerodynamicist assigned to the UTTAS program was Donald Jepson for whom it was said, "had an almost singular passion for improving rotor aerodynamic efficiency." Jepson, together with Jack Landgrebe from the United Aircraft Research Laboratories, focused on understanding the performance effects of vortex operation and on finding the right blade-tip geometry to operate efficiently in the tip vortex region of the preceding blade. He conducted many experiments on the whirl stand with full-scale CH-53 blades to evaluate a variety of blade-tip designs with three, four, five, and six blade rotors.

His experimentation resulted in a unique twist geometry in the tip region characterized by an incidence change, or kick-down, at around 90% blade span. This tip twist configuration, together with an inboard linear twist of minus 18 deg, resulting in an equivalent linear twist of minus 16.4 deg, was selected for the UTTAS blade. Figure 50 shows that twist distribution. As can be seen, twist in the outer 4% of span actually reverses direction and washes out several degrees of equivalent linear twist.

Jepson's reasoning behind this unique shape for the UTTAS blades, referred to as the "beta" tip, was that hover performance would improve because the extreme tip passed outboard of the preceding blade-tip vortex

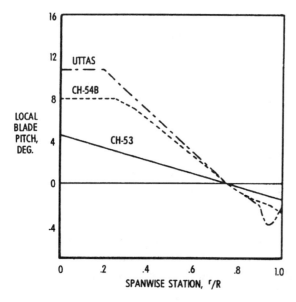

Fig. 50 Equivalent linear twist distribution of the UTTAS and Black Hawk main rotor blade is 16.4 deg, greater than any prior Sikorsky blade.

path. The adverse effect of the vortex interference could then be reduced and lift in the tip sections increased. In forward flight, the twist reversal would reduce the advancing side negative tip loading, which would again improve forward flight efficiency. Several years later advanced computer codes confirmed the validity of Jepson's intuition. The high twist together with the Beta tip twist configuration made the greatest contribution to closing the gap toward an FM of 0.75, but the goal of 0.75 was not yet reached. Two additional aerodynamic design features helped achieve that goal: the cambered airfoil design and the aft swept tip.

The airfoil first selected for the full span of the UTTAS main rotor blade was the cambered SC-1095, designed by Sikorsky to improve performance over a wide range of operating conditions. It helps hover performance in two ways: by generating greater lift because of its higher maximum lift coefficient and by increasing the built-in blade negative twist because of its negative pitching moment. Approximately 1.5 deg of additional twist is generated adding to the built-in twist just shown, which adds another incremental improvement to FM. Sikorsky first used this airfoil on its improved rotor blade (IRB) program for the CH-53D, reviewed in the following sections. During that R&D program, the manufacturing technologies needed to produce the titanium spar were developed. The significant performance improvements of the CH-53D equipped with the improved rotor blades in all flight modes, including maneuvering, made it a logical choice for the UTTAS blade. Measured performance data from whirl stand and flight testing were very timely for the UTTAS program because first flight of the IRB occurred in September 1971 just four months before the Army released its RFP.

The final incremental improvement to FM was provided by the 20-deg aft sweep of the outer 5% of span. The swept-tip feature came from a Black Hawk namesake experimental helicopter that also began its flight testing about the time that the UTTAS program got under way.

That helicopter, designated as the model S-67, was a prototype of an armed attack helicopter built using dynamic components from the company's S-61 model. This prototype was intended to be a candidate to replace the unsuccessful Lockheed AH-56 Cheyenne gunship program that was terminated in 1969. The S-67 was designed to reach a speed of 180 kn using the existing S-61 rotor partially unloaded by the small wing seen in Fig. 51. The design team that created this high-performance helicopter was led by Aristides (Al) Albert, one of Sikorsky's most competent designers, while the program was managed by Ken Horsey who later became the UTTAS program manager. Only one prototype was made by the company, which was designed, built, and flown within one year from go-ahead. As chance would have it, Sikorsky named the S-67 "Blackhawk" many years before the Army selected the name "Black Hawk" for UTTAS. But the new model did in fact have a genetic relationship to the earlier Blackhawk in terms of blade-tip geometry.

Fig. 51 Black Hawk's 20-deg swept tip came from Sikorsky's prototype S-67 Black-hawk. This tip geometry auto-matically changes blade twist during hover and cruise flight in a direction to increase efficiency as a result of the tip's air loads in relation to the blade's torsional elastic axis. (©Igor I. Sikorsky Historical Archives, Inc.)

An aft swept tip was installed on the S-67 because of concern about the adverse effects of high advancing side Mach numbers. The 20-deg swept tip was intended to avoid a phenomenon called submultiple oscillating track (SMOT) that produced variations in blade track at high tip Mach numbers. It functioned as intended on the S-67, but it had other benefits that were of great interest to the UTTAS rotor design. Tip-generated noise was reduced, but more importantly the forces produced at the tip generated moments about the blade's elastic axis. Because of the load offset caused by sweep, illustrated in Fig. 52, these moments resulted in a change in blade twist. This twist change for the UTTAS blade amounted to about one degree negative in hover that further benefited FM.

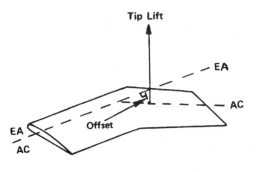

Fig. 52 Forces applied to the swept tip behind its elastic axis produce spar torsional moments to change blade.

The benefits of high twist in hovering flight were well accepted. However prior to the advent of titanium spars, the structural concerns of high twist in cruise flight, including vibratory stress levels and aeroelastic behavior, had to be reconciled.

As mentioned earlier, the higher vibratory stresses in forward flight produced by high twist had limited the amount of twist that could be used on spars made of aluminum because of its fatigue strength, or more accurately, its strain allowable properties. For the UTTAS blade, the concerns about stress levels with high twist and during high-speed flight were resolved by the use of titanium. The vibratory strain allowable properties of titanium are twice those of aluminum, which permitted use of high twist without incurring any fatigue damage throughout the full flight envelope. The absence of any fatigue crack problems on Black Hawk blades after over 20 million blade flight hours is the best confirmation that titanium was the optimum choice for the spar material at the time.

The challenge of controlling the rotor's characteristics in forward flight while striving to achieve maximum hover performance was addressed in the UTTAS blade by several design features. Its titanium spar provided the large increase in strain allowables to cope with the higher stresses generated by high twist during forward flight. Figures 53 and 54 illustrate two important issues of spar material selection [9]. The first is the influence of twist and speed on vibratory flatwise bending strain and the need for high material strain allowables.

Materials such as titanium, graphite, and fiberglass are seen to be good candidates from the strain allowable standpoint. Figure 54, which is based on 12% airfoil thickness, shows that aluminum can achieve a high FM with high twist, or alternatively, a high speed with low twist. Titanium is able to

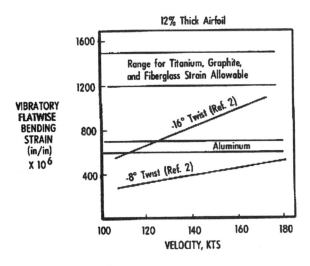

Fig. 53 Titanium's superior strain allowables are needed to withstand the strains of highly twisted blades operating at high flight speeds.

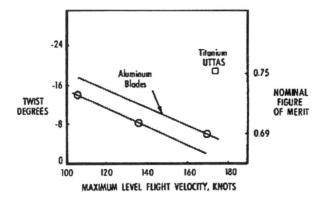

Fig. 54 Aluminum blades can achieve high FM with high twist at low speed or at high speed with low twist but titanium achieves both.

achieve both requirements simultaneously. The thinner SC1095 airfoil increases structural margins further because flatwise strains are reduced by about 20%.

In addition to providing higher strain allowables, titanium offered greater spar torsional stiffness, which is an important design consideration. Because rotor blades are high-aspect-ratio structures, which experience little torsional stiffening caused by centrifugal effects, applied torsional moments, if not properly controlled, can lead to large torsional responses resulting in vibrations or at worst, instability. The high torsional stiffness of the closed-tube UTTAS titanium spar prevents unstable behavior. In addition, the swept tip was found to be effective in controlling the torsional response and in stabilizing the advancing tip.

The final aerodynamic configuration of the UTTAS blade is illustrated in Fig. 55. Also shown is the modification of the SC-1095 airfoil in the outboard region, described in Chapter 7, added during flight testing to improve maneuvering load factor. The initial airfoil shape at the time of UTTAS first flight was the SC-1095 from root to tip. Early into the flight-test program,

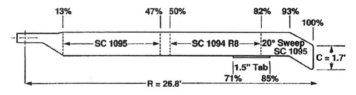

Fig. 55 Final UTTAS main rotor-blade aerodynamic design is shown here with its airfoil distribution as noted. Chapter 7 explains the need for the leading edge contour change that became identified as the R8 modification.

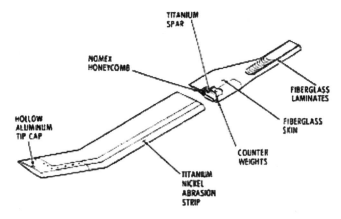

Fig. 56   Main components of the Black Hawk main rotor blade.

the outboard airfoil was modified to the SC-1094 R8. Figure 56 shows the physical configuration and major components of this blade.

TITANIUM SPAR RATIONALE AND CHALLENGE

The use of titanium for rotor and transmission components at Sikorsky began in the late 1950s, largely because of the leadership of its then engineering vice president, Harry T. Jensen. The American Helicopter Society's Reliability award was named in Jensen's honor in recognition of his work in establishing safe-life and fail-safe design criteria.

Jensen recognized early that titanium's properties were an excellent match to the vibratory load environment of helicopter rotor and transmission components. His pioneering work in developing an understanding of titanium's fatigue strength resulted in creation of the database that enabled the changeover from typically steel components to titanium with high confidence. Titanium resulted in significantly increased fatigue lives, reduced component weights, and elimination of corrosion that often became the origin of fatigue cracks with steel and aluminum parts.

Capitalizing on the attributes of titanium for blade spars was an evolutionary next step that began 10 years later, in the late 1960s. Sikorsky's first attempt at building spars from titanium was for its experimental coaxial rotor helicopter named the ABC for advancing blade concept. Immediately following the ABC, and just prior to start of the UTTAS program, the technology of applying titanium to blade spars matured rapidly with the development of the improved rotor blade for the CH-53D Marine Corps transport helicopter.

Of the many properties of titanium, the one of greatest relevance to blade spars of articulated rotors is its high fatigue strain allowable. The benefits of this property become greater as design cruise speeds increase, and titanium's high fatigue strain allowable becomes more relevant than its more familiar fatigue stress allowable. Fatigue strain allowable is the more important structural characteristic because of the mechanisms that produce vibratory blade stresses. As explained in the prior reference,

> The vibratory radii of curvature of a critical blade station is relatively insensitive to the flexural stiffness of the spar in the flatwise direction. As a result, for all things being equal the articulated rotor blade is a constant vibratory strain system. The reason for this is the dominant role centrifugal stiffening plays in establishing the flexural movement of blade sections [9].

Clearly, materials having high strain allowables are the preferred spar materials. Titanium has a fatigue strain allowable double that of 6061 aluminum used in prior Sikorsky rotor blades. This characteristic, together with its strength-to-weight ratio and corrosion resistance, convinced Sikorsky to undertake the challenge of building a titanium spar blade. That challenge was not only to build experimental quantities but to develop the manufacturing processes for volume production as well with emphasis on controlling variability of the processes.

TITANIUM SPAR MANUFACTURING TECHNOLOGY

The titanium-spar rotor blade is of special interest because major advancements in manufacturing technology had to be made in order to realize the benefits in performance, structural integrity, and where the benefits of advanced design innovations required creation of equally advanced tooling and manufacturing solutions. New processes had to be created for building titanium spars in a high-quality, repetitive manner and at acceptable cost in order to justify its use in a high-volume program.

By the early 1970s these processes were finally developed by Sikorsky and have been used to produce titanium rotor blades for Sikorsky's S-65, S-70 and S-76 helicopters. Over 20,000 titanium blades have been produced for these helicopters and all by the same basic processes.

Development of the methods to build a titanium spar began with the ABC coaxial rotor designed by Sikorsky in the 1965 time frame. The idea behind this concept was to achieve higher speeds by forcing the advancing blades of each rotor to carry a greater share of lift thereby delaying the limitation of retreating blade stall. To do this required the bending moment of one rotor to be balanced by that of the other rotor, which suggested use of very rigid rotors more like propellers than helicopter rotors. Close spacing of the two rotors was needed to reduce drag; therefore, the blades had to be very stiff in the flatwise direction. Titanium's strength and modulus made it a logical choice in order to allow close spacing of the two counter-rotating rotors at reasonable weight. Being a new and novel concept, the ABC helicopter

Fig. 57 Sikorsky's first use of titanium blade spars was for the high speed S-69 ABC coaxial rotor concept. Its spars were machined from long titanium extrusions, which was a process acceptable for experimental blades but far too costly for production. (©Igor I. Sikorsky Historical Archives, Inc.)

had many technical challenges, not the least of which was how to build its titanium blades.

Construction of the ABC experimental aircraft, the XH-59A, shown in Figure 57, was funded by several U.S. government agencies along with Sikorsky. Its rotor underwent performance testing in 1970 in the Ames Research Center Wind Tunnel, and the aircraft first flew in 1973.

The blades for the ABC's 40-ft-diam coaxial rotor were made from 17-ft-long 6AL-4V titanium extrusions, machined both inside and out to produce tapered diameter and tapered wall thickness tubes. The spar tubes were then hot formed into an elliptical shape, while twisted, in ceramic hot-forming dies. The end results were spars of very precise airfoils and accurate twist distributions but whose machining operations were costly and very wasteful of titanium. This hot-forming operation was a success that was to be adopted for all subsequent titanium spars. But finding a significantly less expensive way to produce the titanium pre-forms, ready to be hot formed, became the goal.

That goal was achieved by the manufacturing technology developed during the R&D program to develop the new high performance IRB blade for the CH-53D. The performance objectives for that program included the capability for the CH-53D to carry an increase of 3500 lb in payload and to achieve a cruise speed of 180 kn at 38,000 lb gross weight without incurring fatigue damage to the blades. Titanium was selected as the spar material for the reasons already noted. In May 1970 Sikorsky management committed R&D funding to begin work on the IRB for the CH-53D's 72-ft-diam main rotor, in advance of NAVAIR support. First flight of the IRB titanium blades took place in September 1971, which was almost one year before the Army awarded contracts for its UTTAS prototype program. Results of the flight evaluation showed that the aerodynamic and structural performance was better than anticipated with gross weights flown up to 42,000 lb at maximum power with spar stress still within the endurance limits of titanium. The outstanding performance of the IRB proved its aerodynamic design features and its use of titanium as well as the processes developed to build the blades. As a result, data from the IRB program were very timely in justifying Sikorsky's UTTAS design features and material selection to the Army. Three Sikorsky engineers most responsible for the success of the IRB program are pictured in Figure 58. Their accomplishments were recognized by the United Aircraft Corporation.

The improved rotor blade program, despite its understated title, was an enormous success both in demonstrating the benefits of its aerodynamic innovations and in developing and demonstrating an acceptable manufacturing process. The blades for the CH-53D's rotor required titanium spars 33 ft long, and the challenge was to find a method that would economically produce a pre-form of this length ready to be hot formed to the desired shape and twist. Initially, extrusions were used that weighed 5400 lb each and machined down to 200 lb to build eight prototype blades while the search for an acceptable process was underway [10]. These spar extrusions were successfully extruded to the full 33 ft length after the right thermomechanical working processes were developed to achieve acceptable grain microstructure. Initial attempts to extrude titanium to this length were failures. Although never considered for production blades, these extrusions were necessary to be able to quickly manufacture experimental blades while several potential production processes were being explored.

Three other methods for producing long hollow titanium tubes were tried. Cold tube reducing by a rolling process was not successful because of surface

Fig. 58   Standing with the first completed IRB blade are Bill Paul, left, who convinced Sikorsky and NAVAIR management of the potential benefits of this new technology with Bob Zincone who successfully directed the design efforts and Les Burroughs who directed creation of manufacturing process suitable for producing titanium spars. The three were awarded United Aircraft Corporation's George Meade Gold Metal Award for outstanding achievement in developing the titanium/composite rotor blade. (©Igor I. Sikorsky Historical Archives, Inc.)

Fig. 59 Titanium flat sheet is cold formed into open tubes in Sikorsky's 2000-ton hydraulic press. (©Igor I. Sikorsky Historical Archives, Inc.)

tears created during the initial rolling passes. Hot tube reducing produced better results, but surface laps and tears were not eliminated. The third method was successful and was adopted for manufacture of all Sikorsky titanium spars. This process starts with cold forming an annealed flat titanium sheet using the 40-ft 2000-ton hydraulic press shown in Fig. 59.

Cold forming is performed in stages, as shown in Fig. 60, ending as an open tube ready for plasma arc welding.

The C-section tube is clamped and plasma arc welded along its entire length in a single welding pass producing a closed tube. Figure 61 illustrates the capstan weld mill with an open tube ready to be welded in a controlled atmosphere.

The welded tube is then hot creep formed into an elliptical section in heated, ceramic matched dies during which the high twist is formed. Figure 62 is a close-up of the ceramic die cavity in which the welded tube is

Fig. 60 Four successive steps in cold-forming titanium sheet to the open tube shown uppermost, which is ready to be welded to a closed shape. (©Igor I. Sikorsky Historical Archives, Inc.)

Fig. 61 Cold-formed open tube is plasma arc welded in an inert atmosphere. (©Igor I. Sikorsky Historical Archives, Inc.)

inserted with the weld line positioned in a low-stress area. Prior to bonding the skin assemblies, the spar is shot peened and subjected to a Picatinny process surface pretreatment [11].

The titanium-spar building process outlined has been well refined and used to build thousands of rotor blades for the Sikorsky S-70, CH-53D/E, and S-76 models.

The aerodynamic design features of the Black Hawk rotor blade were essential to achieving the Army's performance requirements while its titanium spar provided the structural basis for these features. After over a quarter-century of service experience including combat, during which over 20 million blade flight hours have been accumulated, every performance, fatigue life, and ballistic tolerance claim of the titanium/composite blade has been met.

Fig. 62 Heated ceramic dies, shown prior to loading a welded tube, hot form the round titanium spar tube into an airfoil shape with twist formed at the same time. Internal gas pressure keeps the spar from collapsing in its heated condition. (©Igor I. Sikorsky Historical Archives, Inc.)

ELASTOMERIC MAIN ROTOR HEAD

The commonly held perception of earlier generation rotor systems was that they were complex, unreliable, maintenance intensive, and vulnerable to combat damage. Generally that was a correct perception. Low maintenance or long time between overhauls periods never distinguished earlier rotors of the fully articulated configuration, typical of larger multiblade helicopters. Rotors in general tended to drive the helicopter's maintenance burden, and all heavy maintenance of rotors of necessity had to be done at the depot level. But the technology of the elastomeric bearing has changed perceptions by achieving a breakthrough in rotor design of the UTTAS rotor head. That design not only met the low maintenance and high reliability requirements, but it also achieved very high ballistic survivability as well as compactness needed for air transport. It also permits on-aircraft replacement of all bearings and components eliminating the need for depot overhaul.

In selecting the UTTAS rotor design, consideration was given to the likely rotor design approach that competition would offer. It was Sikorsky's assessment that Boeing Vertol would likely base its rotor design on the rigid-rotor concept recently developed by the German company MBB for its BO-105 helicopter. That was a publicized relationship that stressed the virtues of the BO-105 rotor system in terms of high control power and simplicity. On the surface the rigid rotor seemed like a good candidate to meet the Army's most critical requirements. The rigid rotor's inherently high control power was well suited to the maneuver requirements while its compactness helped the overall air transport solution. Furthermore, the rigid rotor's elimination of bearings requiring lubrication offered important maintenance advantages for UTTAS.

However attractive the rigid-rotor concept appeared on the surface, Sikorsky was not convinced that an adequate knowledge base existed at that time with regard to the aeroelastic and structural considerations of the rigid rotor when applied to a main-rotor application. At the same time, Sikorsky in conjunction with the United Aircraft Research Laboratories was developing the bearingless crossbeam tail rotor for UTTAS described in this chapter. In developing the crossbeam tail rotor, a good understanding was gained regarding the aeroelastic stability of bearingless rotors as well as the best material selection. However, extrapolating that understanding to the main rotor with its far greater blade motion requirements as well as far more influential impact on aircraft vibrations was thought by the company to be too great a risk for the UTTAS program.

The most important factor behind Sikorsky's design choice of the UTTAS rotor was the emergence of elastomeric bearing technology in the right size range. That technology had the promise of totally eliminating the maintenance burden historically associated with articulated rotors caused by the lubrication of conventional bearings. It also offered a degree of design flexibility not achievable with earlier articulated rotors that used metallic antifriction bearings to provide blade flap, lag, and pitch degrees of freedom.

The breakthrough in elastomeric bearing technology came from a U.S. Navy-sponsored program whose objective was a large-scale demonstration of elastomeric bearings applied to helicopter main rotors. The success of this program placed new and compelling design options on the table for the UTTAS rotor design. In 1970, only two years before the Army released its RFP for UTTAS, the Navy and Sikorsky began development of a new fully articulated main rotor head for the Marine Corps CH-53D helicopter. That new rotor head was based on using elastomeric bearings to completely replace the antifriction bearings used in this helicopter up to that time.

The objective of the Navy program was to greatly reduce maintenance of the CH-53D main rotor while improving its reliability. All lubrication requirements were to be eliminated in order to finally solve the persistent lubricant leakage problem that was typical of oil-lubricated bearings. This elastomeric rotor went through extensive bench and whirl testing and achieved first flight in the CH-53D in early 1972 almost at the exact time when industry was preparing its UTTAS proposals.

The elastomeric bearings, designed to react the CH-53D's centrifugal force of 83,000 lb, were so successful that Sikorsky made the decision to apply that technology to UTTAS whose centrifugal force was 70,000 lb, well within the value demonstrated.

The Army's maneuverability requirements for UTTAS were achieved by locating the rotor's virtual flap hinge 15 in. from the centerline of rotation. That offset, equivalent to 4.7% of rotor radius, was selected to produce the control power needed to generate required aircraft maneuvering rates. The maneuver capability achieved met all requirements and is said by pilots to provide exhilarating pitch and roll agility.

After selecting the elastomeric bearing approach, design of the main rotor head focused on achieving substantial improvements in reliability, maintainability, and ballistic tolerance over prior Sikorsky rotors. The air transport requirement mandated reducing rotor height, and several bearing arrangements were studied to achieve as compact a rotor head as possible. What evolved was a design that made innovative use of elastomeric bearings to create a rotor that more resembles a propeller hub than a helicopter rotor as illustrated in Fig. 63.

In the CH-53D elastomeric rotor, a single spherical bearing provides all blade motions including pitch change, flap, and lag motions. Pitch change requires the largest torsional deflection of the bearing. However in the UTTAS rotor, the pitch motion is split between two elastomeric bearings, one spherical and one cylindrical. The spherical unit accommodates all blade flap and lag motion while the combination of this spherical bearing together with the

Fig. 63 UTTAS compact propeller-shaped rotor head with internal elastomeric bearings. Its titanium hub provides ballistic and environmental protection to the elastomeric elements. (©Igor I. Sikorsky Historical Archives, Inc.)

cylindrical bearing, acting as two torsional springs in series, provides all pitch change motion.

This unique bearing configuration is shown in Fig. 64. The objective of this bearing arrangement was to shrink the size of the spherical bearing so that both bearings could be fitted within a rotor hub, thereby making the rotor head more compact and aerodynamically cleaner. Figure 65 shows the major components of the Black Hawk main rotor assembly as installed on the aircraft.

That design also helped protect the bearings from ballistic damage, although they were later found to be highly tolerant of projectile penetration by live-fire testing to 23-mm armor-piercing incendiary (API). Its unique design shows the freedom that the elastomeric concept can give designers in tailoring the rotor design to achieve more than the traditional helicopter design requirements.

The development history of the UTTAS elastomeric rotor has been well described by its Sikorsky designer Robert Rybicki [12]. In his referenced paper he describes the unexpected technical as well as manufacturing problems experienced during that development. Both the design and material of the metal shims that separate the rubber laminations were found to have a profound effect on bearing life. The reason is that shim design not only affects

Fig. 64 UTTAS spindle assembly showing the black cylindrical bearing for pitch change on the far left and the spherical bearing further outboard to the right for flap and lag motion as well as pitch change. (©Igor I. Sikorsky Historical Archives, Inc.)

shim stresses but also the stresses in the elastomer material. This was first revealed in a dramatic bearing failure that occurred on Sikorsky's hub and shaft test fixture that subjects an entire rotor assembly to a range of forces and motions far greater than could be applied in flight operation. During testing in this fixture, and fortunately before first flight of a UTTAS prototype, one of the spherical elastomeric bearings experienced a total collapse caused by a shim fatigue failure. This failure was so severe that it threatened Sikorsky's UTTAS program because the company was totally committed to its elastomeric rotor. Through good engineering, the failure was traced to the very high amplitude of blade flapping simulated in this test fixture. That flapping produced shim vibratory bending stresses which were higher than the initial stainless-steel alloy was capable of withstanding. An alloy having greater fatigue strength was substituted, which completely solved the problem in time for first flight.

It was found that unique loading conditions, such as static ground conditions, had a strong effect on the life of elastomeric bearings. Static droop stop loads, with the aircraft parked on the flight field, can produce elastomer separation because of hydrostatic tension applied to the unloaded side of the bearing. Similarly, asymmetric loads applied during automatic blade folding as with the SH-60 Seahawk must be considered during bearing design. In addition, ground conditions of loading such as blade start-up and shutdown

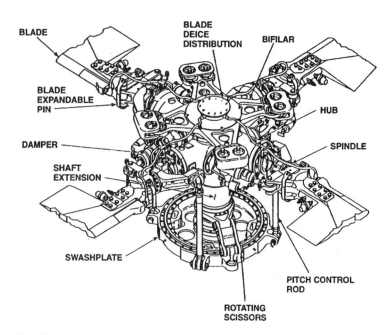

Fig. 65   Major external components of the Black Hawk main rotor head.

loads, on-off centrifugal loads, and droop stop loading have been found to be more important than earlier expected.

The application of elastomeric bearings to helicopters has made an enormous improvement in all rotor head attributes especially in reliability and maintainability, the two areas where improvements were most needed. The fact that rubber bearings do not need any form of lubrication while they are uniquely suited to the small-amplitude oscillatory motions associated with rotor-blade articulation have made elastomeric bearings ideally suited to helicopters. Not only has maintenance been nearly eliminated, but also replacement of the elastomeric bearings is now field level task using common tools. With prior-generation antifriction bearing rotors the only way to replace failed bearings was by removing the entire rotor and sending it back to depot for complete teardown and overhaul. However with the Black Hawk rotor, a single failed or ballistically damaged bearing can be replaced in the field and on the aircraft. This ability has reduced support costs by reducing the spare rotor assemblies needed, and it has further increased aircraft availability.

To appreciate the major benefits that elastomeric technology has provided to aircraft reliability and maintenance, it is helpful to understand the failure modes and dependence on lubrication of prior metal bearing technology. Multiblade articulated rotors have typically used conventional anti-friction bearings to provide blade flap, lag, and pitch angular motions. These bearings, designed for continuous rotational motion, are not well suited to the small-amplitude oscillatory motions typical of helicopter rotor applications. But until the creation of elastomeric bearings, there were no practical alternatives to conventional metallic bearings.

The basic problem with ball- and roller-type bearings was their mode of failure when they were forced to rotate back and forth through small angles. In continuous rotation applications, their failure mode is typically one of fatigue involving spalling of the inner or outer race as a result of vibratory subsurface shear stresses. The statistical characteristics of bearing life for this failure mode are well understood and predictable. However, when used in rotor heads, the predominant failure mode is not surface fatigue but surface wear caused by iron-oxide debris being ground back and forth over the ball or roller-to-race contact area. Bearing life for this failure mode, referred to as fretting corrosion, has not been predictable with confidence because of the many variables influencing the wear phenomenon. These include surface compressive stresses, type of lubricant, amplitude and frequency of the oscillatory motion, and other factors even less understood. Failure of these metallic bearings, characterized by relatively deep indentations in the races, similar to brinelling, often produced aircraft vibrations and sometimes roughness in the flight controls. Those effects, plus the very burdensome maintenance actions needed to prolong bearing lives, were the Achilles heel of earlier rotor systems.

Until the 1960s, helicopters used grease to lubricate rotor system bearings, and greasing was required on a daily basis to purge out the abrasive iron oxide products of fretting corrosion. Sikorsky's five-bladed H-37 (S-56 helicopter) had over 30 grease fittings in its main rotor, which required daily re-lubrication with a grease gun to purge out the fretting debris. That meant not just topping off the grease supply but continuing to pump in grease until the old reddish grease, only a day old, was expelled and clean new grease could be seen. This was a very labor-intensive maintenance procedure.

During the 1960s, Sikorsky introduced the use of oil lubrication of the blade hinge bearings to eliminate the burden of daily greasing. This was a major step forward, but it required development of seals having special features plus fungicide properties to prolong seal life. However, oil leakage from seals and oil reservoirs was never completely corrected, and the hoped-for maintenance benefits were not fully realized. Worst of all, when oil leaked from a rotor head rotating at full speed, it was instantly noticed by nearby equipment and people. Technology of metallic antifriction bearings seemed to have reached a limit for helicopter rotors, and it was time for a new approach.

Later in that decade, development of elastomeric bearings made of natural rubber laminates and metal shims, and applicable to applications requiring small angular motions, began to show promise for helicopter rotor applications. During that decade, all major U.S. helicopter manufacturers began to experiment with elastomeric bearing rotors, but Sikorsky demonstrated the largest step forward in this technology with the CH-53D program mentioned earlier. In conjunction with the Lord Manufacturing Corporation, Sikorsky moved rotor technology a major step forward by demonstrating feasibility of the elastomeric rotor concept at a large scale and by successfully putting this rotor into production and fleet operational service. This new technology was in time to benefit the UTTAS program and has been incorporated in all Black Hawk derivatives as well as in other Sikorsky models.

BEARINGLESS CROSSBEAM TAIL ROTOR

The Black Hawk crossbeam tail rotor was a dramatic departure from past Sikorsky design practices and represents a very successful application of advanced composite materials in significantly reducing rotor weight, complexity, and maintenance. The crossbeam name comes from the use of two spars, each of which is continuous from one blade tip to its opposite tip. The two spars are stacked together and spaced 90 deg to each other as shown in Fig. 66.

With this arrangement, each blade's centrifugal load is internally reacted by that of the opposite blade, thereby relieving the tail-rotor hub of large loads. The major innovation of this rotor concept was the application of the

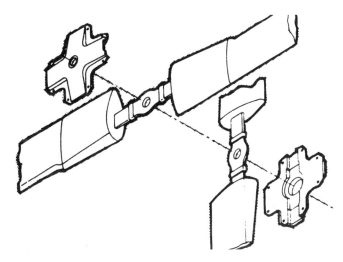

Fig. 66   **Black Hawk tail rotor contains no bearings. All pitch change motion is provided by elastic deformation of its graphite spars. Two separate paddle assemblies are bolted together by titanium plates to form the four-bladed rotor. The pitch control system passes through the center hole shown.**

unique structural properties of fiber composite materials to provide sufficient torsional flexibility so as to eliminate the need for pitch change bearings. The design challenge was to achieve the desired torsional properties while providing an aeroelastically stable rotor throughout the aircraft's flight envelope.

Prior to the UTTAS competition, Sikorsky tail rotors were of the semi-articulated configuration that permitted blade flapping and pitch change motions but were stiff in the in-plane direction. Conventional antifriction bearings provided blade flap and blade pitch change motion and were typically roller and ball bearings. All bearings required oil or grease lubrication, similar to earlier generation main rotors, thereby adding to the rotor maintenance burden. However, the crossbeam tail rotor totally eliminated bearings and achieved a new level of simplicity, resulting in greatly improved reliability and freedom from maintenance. By the same token, ballistic tolerance was also significantly improved. The conventional tail rotor used on the Sikorsky S-61 helicopter is the same size as the Black Hawk rotor, but it is 40% heavier and has more than twice the number of parts.

The concept for the crossbeam rotor originated at the United Aircraft Research Laboratories (UARL) during the late 1960s when the properties of filament composite material became understood. The pioneering work done at UARL by M.C. Cheney in applying the unique anisotropic properties of fiber-reinforced composite materials to helicopter rotors formed the basis of Sikorsky's development of the crossbeam tail rotor known then as the XBR rotor [13]. The evolution of the UTTAS tail rotor at Sikorsky is described by

Bill Noehren and Ron Fenaughty in their AHS paper [14] in which they emphasize structural design and aeroelastic stability.

The application of graphite-epoxy composite material to the tail blade spar permitted attainment of properties that were not achievable with metal structures. Proper orientation of the graphite fibers was a key design tool for optimizing elastic properties of the spar. Although boron fibers were initially considered for the spar, graphite was ultimately selected because of cost and availability considerations. There was some initial concern about damage tolerance of graphite laminates, but that was resolved by using scrim cloth to protect the spar from handling damage.

Graphite was chosen over fiberglass because of its higher ratios of fatigue strain allowables to density, both in bending and torsion, and its high bending-to-torsion stiffness ratio. Low torsional stiffness was an especially important parameter in order to keep pitch control loads as low as possible. Because of these favorable ratios, graphite produced a much lighter spar than would have been possible with fiberglass.

Ensuring aeroelastic stability throughout the tail rotor's thrust and flight speed envelope was a primary design requirement in addition to achieving a high rotor FM to match that of the main rotor.

Proper placement and separation of blade natural frequencies over the blade pitch angle range was achieved by fine tuning the spar's geometry and fiber orientation. In addition, the airfoil covering the spar was mounted at an angle to the spar, that is, the airfoil's chordwise axis is not coincident with the spar's chordwise axis. By mounting the airfoil at an angle to the spar, as shown in Fig. 67, maximum separation was achieved between the first edgewise and flatwise bending modes of the blade over the operating pitch range.

Extensive work was done to develop the analysis techniques needed to predict accurately stable operation throughout the flight envelope.

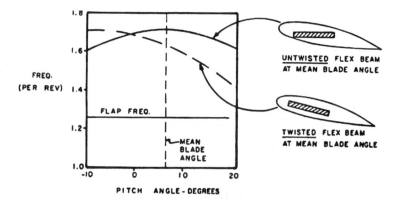

Fig. 67   Airfoil cover is mounted at an angle to the spar to achieve maximum separation of blade bending modes.

The accuracy of these techniques was then validated by a series of rotor test stand, wind tunnel, and flight tests of a full-scale tail rotor prior to first flight of the UTTAS prototype. Analytical methods to reliably predict performance and aeroelastic characteristics of the crossbeam rotor concept were developed by UARL with early support from NASA Langley and the Army. This work included extensive small-scale model testing to develop confidence prior to proceeding with aggressive full-scale stability testing.

In 1973, the first full-size UTTAS tail rotor began operation on a unique test stand at Sikorsky that simulated yawing flight by precessing the rotor as well as simulating sideward flight to 35 kn by blowing on the rotor disc. During whirl testing, rotor dynamic characteristics were successfully demonstrated by a simulated ballistic severance of a blade pitch change push rod. An explosive charge, strapped to one of the four push rods, was detonated while the rotor was whirling, thereby removing all blade torsional restraint from the control system. The blade proved to be well behaved with no tendency toward instability or excessive response. This test was repeated at a number of simulated flight conditions to ensure stable response throughout the flight envelope.

Following these tests, the entire UTTAS tail assembly including tail pylon, tail rotor, and tail gear box was installed and operated in the 18-ft low-speed wind tunnel at UARL for extensive testing prior to first flight. This was thought to be the ultimate in modeling because the rotor, control system, and airframe structure were all totally representative of the UTTAS aircraft. The final testing performed before first flight of UTTAS was actual flight testing on a Sikorsky S-61 helicopter with the installation shown in Fig. 68. The results of these tests continued to confirm the performance and stability of the crossbeam tail rotor and helped to establish safe operational clearance for the first flight of the UTTAS prototype.

Fig. 68 Flight risk reduction of the first UTTAS crossbeam tail rotor on an SH-3H. (©Igor I. Sikorsky Historical Archives, Inc.)

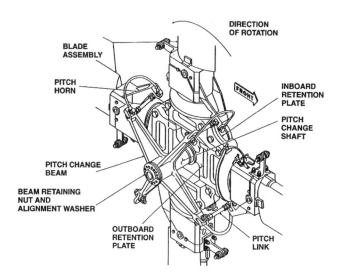

Fig. 69   Major components and assemblies of the crossbeam tail rotor.

The focus on analytical development, together with full-scale wind tunnel and flight testing, resulted in the crossbeam tail rotor being the most stable and highest performance tail rotor that Sikorsky has ever produced. The millions of successful Black Hawk flight hours confirm that all design objectives were achieved and that technology has become a new design standard for tail rotors. Figure 69 illustrates the UTTAS and, later, Black Hawk tail rotor assembly.

CANTED TAIL ROTOR

The Black Hawk's tail-rotor installation is one of the aircraft's most distinguishing design features. Its tail-rotor's axis is not only inclined 20 deg in the up direction, but the rotor is located on the right side of the tail pylon instead of the left side typical of U.S. helicopters. Both features were aimed at helping to meet specific Army requirements, and both have provided the intended benefits. These are discussed next together with the flight control system changes required to compensate for the yaw-to-pitch coupling resulting from the tail-rotor's canted thrust axis.

The idea of inclining the tail-rotor's thrust in order to generate added lift is a matter of simple physics. The canted tail rotor is not so much of a technology achievement as it is a clever design innovation to solve a specific problem. In the case of UTTAS, that problem was how to make the aircraft smaller in order to be air transportable without major disassembly. The canted tail rotor resulted in a more compact aircraft in two ways: first, by reducing the lift required of the main rotor, thereby permitting a smaller main rotor diameter; and second, by permitting a shortened fuselage nose because the aircraft's c.g. could be moved aft to coincide with the center of lift of both rotors.

However a less obvious benefit to the Black Hawk is that the increment of lift supplied by the tail rotor is generated at less power per pound of lift than is the lift of the main rotor. The net result is that with a canted tail rotor more total lift can be produced for the same installed power than is possible with a conventional tail rotor, other factors being equal. This makes it an attractive design option for any single rotor helicopter.

The 20 deg of upward inclination increases the total thrust required of the tail rotor by only 6.5%, which is the cosine of the cant angle; however, 34% of its thrust becomes available as a lifting force, which is the sine of the cant angle. For the Black Hawk, this lift component equals approximately 400 lb in hovering flight. However, to produce this lift requires only an additional 22 hp, which is equivalent to 18 lb per horsepower. This lift-to-power ratio is about three times greater than that of the main rotor, which means that the main rotor diameter could be reduced by about 1.5 to 2 ft because of the contribution to total lift provided by the canted tail rotor. This reduction helped to solve the air transport problem without having to sacrifice aircraft performance, which would have been the case if the main rotor were reduced in size without benefit of the canted tail-rotor's lift contribution.

Helicopters designed in the United States typically have main rotors turning counterclockwise as viewed from above. As a result, tail rotors are normally placed on the left side of the vertical pylon where they function as pusher rotors to counter main rotor torque. This tends to improve tail-rotor efficiency by avoiding the losses associated with downwash against the vertical pylon. However, to improve survivability, Sikorsky located the UTTAS tail rotor on the pylon's right side where it functions as a tractor rotor. Combat survivability is improved in the event that ballistic damage would cause separation of the tail rotor from the airframe. In that instance, a traditional pusher tail rotor could contact the pylon and cartwheel into the main rotor. On the other hand, with a tractor installation, the tail rotor would fly cleanly away with little chance of airframe or main rotor contact. The tractor configuration also creates a safer environment for troops and maintenance personnel because of the greater distance between the tail-rotor blade tip and the ground. Finally, the UTTAS design simply looked better with its canted tail rotor located on the right side of the pylon. The slight loss in performance as a result of the vertical drag already mentioned was accepted as a good trade in view of the substantial benefits.

One aspect of the canted tail-rotor concept that needed to be considered is the aircraft pitch response when rudder inputs are made. Pedal inputs for yaw maneuvers produce a change in tail rotor thrust and therefore a change in its lift component, which generates an aircraft pitching moment. Flight testing had demonstrated that coupling main-rotor longitudinal cyclic pitch to pedal motion easily compensates for this pitching moment. The amount of main rotor longitudinal cyclic coupling required to cancel the lift moments generated by the tail rotor is easily predicted.

Fig. 70 Canted tail-rotor demonstration on a CH-53A to evaluate the control de-coupling solution as well as flight performance. The configuration shown in this picture was adopted for the larger CH-53E. (©Igor I. Sikorsky Historical Archives, Inc.)

The potential risk issues were examined by flying a canted tail rotor on three different Sikorsky helicopters prior to and during the UTTAS design phase. The first test was performed on an S-61R helicopter in December of 1969 at flight speeds to 115 kn and gross weights to 17,000 lb with a 20-deg pusher tail rotor (on the left side). During these flight tests, the compensation of aircraft yaw-to-pitch axis coupling by mixing yaw with longitudinal controls was demonstrated.

The second test was performed on a CH-53A in October of 1971 at speeds to 150 kn and gross weights to 35,000 lb with a 20-deg canted tail rotor also mounted on the pylon left side as shown in Fig. 70. Again all control coupling dynamics were accurately corrected.

The last flight evaluation of the canted tail rotor was performed on an S-58T helicopter flown in June of 1973, which was about a year prior to the UTTAS first flight. This S-58T demonstration was the first to have the 20-deg canted tail rotor mounted as a tractor (on the right side) as in the UTTAS configuration.

This last evaluation confirmed the feasibility of both the cant angle and tractor innovations with hardware representative of the UTTAS size. This combined flight experience on three aircraft effectively eliminated risk of the unique tail-rotor installation on the UTTAS.

The canted tail-rotor concept has proven its value on all versions of Sikorsky's CH-53E heavy transport helicopter and on all Black Hawk models and derivatives. It has been adopted for new Sikorsky designs and could become the standard for future single-rotor helicopters. Sikorsky's David S. Jenney is credited with recognizing the value of this concept and promoting its benefits first for the CH-53E and then for the UTTAS. Without Jenney's persuasive technical arguments, adoption of the canted tail rotor by Sikorsky would undoubtedly have been delayed.

Chapter 5

DESIGNED TO SURVIVE

The YUH-60A UTTAS prototype was the first U.S. military helicopter to be designed from the ground up to survive in a low-threat ground-fire environment. Additionally, it was designed to have significant structural tolerance in mid- to high-intensity threat environments. It was also the first U.S. military helicopter to be designed from the ground up to protect its flight crew and cabin occupants in the event of crash landings. Both requirements were new to helicopter design in the 1970s era, and both reflected the Army's combat experience in Vietnam. The extent to which UTTAS achieved these requirements is likely to become the Black Hawk's most enduring legacy. This chapter describes the many unique design features that have set new standards for helicopter survivability. Throughout the aircraft design, innovative design solutions helped achieve these standards without incurring excessive weight or cost penalties.

CRASHWORTHINESS DESIGN

Because of the protection that its robust design gives to occupants in serious accidents, Black Hawk models have experienced far fewer occupant fatalities and serious injuries from hard landings and crashes than would have been the case with earlier generation helicopters. Through examination of numerous wreckages, the Army has judged that many pilots and cabin occupants have survived accidents that were felt to have been non-survivable by their severity. Several such examples are described next. This record is a strong validation of both the Army's "Crash Survival Design Guide" and of UTTAS design innovations that were created through the use of that guide.

When UTTAS was designed in the early 1970s, crashworthiness was a new engineering discipline and one that was not high on the list of design priorities. As was traditional in that time period, flight performance, maneuver capability, weight reduction, and other traditional attributes were the subjects on which design engineers focused their attention. However, because of the Army's specifications reinforced by excellent Black Hawk mishap experience, crashworthiness considerations have now forever changed design priorities. Most importantly, the well-proven success of this new engineering discipline has captured the attention of helicopter operators worldwide, ensuring that the priority of crashworthiness design will remain high for both military and civil designs. Paying modest weight and performance penalties to achieve a substantial survivability payoff has become an accepted tradeoff that has extended as well to design of commercial helicopters.

The Army Safety Center, after studying the accident experience of many Army helicopters operating during the Vietnam conflict, concluded that improved design features could have significantly reduced injuries, fatalities, and aircraft damage. During the 1960s, the Eustis Directorate of the U.S. Army Air Mobility Research and Development Laboratory contracted with the AvCIR Group of the Flight Safety Foundation to define the Army aircraft environment and to develop design concepts and criteria to reduce injuries, fatalities, and damage. What followed were crash investigations, aircraft crash tests, and design studies leading to creation of the Army's USAAMRDL Technical Report 71-22 "Crash Survival Design Guide" [15]. Adherence to this guide was required by the Army in its UTTAS request for proposal in 1972 and was a primary reference during design of Sikorsky's YUH-60A to achieve an exceptional level of crashworthiness.

The design innovations for UTTAS have proven to be effective in protecting occupants at a modest cost in additional weight. The aircraft's high-performance margins permitted the weight of its crashworthiness features, estimated to be approximately 300 lb, to be accepted with minimal compromise. Technology advancements and clever design approaches promise to achieve even greater protection at less weight for future helicopter designs.

The crashworthiness design discipline was very immature in that earlier time frame, and Sikorsky recognized that it lacked adequate in-house capability. As a result, the company elected to add several recognized experts to its team. J. W. Turnbow and S. H. Robertson, who were major contributors to TR 71-22, became an essential and integral part of the UTTAS engineering effort at Sikorsky prior to award of the prototype contract. Later in the UH-60A program, a third crashworthiness pioneer, Stanley P. Desjardins, made significant contributions by development of the crashworthy crew seats with load-limiting stroking capability. These three experts contributed significantly to the Black Hawk's unique crash survival characteristics that have been tested many times during its long service history both in training and during combat operations.

The influence of these pioneers in effectively teaching Sikorsky engineers the holistic aspects of helicopter crashworthiness design has been extremely effective in creating an in-house capability. Chief among those trained was Brian L. Carnell, a senior Sikorsky structures engineer who became the key motivator for creating the Black Hawk's crashworthiness features.

The Black Hawk helicopter's most significant crashworthiness design features [16] are illustrated in Fig. 71. To be both effective in protecting

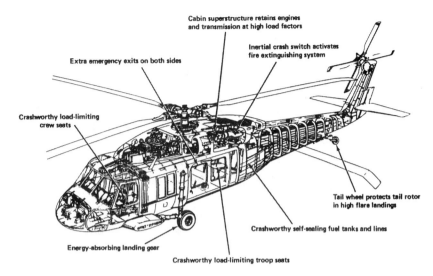

Fig. 71   Crashworthiness features designed into the Black Hawk at the start of the UTTAS program.

occupants and to be as weight efficient as possible, all features had to be designed into the helicopter at the inception of the design process.

The Army's specific requirements for crashworthiness were intended to encompass 95% of helicopter accidents judged to have been survivable. One definition of a survivable accident is as follows:

> one in which the forces transmitted to the occupant through seat and restraint system do not exceed the limits of human tolerance to abrupt accelerations and in which the structure in the occupant's immediate environment remains substantially intact to the extent that a livable volume is provided for the occupants throughout the crash sequence [17].

However, survival requires more than controlling the applied forces and retaining occupant living space. Additional critical survival requirements include the following: 1) the need to restrain high mass items, 2) provisions for adequate occupant restraint systems, 3) availability of adequate emergency evacuation means, and finally, 4) provisions to prevent postcrash fires. The ways that these requirements were met are described next.

Mishaps experienced by the Army from the time that the UH-60A entered service in 1979, through an 11-year period to 1990, have proven the very real benefits of these design features as documented by Army medical personnel [18].

Absorption of crash energy over the longest possible distance was the primary approach to reducing decelerations and occupant crash forces. The

Black Hawk landing gear was designed to absorb most of the energy in crashes of predominant vertical velocity up to the Army's requirement of 42 fps. However, during vertical drop testing, the landing gear did not fully achieve its design goals with the result that the recognized vertical impact velocity for the aircraft is 38 fps instead of 42 fps. The landing gear decelerates the aircraft to an average of 9 g through a distance of 23 in. This prevents fuselage ground contact at sink speeds of up to 35 fps (2100 ft/min). At higher sink speeds, structural deformation of the seats and airframe provides protection for the occupants. This gear is unique in having two air-oil struts, one above the other, to absorb energy; its lower unit functions during normal landings of up to 10 fps during which its upper unit is mechanically prevented from stroking. In very hard landings that exceed 10 fps, the motion of the lower unit's piston releases a locking device enabling the upper unit to stroke and continue to absorb energy during a heavy or crash landing. Load-limiting relief valves in both stages limit the load factor to 18 g. Figure 72 illustrates the operation of the lower and upper struts during a crash sequence. Because the oleos are separate, if the first stage sustains battle damage, the second stage is still triggered and is capable of functioning for normal landings.

The crew and troop seats contribute significantly to survival by absorbing energy during a crash to reduce forces applied to the occupants' spinal column. Both pilots' seats contain two-stage struts that can stroke 12 in., limiting 50th-percentile occupants to a $14\frac{1}{2}$-g load factor. Troop seats can stroke 10 in. and limit loads to the same $14\frac{1}{2}$-g level. They do this by wire-bending energy absorbers attached at the rear of the seat frame up to the cabin ceiling shown in Fig. 73. Figure 74 shows the aircrew and troop seats before and after a predominantly vertical crash.

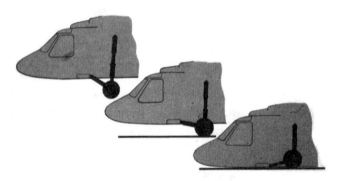

Fig. 72   Two-stage main landing gear oleo strut provides most of the energy absorption to limit loads on the occupants. Sequential stroking of the oleos takes place until fuselage contacts ground.

Fig. 73   Brian Carnell, who led the Black Hawk crashworthiness design effort, strapped in a troop seat supported by energy-absorbing reels attached to the cabin ceiling. (©Igor I. Sikorsky Historical Archives, Inc.)

The airframe structural arrangement focused on maintaining a protective shell around the occupants capable of restraining high-mass components, maintaining 85% of cabin living space in the 38-fps crash, and limiting load buildup in crashes with a high forward speed component. Figure 75 illustrates the longitudinal keel beams, rounded up at the cockpit nose to minimize plowing in nose-down crashes and to help the aircraft skid along the ground so as to minimize decelerations.

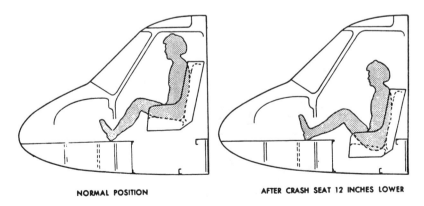

NORMAL POSITION   AFTER CRASH SEAT 12 INCHES LOWER

Fig. 74   Pilot and copilot seats can stroke 12 in. and limit spinal loads to survivable levels. All troop seats contain energy-absorbing devices to limit occupant loads similar to the crew seats.

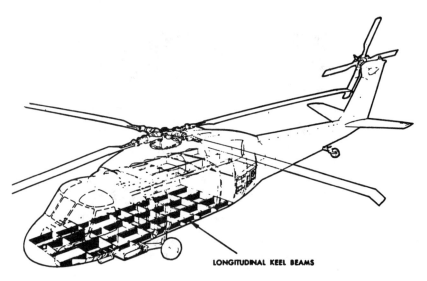

Fig. 75 **Longitudinal keel beams help prevent plowing of the ground in mishaps with high forward velocity.**

Figure 76 shows the mainframes and overhead beams that constitute the cabin structure. This structure was designed to restrain the heavy overhead engines, main transmission, main rotor, and secondary systems to combinations of 20-g forward, 20-g downward, and 18-g sideward load factors. All structural members are aluminum providing high ductility and energy absorption.

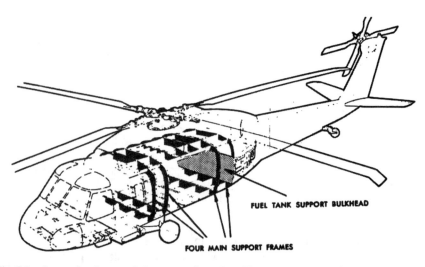

Fig. 76 **Large fuselage mainframes and overhead beams prevent engines, transmission, and rotor from penetrating living space in high-vertical-velocity mishaps.**

Ductility permits the kinetic energy of the high-mass items to be absorbed without building up high load factors while energy absorption minimizes structural damage and injuries caused by dynamic springback.

Prevention of postcrash fires was achieved by designing the fuel system, shown in Fig. 77, and other flammable fluid systems to minimize leakage in crashes and by locating possible ignition sources away from potential fluid spillage areas. The crashworthy fuel cells were required by specification MIL-T-27422B to sustain a free drop from 65 ft, full of water to normal capacity, without leaking. Successfully passing this very stringent test required significant development work on the part of the fuel-cell manufacturer. After each of six successive drop tests, the cell exhibited slight leakage in corner and in fitting attachment areas. After each test, design and manufacturing improvements were incorporated, and finally the seventh drop was a complete success, and its design became the production standard.

All fuel lines in the Black Hawk suction fuel system are self-sealing flexible hoses. They are connected by self-sealing breakaway valves and routed away from the fuselage sidewalls and underside that suffer the most damage in a crash. LTC Shanahan [18] reports that during the 11-year period of data evaluation there had not been a single fatality caused by thermal injury in Black Hawk crashes. He further reported, "the system has performed exceedingly well under crash conditions well in excess of structural design limits including several crashes with vertical velocities exceeding 18.3 mps (60 fps)."

Survivors of crashes involving Black Hawk and its derivative models have expressed many very positive comments about its design. But the simple heartfelt comment by Chief Warrant Officer Michael Durant captures the feelings of many crewmen. In 1995, a rocket-powered grenade brought down

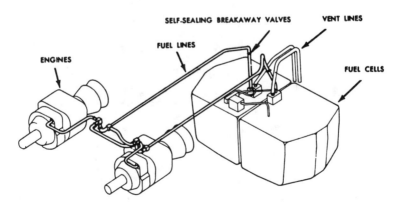

Fig. 77 Probability of postcrash fires has proven to be low because of the effectiveness of the crashworthy fuel cells, self-sealing breakaway valves, and routing of the suction fuel system lines.

CWO Durant's UH-60 during operations in Mogadishu, Somalia, which were made famous by the book *Black Hawk Down* [19]. During an interview several years after the crash of his helicopter, pilot CWO Michael Durant said, "I owe my life to the design of this aircraft" [20].

The extent to which the design features just outlined enhanced survivability can be appreciated by a graphic review of the aircraft damage and survivor status described in the following mishap descriptions. They were provided by the U.S. Army Safety Center at Fort Rucker and are used with permission.

MISHAP NUMBER 36 (FIG. 78)

Time 0833 in April 1994
Model: UH-60A
Classification: Partially survivable
Category: Loss of power of both engines
EVENTS.   During a simulated combat training mission over the mountains in the western United States, the aircraft landed on a confined area of a mountain ridgeline. When taking off from this area over rough, rugged terrain, the aircraft lost power from both engines. Low-engine rpm lights came on, and the low-rotor rpm audio warning sounded. The pilot leveled the aircraft as it impacted down the slope on the 35- to 40-deg sloping ridge. The aircraft came to rest on its right side, still heading down the slope. The two pilots exited through the left cockpit door, and the two cabin occupants exited through the left gunner's window.

Fig. 78   Mishap 36: impact on 40-deg slope after total power loss. Estimated 55-fps horizontal and 5-fps vertical impact speeds. No fuel spilled and no fire or loss of living space. Four occupants, two minor injuries, and two uninjured. Condition of rotor blades indicates low rotor speed at impact. (U.S. Army photo, used with permission.)

TERRAIN TYPE. The terrain type was a ridgeline in mountains at an altitude of 4500 ft. At the impact spot, the slope of the ridge was 35 deg downward, and the sod surface was covered with rocks and boulders.

ESTIMATED IMPACT VELOCITY. The impact velocities relative to the ground were 5 fps vertical and 55 fps longitudinal. The aircraft attitude relative to the ground at the first impact was 25 deg nose up with no roll or yaw. The aircraft then nosed down and impacted in a 10-deg nose-down attitude. The inertia loads were estimated to be low.

STRUCTURAL DAMAGE. The aircraft was significantly damaged. In the second impact, the windshields and nose chin bubbles shattered with major damage to the nose area below the pilot's foot pedals. There was little loss of living space, the exception being that for the right rear troop seat. It was torn from the aircraft and caused the accident to be classified as partially survivable. The tail wheel and main landing gear were torn from the fuselage. All four main rotor blades sustained extensive damage when they impacted and dug into the rock piles on the slope. Most of the damage to the fuselage was on the right side because of the rollover. The cockpit and cabin doors on that side were torn from the aircraft.

Postcrash fire: No fire occurred.
Number onboard: 4
Injuries: 2 minor injuries

Both pilots suffered minor injuries. One pilot had a shoulder muscle strain when the displacing cockpit door struck it. The other pilot suffered a lower back muscle strain because of excessive motion. No stroking of the crew seats occurred.

MISHAP NUMBER 37 (FIG. 79)

Time 2145 in July 1994
Model: MH-60L
Classification: Partially survivable
Category: Loss of power from one engine

EVENTS. After taking off on a nighttime training mission and approximately 250 ft above the ground, the crew heard an unusual whining sound, followed by a loud pop. The crew assessed the sounds to be a malfunctioning engine and pulled its power control lever to idle. The rotor rpm dropped to 60%, and the aircraft continued its descent. The crew leveled the aircraft and pulled full collective in an attempt to cushion the landing. It then hit the ground hard in a tail low attitude with low rotor rpm and was severely damaged.

TERRAIN TYPE. The terrain was a level ground live-fire range impact area with numerous holes from live ordnance explosions with brush growth around 5 ft high scattered throughout the area.

Fig. 79   Mishap number 37: Impacted ground at estimated 25-fps horizontal speed and 50-fps vertical speed. No fuel spilled and no fire, some loss of living space. Three occupants, two major and one minor injury. (U.S. Army photo, used with permission)

ESTIMATED IMPACT VELOCITY.   The ground speed at impact was 25 fps, and the vertical speed was 50 fps. The aircraft attitude at impact was 10 deg nose up, 5 deg rolled right, and yawed 10 deg to the left. The impact forces were estimated to be 25 g down, with lateral and longitudinal loads of 1.3 g.

STRUCTURAL DAMAGE.   The aircraft impacted the ground in a tail low attitude causing the tail wheel and stabilator to contact the ground first. This impact separated the tail cone at the transition section and the tail rotor pylon from the tail cone near the tail wheel. The main landing gear also separated from the fuselage. Two main rotor blades and the tail rotor blades were torn free, damaged by the tree and ground strikes. There was some loss of living space in the cockpit and the cabin because of the collapse of the roof. However, the Robertson internal auxiliary fuel tanks installed in the rear of the cabin supported the aft portion of the cabin roof structure.

Postcrash fire: No fire occurred.
Number onboard: 3
Injuries: 2 major, 1 minor

One pilot suffered simple fractures of a bone in a foot when it struck a pedal and his left wrist when it struck the collective control stick. The other pilot suffered a broken jaw when his seat rotated forward and his head struck the cyclic control stick. The crew chief suffered a bruised hip when he was thrown from the gunner's seat.

MISHAP NUMBER 55 (FIG. 80)

Time 0704 in April 1999
Model: UH-60L

Fig. 80   Mishap number 55: impacted trees at 80 kn with vertical speed estimated to be 67 fps. Fuselage broke into four sections. No fuel was spilled, and there was no fire. Five occupants aboard and all five sustained major injuries. (U.S. Army photo, used with permission.)

Classification: Nonsurvivable

Category: Inadvertent flight into ground

EVENTS.   The aircraft was on a daytime field training mission, flying at approximately 80 kn and less than 50 ft above the highest obstacle. It descended and crashed through 75-ft tall trees and impacted the ground. The aircraft was destroyed.

TERRAIN TYPE.   The terrain was flat with a mixture of hardwood and pine trees.

IMPACT SEVERITY.   The ground speed at impact was 127 fps, and the vertical speed was 67 fps. The aircraft was in a level flight attitude with no yaw.

STRUCTURAL DAMAGE.   The aircraft was broken into four main sections with no protection of any living space. The forward cabin, with the cockpit still attached, came to rest inverted with the left side crushed. The main and tail rotor blades were destroyed by tree and ground strikes. All landing gears and the tail rotor gearbox were torn free from the aircraft structure.

POSTCRASH FIRE.   The two main fuel cells separated from the aircraft, and the breakaway valves functioned as designed, preventing fuel spillage and post-crash fire.

Number onboard: 5

Injuries: 5 major injuries

One pilot suffered a spinal compression fracture. The other pilot suffered a fractured ankle when it struck a foot pedal. The crew chief had fractures of a leg and ribs when he hit the structure. One crewmember had a fractured thigh, and the other crewmember had fractures of the nose, upper arm, lower leg, and dislocated hips caused by impact with the structure.

MISHAP NUMBER 59 (FIG. 81)

Time 2210 in February 2000
Model: UH-60L
Classification: Partially survivable
Category: Inadvertent flight into ground

EVENTS.   The aircraft took off on a night-vision training mission and, at the beginning of the ascent, made an unintentional left turn, then descended to a cross-slope ground impact. A main rotor blade hit the ground and began to disintegrate. The other blades flexed downward and impacted the tail-rotor drive shaft fairing, the nose of the aircraft, penetrating the cockpit, and the top of the cabin. The aircraft rolled left 200 deg and yawed left 90 deg, coming to rest on its left side.

TERRAIN TYPE.   The terrain was desert sod with a 3-deg slope.

ESTIMATED IMPACT VELOCITIES.   The ground speed at impact was 59 fps, and the vertical speed was 27 fps. The aircraft attitude at impact was 5 deg nose down and 20 deg roll to the left with no yaw angle. The inertial loads were estimated to be 11 g up, 5 g aft, and 2 g lateral.

STRUCTURAL DAMAGE.   The nose section and crew compartment were torn on both sides and badly crushed and were barely hanging on to the main fuselage. The tail cone was broken off the transition section but remained attached by some sheet metal and some wires. The tail cone broke at the attachment point

Fig. 81   Mishap number 59: contacted ground during night-vision training mission. Impact speeds estimated to be 59 fps horizontal and 27 fps vertical. No fuel was spilled, and there was no fire. Seven occupants, two suffered major and five sustained minor injuries. (U.S. Army photo, used with permission.)

of the tail landing-gear yoke. The left-side door was torn off and broken in two. On the right side, the stub wing and main gear drag beam, wheel, and tire were torn away from the aircraft, and the shock strut was buckled and broken at the lower attachment point. The tail-gear yoke was broken off, the tail wheel was broken, and the tire was deflated. The fuselage mainframes on the right side were damaged. The aft cabin frame was buckled several inches on the right side.

Postcrash fire: There was no fuel spillage from the main fuel cells, which remained relatively intact. No fire occurred.

Number onboard: 7

Injuries: 2 major, 5 minor

The copilot in the left seat suffered a major injury, a multiple compound fracture of the right leg. The pilot in the right seat had only minor injuries. In the cabin, the crewmember in the right-hand crew chief seat suffered major injuries, spinal damage, a right arm fracture, and a left shoulder separation. The other two crew and two passengers suffered only minor bump and bruise injuries.

From an examination of the mishaps just described, together with other Black Hawk accidents, it is apparent that the Army set the right design requirements and the right priority for crashworthiness. Army engineers, Sikorsky designers, and crashworthiness consultants can take great pride in their innovative designs and especially in knowing that many lives of aircraft crewmembers and occupants have been saved and their injuries lessened. They have set new standards and priorities for future military and commercial helicopter design.

BALLISTIC DESIGN

As with crashworthiness, UTTAS was required to address survivability against combat ballistic threats when its design first began. Special design innovations and materials were incorporated early in the design process to defeat threats specified by the Army. When the small arms and higher threats up to 23-mm high-explosive incendiary rounds were specified in the 1972 timeframe, the new emerging threat from rocket-propelled grenades (RPG) was not yet recognized.

Beginning in the 1990s, Black Hawk and other military helicopters have been found to be vulnerable by shoulder-fired RPG weapons. As a result, development of an antiweapon system to defeat RPGs is underway, but current survival tactics concentrate on operational flight procedures. This emerging RPG threat is discussed at the end of this chapter.

A significant reduction in battlefield vulnerability was achieved in the UTTAS design without incurring an excessive weight penalty. Figure 82

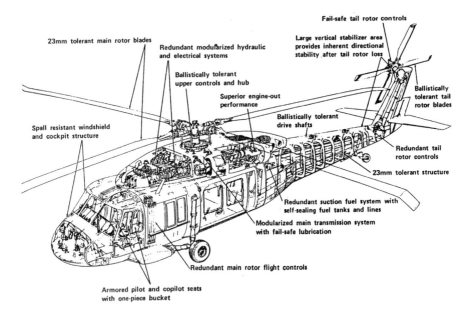

Fail-safe tail rotor controls

23mm tolerant main rotor blades

Redundant modularized hydraulic
and electrical systems

Large vertical stabilizer area
provides inherent directional
stability after tail rotor loss

Ballistically tolerant
upper controls and hub

Ballistically
tolerant tail
rotor blades

Superior engine-out
performance

Spall resistant windshield
and cockpit structure

Ballistically tolerant
drive shafts

Redundant tail
rotor controls

23mm tolerant structure

Redundant suction fuel system with
self-sealing fuel tanks and lines

Modularized main transmission system
with fail-safe lubrication

Redundant main rotor flight controls

Armored pilot and copilot seats
with one-piece bucket

**Fig. 82   Key design features that enhance Black Hawk's battlefield survivability are
highlighted.**

illustrates this helicopter's most significant design features for improving
battlefield staying power in a high threat environment. Its design illustrates
the significant gains that can be achieved when survivability is seriously
considered early in the aircraft design process while the configuration is
still fluid and while component locations can be optimized to achieve the
best separation and structural protection. By the early application of good
design practices, excellent ballistic tolerance was achieved without need
for any parasitic armor other than for the cockpit crew seats.

Training of the designers of all aircraft subsystems was accomplished
under the leadership of engineers Dave Fansler and Stan Okarma. They
trained and motivated designers to find the unique design approaches
described in this chapter to meet the ballistic requirements with minimal
weight penalty.

Systems designers were encouraged to incorporate redundancy of critical
components, structural shielding, and by physical separation of flight-essential
elements. Examples of wide separation to avoid single hit disablement of
redundant or multiple systems include engine placement 5 ft apart, protected
locations of the secondary power modules and control system routing. The
UTTAS cockpit was configured to locate the crew seats 4 ft apart on centerline for the same reason.

Figure 83 illustrates how new technology for both the rotor head and transmission system benefited several key aircraft attributes simultaneously.

Fig. 83 UH-60A main gearbox with all lubrication lines internal and with its elastomeric rotor is far simpler than the prior-generation SH-3H with its web of oil lines to both rotor and transmission. (©Igor I. Sikorsky Historical Archives, Inc.)

On the right is the Black Hawk main rotor and gearbox assembly. Shown on the left is the prior-generation assembly for the Sikorsky S-61 designed 20 years earlier.

Both assemblies are comparable in power transmitted, engine-to-rotor reduction ratio, and aircraft gross weight.

The S-61 five-blade fully articulated main rotor contains conventional antifriction bearings that are oil lubricated from the central reservoir seen mounted above the rotor. The Black Hawk four-blade rotor is designed around elastomeric bearings requiring no lubrication. The S-61 main gearbox has four stages of reduction to accomplish what Black Hawk gearbox does in only three stages. A major improvement from the ballistic tolerance standpoint is the use of internally cored oil passages for the Black Hawk gearbox as compared with the external plumbing visible on the S-61 gearbox and rotor head to supply oil lubrication to various locations.

One of the most significant technology improvements was achieving the capability of the Black Hawk gearboxes to operate for 30 min after loss of all lubricants. Chapter 4 outlined some of the design innovations used to provide this capability, which included incorporation of special materials, bearing clearances, and oil "dams" around critical bearings. It noted that a test of 60 min at a power corresponding to speed for best range was required by the Army to prove the 30-min capability.

Selection of the right materials to help defeat the specified threats was an important aspect of Black Hawk vulnerability reduction. Included in this selection were electroslag remelt steels for hydraulic servo components, spall-resistant cockpit windshield panels, ballistically tolerant bearing liner materials, self-sealing fuel components, and main and tail rotor-blade spar materials. Design innovations that permit vital systems to continue to function after ballistic impact, noted next, were developed and patented: 1) flight control bellcranks designed with redundant connections and pivots to permit operation after ballistic damage to any one of the three pivot axes; 2) preloaded quadrant spring arrangement that allows either cable to fully control tail rotor pitch following loss of the mating cable; 3) spring-loaded tail rotor servo valve so as to position pitch to the cruise flight setting in case all yaw control from pilot to tail rotor is lost; 4) transmission bearing and gearing technology to allow extended continued flight after loss of all lubricants; and 5) robust rotor-blade and rotor-head titanium components and elastomeric bearings that have demonstrated continued operability after ballistic impact through both live-fire testing and actual combat experience.

Not all of the new technologies designed into the UTTAS prototype lived up to the promise suggested during initial laboratory testing. The most notable example relating to survivability was the use of grease lubrication for gearboxes in place of oil. Sikorsky's proposal for the UTTAS prototype program envisioned use of a specially developed grease for lubrication of tail and intermediate gearboxes. The motivation for using grease was to reduce the likelihood of losing all lubricant as a result of battlefield damage of the housings. Field maintenance would also benefit. Both gearboxes were intended to be "sealed-for-life" units such that periodic checks of lubricant levels would no longer be needed.

However as outlined in Chapter 3, during the initial phase of the UTTAS test program, an overtemperature situation occurred in the intermediate gearbox during operation of the ground-test vehicle. In addition, several unexplained instances of gear hardness loss were experienced during bench development testing. As a result of this experience, the decision was made to quickly change back to traditional oil lubrication.

Reduction of detectability was another important aspect of design to achieve a high level of combat survivability. Development of an infrared suppression kit to reduce engine signature as well as exhaust visibility greatly reduced detectability. The infrared suppression kit was originally designed to reduce signatures at flight speeds of above 80 kn. However the Army later tightened its requirement to provide suppression down to hover conditions, and this was achieved by a redesign of the suppressor.

Noise levels of the main rotor blades were reduced below the levels of contemporary helicopters by the aft swept tips and a moderate blade-tip speed of 700 fps. Cockpit windshield shaping to reduce glint, plus conductive coatings in the windshields and cockpit skin to reduce radar cross section, also helped reduce detectability.

Analysis of helicopter combat damage in Southeast Asia during the Vietnam conflict [21] indicates that ballistic damage to engines, fuel systems, and flight controls caused most crashes and forced landings. The significant contribution to those statistics by engine damage would have been expected for single-engine helicopters and especially for those underpowered aircraft of that era. However, the rate of mishaps of dual-engine helicopters, following loss of one engine, was surprisingly high. That was because of the relatively low power margins of certain twin-engine machines when operating in the temperatures experienced in SEA. The result was that flight in the combat landing zone often forced the helicopter to operate in the "avoid" region of its height-velocity curve.

Low power margin results in a large avoid region extending from sea level to over 500 ft altitude and out to speeds of 30 kn or higher. Single-engine flight anywhere within this envelope is not possible. Thus the combat loss of one engine while flying in this region made recovery nearly impossible with the remaining engine.

The high UTTAS power margin, created by its design for hot and high ambient conditions, greatly reduces the avoid area of the height-velocity curve to below 100 ft altitude out to approximately 20 kn. It provides a very high probability of continued flight in the event that one engine is disabled during landing or takeoff.

Design of the UTTAS fuel system focused on achieving high levels of both crashworthiness and ballistic tolerance, and in fact these Army requirements had complementary effects on each other. The Army, based in part by the excellent service record of the Navy's CH-53 series that pioneered suction systems using engine-mounted fuel pumps, mandated the use of a suction system for UTTAS. Its major benefit is avoidance of sprayed fuel and consequent fire in the event of fuel line damage. For the Black Hawk all fuel lines are self-sealing so as to avoid engine flameout from ingesting air in case a suction line is ballistically damaged. The self-sealing capabilities of its fuel cells provide full protection against many projectiles. In addition, these cells have been shown to provide good protection against fires and hydraulic ram damage against 23- and 30-mm high-explosive-incendiary (HEI) threats.

The UTTAS flight control system design focused on providing the largest possible separation between pilot and copilot controls and keeping them separate until joining was necessary at the controls mixing unit. Plastic troughs located under the horizontal control rods running below the cockpit floor prevent jamming against fuselage structural members in the event that the control rods were severely damaged. Figure 84 shows the controls run from cockpit to rotors.

A unique preloaded quadrant located in the tail rotor pylon enables the pilots to maintain full control of the tail rotor even if one of the two cables is severed. In effect, the single remaining cable can be "pushed" as well as pulled by the automatic action of the spring-loaded quadrant when it senses loss of the normal cable tension. Figure 85 illustrates components of this quadrant assembly.

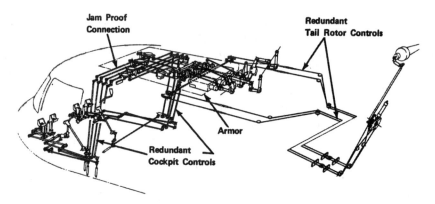

Fig. 84   Separation of pilot and copilot flight control runs was a prime design objective as noted in this sketch.

Figures 86 and 87 show what happens in the event of severance of one cable.

In the event of severance of both cables, a centering spring designed into the tail-rotor control servo positions the servo valve in the proper position to apply a cruise flight tail-rotor pitch setting for return to base. This centering spring is shown in Fig. 88.

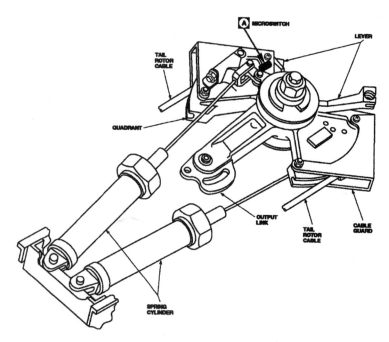

Fig. 85   Preloaded tail-rotor control quadrant allows full control even if one of the two control cables were severed by a projectile.

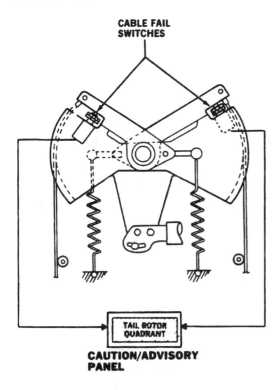

CABLE FAIL SWITCHES

TAIL ROTOR QUADRANT

CAUTION/ADVISORY PANEL

Fig. 86 Tail rotor control quadrant shown in normal flight condition.

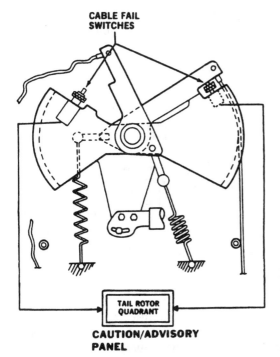

CABLE FAIL SWITCHES

TAIL ROTOR QUADRANT

CAUTION/ADVISORY PANEL

Fig. 87 Quadrant configuration after severance of one cable. The remaining cable held in tension by its spring allows complete control of tail-rotor pitch, and the crew is advised of the severed condition.

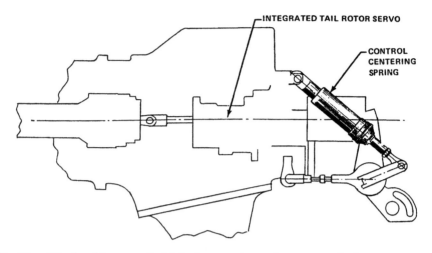

Fig. 88   If both cables were disabled, the centering spring commands the control servo to the proper tail-rotor pitch setting to permit cruise flight to a safe landing zone.

Another design innovation introduced in the UTTAS flight control system to improve ballistic tolerance was the tripivot bellcrank concept shown in Fig. 89.

Conventional flight control bellcranks, consisting of an input connection, a pivot axis, and an output connection, have been susceptible to jamming by ballistic damage to the pivot point. Because of the large number of such bellcranks in a mechanical control system and their relatively small size compared to the threats, they contribute measurably to vulnerable area. Extensive use of tripivot bellcranks in the H-60 series helicopters has significantly improved tolerance to small arms fire.

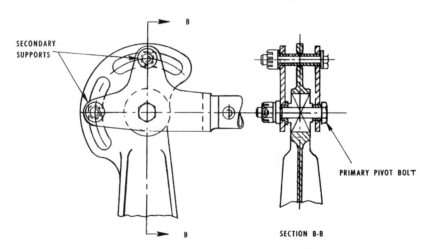

Fig. 89   Unique tripivot concept is used throughout the Black Hawk flight control system. By providing secondary pivot supports, this arrangement permits full bellcrank motion if any one of the three pivots becomes jammed by a projectile.

CREW PROTECTION

Creative design innovations to improve helicopter flight crew protection from ground fire, as well as to enhance crash survivability, were initiated several years before the UTTAS program. One such program was for the Army CH-54 flying crane helicopter for which Sikorsky was awarded a contract to develop new armored, crashworthy cockpit seats. That development effort led to design concepts that formed the basis of the early UTTAS crew seats.

Figure 90 is one of Sikorsky's first experimental designs of the CH-54 seats showing the movable side armor panels similar to what later was developed for the UTTAS cockpit. The energy-absorbing concept developed for this seat was the predecessor to the initial UH-60 crew seats.

The ceramic-composite seat pans produced by the Carborundum Company for the Skycrane project weighed approximately 9 lb/ft^2 compared to 13 lb for the dual hardness steel then used for the Navy's CH-53D helicopters. That significant weight saving led to selection of boron carbide for the UTTAS crew seats.

The evolution of the energy-absorbing solution used on the UTTAS prototypes and early production Black Hawk helicopters is an interesting story

Fig. 90   Sikorsky engineer Dave Fansler seated in a mock-up of an armored and crash-survivable crew seat designed under Army contract for the CH-54 Skycrane in the mid-1960s. (©Igor I. Sikorsky Historical Archives, Inc.)

of adapting a commercial solution to new military requirements. Energy-absorbing units called "Torshocks" were used by the California Highway Department to support guardrails so as to provide a cushion for errant drivers who happened to hit the rails. After an impact, the highway crew would pull the guardrail back into place without having to replace the Torshock absorbers. The configuration of the Torshock, developed by the ARA Company, was simply two tubes separated by a rolling wire torus. The diameter of this wire controlled the amount of kinetic energy absorbed and the stroking load when applied to seat design.

Six Torshock struts supported the armored bucket and allowed the seat and occupant to move downward, forward, and sideward in response to dynamic loads occurring during a crash impact. These six struts can be seen in Fig. 91.

Later in the UH-60 program, a new crew seat was designed and qualified by Simula, Inc., now part of Armor Holdings, Inc. Its configuration is shown in Fig. 92.

In the Simula seats, the armored bucket is supported by four bearing assemblies mounted to two vertical support tubes that provide normal seat adjustment as well as crash energy absorption. During high vertical sink

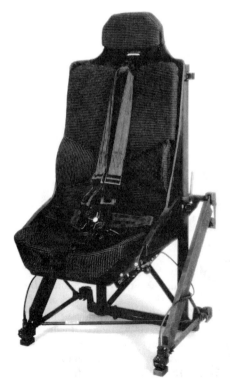

Fig. 91   Initial Black Hawk crew seats were supplied to Sikorsky by the Army as government furnished equipment. The seat made by Simula is shown in this figure.

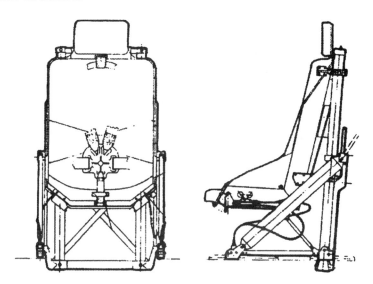

Fig. 92   Simula became the prime crew seat supplier in 1993 and has produced over 4000 seats for the UH-60 and its derivative models.

speed accidents, the seat moves down the support tubes with motion controlled by two inverting-tube-type energy attenuators. A minimum of 12 in. of stroke is provided at a load factor of 14.5 *g* based on average crew-member weight. A cavity in the cockpit floor accommodates this stroking for the full seat adjustment range. The seats are equipped with restraint systems with lap belt, shoulder harness with inertia reels, and lap belt tie-down straps all using low-stretch webbing. A single-motion rotary-type buckle is on the end of the lap belt tie-down strap to ensure that the strap is always used. This restraint system prevents the occupant from sliding under the lap belt in a crash while still allowing quick release for emergency exit.

The ballistic threat that the UH-60 crew seats can defeat remains classified, but crew torso protection was paramount in the Army's specification. Protection from the lower hemisphere minus 15 deg was specified and provided by the curved one-piece seat bucket plus the movable side armor wing. The geometry of this wing evolved during the early UTTAS design process while an experienced Army pilot in a position of authority was evaluating it.

During the Army review of the full-scale wood UTTAS mockup in September 1973, the UTTAS project manager, Brigadier General Leo Turner, sat in the pilot armored seat to evaluate internal and external visibility. While in the seat, General Turner asked for a saw for cutting wood. With saw in hand, he proceeded to cut away parts of the armor wing until he felt that a satisfactory compromise between protection and visibility was achieved, and that became the accepted configuration.

EMERGING THREAT TO HELICOPTERS

The RFP for the UTTAS stressed the importance of surviving in an environment that included 7.62-mm (0.30-cal.), 12.7-mm (0.50-cal.), and 14.5-mm threats. A not-to-exceed vulnerable area limit was required for the 7.62 mm with a desired reduction for the higher threats worded in the RFP as follows: Flight-essential systems shall also be configured to minimize the vulnerability for impact by a 12.7-mm API at 1600 fps (feet per second) and for impacts by a 23-mm HEI (high explosive incendiary) at 1600 fps. In addition, the 30-mm HEI, 37-mm HEI, and 57-mm HEI threat effects and the blast and fragment effects from proximity fused shell and missiles shall be minimized [6].

The primary large threat to UTTAS envisioned during the 1970s was the Soviet ZSU-23-4 "Shilka" 23-mm anti-aircraft gun, shown in Fig. 93.

The ZSU-23-4 has the capability to both acquire and track low-flying aircraft targets, with an effective AA range of 2500 m. Whereas, its guns have a cyclic rate of 800 to 1000 rounds per minute each, they normally fire in bursts of 2–3 rounds per barrel to reduce ammunition expenditure. The crews were known to mix the ammunition at a ratio of three HEI rounds to one API.

With this in mind, the emphasis was placed on minimizing the vulnerability of the UTTAS to the 23-mm projectiles. Tolerance to these threats was achieved primarily through component redundancy and separation. During the early stages of the UTTAS design, the main emphasis on 23-mm tolerance was placed on the airframe structure, particularly the tailcone.

Sikorsky began testing tailcone structure tolerance against the 23-mm threat at the Ballistic Research Laboratory (BRL) in Aberdeen, Maryland. The only tailcones available were those of the S-61 vintage. Many tests were

Fig. 93   1970s vintage Soviet ZSU-23-4 23-mm anti-aircraft weapon.

conducted, and many tailcones were repaired. Finally, it was decided that the "floating frame" concept offered the most tolerant structure to the 23-mm threat. This system resulted in maximum separation of the main load-carrying longerons, providing good tolerance to this threat for about 90% of the tailcone so that structural design approach was incorporated in UTTAS.

To date, there has been only one reported 23-mm hit on a Black Hawk. During the Granada operation in 1983, a 23-mm projectile came through an open cabin door and impacted the main transmission. The aircraft made an emergency landing and was later destroyed by U.S. forces. There have been hits from the RPG weapon. The RPG-7 was adopted by the Soviet Armed Forces in 1961 and is the weapon of choice for many infantryman and guerrillas around the world. At least seven countries manufacture this weapon. The RPG-7, shown in Fig. 94, is a shoulder-fired, muzzle-loaded, antitank, and antipersonnel grenade launcher, which launches a variety of fin-stabilized, oversized grenades from a 40-mm tube.

The largest grenade this weapon can launch is the 85-mm antitank projectile. During the conflict in Mogadishu, Somalia, in October 1994, two U.S. Army Black Hawk helicopters were shot down by RPGs. It has never been determined what size grenade was used. Both helicopters were hit in the tailcone area.

During a training flight in Turkey, a Black Hawk helicopter was hit in the fuselage transition section by an RPG sustaining the damage shown in Fig. 95. Sensing a loss of hydraulics to the tail rotor, the pilots made an emergency landing. The crew chief repaired the hydraulic line, and the air-craft was flown back to its base.

Surviving a direct RPG hit as did the Black Hawk in Fig. 95 and then return-ing to base are most unusual. But at the small arms end of the threat spectrum, Black Hawk survival is more the norm. During the earliest UH-60A combat experience, in the Granada Operation in October 1983, one aircraft sustained a large number of hits while flying nap of the Earth. Figure 96 illustrates those shotlines superimposed on a Black Hawk photograph.

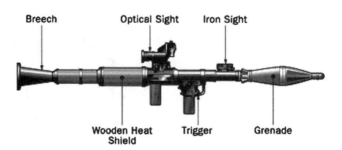

Fig. 94   RPG-7 has a maximum effective range of 300 m against moving point targets. It normally self-destructs after a 4.5-s flight. This equates to a flight of approximately 920 m. It is widely reported that this weapon has only a 50% hit probability.

Fig. 95   RPG strike to the fuselage transition section shown in this photograph taken on site did not cause catastrophic structural damage, nor were the adjacent fuel cell cells badly damaged. This Black Hawk flew back to base after local repairs were made by its crew. (©Igor I. Sikorsky Historical Archives, Inc.)

The pilot reported that he was in the process of resupplying troops in battle and flying nap of the Earth. While coming over a ridge, he surprised a large group of unfriendly people who began shooting at his Black Hawk. The pilot was hit in the leg but managed to fly back to base.

Examination of the aircraft revealed at least 29 hits that were estimated to be caliber 7.62 mm fired from AK-47 type weapons. All hits were from the lower hemisphere and the highest elevation was estimated to be plus 2 deg indicating a roll attitude at the time. The shotlines shown in Fig. 96 would indicate that the small arms fire was directed at the cockpit.

Fig. 96   Trajectories of 29 small arms ground fire sustained by a Black Hawk during the 1983 Granada Operations. (©Igor I. Sikorsky Historical Archives, Inc.)

SURVIVABILITY ASSESSMENT

While the results of the Army's live-fire ballistic testing remain classified, available data from military operations show conclusively that Black Hawk survivability goals, established by the Army in 1972, have been achieved. Combat experience shows that the UH-60 meets and in many cases exceeds the Army's requirements for flying safely for 30 min after ballistic damage from the primary threats. The most significant factor that made this possible was the need to include the requirements for both crashworthiness and ballistic tolerance as part of the aircraft design process at the beginning of the UTTAS program.

Assigning the same design priorities to survivability as has been historically set for aircraft performance, weight, reliability, and other key attributes was done for the first time in this program. This new approach clearly stimulated design creativity as it acknowledged and gave equal weight to a new design discipline supported by specialized training as well. The overall result for the Black Hawk and its many derivatives has been that unprecedented survivability is achieved with a reasonably small penalty in weight and system cost. For the helicopter industry, Black Hawk operational experience has helped set achievable design standards for survivability for new military and civil helicopters.

Chapter 6

DRAWING BOARD TO FIRST FLIGHT

1972 was an especially upbeat year for Sikorsky employees as well as for the local community. Winning a position in the UTTAS program generated enormous hope for the company's future. That critical win offered the possibility of finally reversing the 15-year decline in helicopter production and a long succession of employee layoffs. It was also an upbeat period because the UTTAS contract was the first win of an Army helicopter competition by Sikorsky in many years. Sikorsky earned a place in the UTTAS program by bringing together strong leadership, clear strategies, the right technologies, and creative design solutions. It offered the Army a new technology helicopter that met all requirements, and the program was priced right. It was an offer that the Army could not refuse.

Having won a share in the prototype program, the company's focus was now to design, build, and demonstrate a helicopter better than that of its competitor. With Bell now out of the UTTAS picture, Sikorsky and Boeing Vertol were left to battle for the ultimate award. Winning the production award was the new goal that would conclude a 52-month competitive effort. There was no doubt that the Army's selection of the single sole-source contractor to produce Black Hawk aircraft would shape the U.S. helicopter industry for decades to come. The motivation to develop a successful prototype could not have been higher for both companies. Aggressive goals were set to achieve first flight of the UTTAS prototypes well ahead of contract schedule in the hope that the Sikorsky YUH-60A would fly before the Boeing Vertol YUH-61A.

As the UTTAS program turned out, the Sikorsky prototype did indeed fly both first and earlier than scheduled by contract. In retrospect, designing, building, and getting UTTAS ready to fly were the easy parts of the job. Getting it to fly right was by far the hardest part of the program, and the difficulties were totally unexpected.

The UTTAS basic engineering and development (BED) phase officially started on 30 August 1972 when Sikorsky president Wes Kuhrt and AVSCOM's Maurice Schneider signed the contract. It was a cost-plus-incentive-fee contract for just under $62 million with the main hardware deliverables being three flight-test aircraft, one ground-test vehicle and one static-test article.

The contract was a large document containing a total of 2307 pages. Of these, 437 pages described the aircraft specification, 575 pages specified the qualification work to be performed, and 600 pages were devoted to the various statements of work.

The extent to which the helicopter contracting process has matured can be judged by comparing the UTTAS contract with the contract signed by Igor Sikorsky for the XR-4 prototype helicopter 31 years earlier in 1941 with the Army Air Corps. That contract contained only a single page of specifications for the helicopter that ended up creating a whole new industry. The Sikorsky XR-4 helicopter, Fig. 97, achieved first flight 10 months after contract signing in March 1941. Four months later it was flown to Wright Field in Dayton, Ohio, for acceptance. Seven months after that flight acceptance, the Army Air Corps awarded Sikorsky the very first contract ever to produce more than just a single helicopter.

Within five years, nearly 500 R-4, R-5, and R-6 helicopters had been delivered to the government. This significant production buildup signaled that the helicopter was here to stay, and it became part of the aviation community.

For the UTTAS program, the schedule to build the YUH-60A prototypes, although nowhere near as aggressive as the XR-4, was a challenge heightened by the competitive nature of the program. Table 2 shows the key milestones of the UTTAS program from prototype to production awards.

Flight operations were scheduled to start 26 months after contract award, which was two months ahead of the contract. Factory completion and roll out of the first prototype were planned to occur two months before first flight. That accelerated date for roll-out of the first flight aircraft established the setback schedules for every supporting operation. Those operations included each final assembly position, loading of airframe fixtures, completion of individual parts and sub-assemblies, on-shelf dates for raw material and purchased parts, fabrication of tooling, and the schedule planning for release of drawings.

Fig. 97 Sikorsky R-4, shown next to the Black Hawk, was the first helicopter to be used in service by the U.S. Army Air Corps and the first in the world to enter production. A peak rate of 10 R-4s per month was achieved during WWII. (©Igor I. Sikorsky Historical Archives, Inc.)

Table 2 Sequence, timing, and duration of all major milestones and activities of the UTTAS basic engineering development program from award of the prototype contract to award of the production contract

Activity	Start	Complete	Start months after contract	Finish months after contract	Duration, months
UTTAS BED phase contract	8/1972	12/1976	0	52	52
Basic design data preparation	8/1972	1/1973	0	5	5
Army preliminary design reviews (PDR)	11/1972	3/1973	3	7	4
Cost/schedule control system (SPOTS) training	9/1972	10/1972	0	2	2
Army and Tri-Service validation of SPOTS	1/1973	3/1973	5	7	2
Army mock-up review	9/1993	10/1973	12	14	2
Drawings release (before major design changes)	2/1973	2/1974	6	18	12
Army critical design reviews (CDR)	11/1973	12/1973	15	16	1
Tooling and fabrication (before major design changes)	2/1973	5/1974	6	21	15
Roll-out of first flight-test aircraft		7/1974		22	
Pre-flight acceptance testing—main and tail rotors	5/1974	8/1974	21	24	3
Pre-flight acceptance testing—transmissions	7/1974	8/1974	23	24	1
Pre-flight acceptance testing—ground-test vehicle	8/1974	9/1974	24	25	1
Army safety-of-flight reviews	8/1974	9/1974	24	25	1
Flight testing of first YUH-60A (S/N 21650)	10/1974	3/1976	26	43	17
Flight testing of second YUH-60A (S/N 21651)	1/1975	3/1976	29	43	14
Flight testing of third YUH-60A (S/N 21652)	3/1975	3/1976	31	43	12
Flight testing of company owned S-70	5/1975	12/1976	33	52	19
Army preliminary evaluation (APE)	1/1976	3/1976	41	43	2
Army acceptance of three YUH-60As		3/1976		43	
Army government competitive testing (GCT)	3/1976	11/1976	53	51	8
Army letter of instruction for prod. proposal		2/1976		42	
Submission of production proposal		5/1976		45	
Negotiation of production contract	8/1976	11/1976	48	51	3
Best and final offer		11/1976		51	
Production contract awarded to Sikorsky	——	12/1976	——	52	——

Laboratory test equipment and facilities were scheduled according to aircraft hardware availability as were flight instrumentation and data telemetry facilities. This work consumed the first two contract years during which milestones were achieved on the accelerated schedule. Preliminary and critical design reviews with Army personnel were completed followed by release of approximately 2500 drawings. Aircraft tooling, work instructions, fabrication of components, and delivery of the purchased bill of material all met the planned schedule. Assembly of the static-test article, the ground-test vehicle, and assembly of the three flight-test aircraft encountered no major problems.

Interaction with Army personnel during the UTTAS program impressed Sikorsky engineers with how far the Army had progressed in rotorcraft technical expertise during the preceding decade. From the author's perspective, the center of gravity of government helicopter knowledge moved from the Air Force at Wright Patterson AFB during the 1950s, and to the Navy at the Bureau of Aeronautics during the 1960s, and to the Army at the Aviation Systems Command during the 1970s.

DESIGNING (CS)²

The UTTAS helicopter was not the only contract deliverable that needed to be designed and tested. During that time period, the government required its contractors to have a validated cost schedule control system, $(CS)^2$, particularly for cost-type contracts where costs incurred by the contractor were reimbursed by the government. In such systems, all planned work was broken down into relatively small manageable work packages with assigned managers, schedules, and budgets. Actual performance against the cost and schedule plans was continuously measured and variations reported to management and to the customer. With that information, the "health" of the program could be judged and the need for corrective action determined before the problems became unmanageable and the holes became too deep.

James E. Campion

Sikorsky developed its own program to meet $(CS)^2$ requirements under the leadership of Jim Campion from the company's finance department, who was appointed UTTAS cost/schedule manager. Campion's task was to develop a system that would be used and relied upon by managers to force corrective actions when needed. After training all users, this system had to be validated by the Army as well as by a Tri-Service team. Without such validation Sikorsky could not win the production award no matter how well its prototype aircraft might have performed nor how attractive its production proposal might have been judged.

That fact encouraged senior management involvement, which helped sell the system internally. It needed to be sold first to the finance organization whose culture was not based on nearly instant visibility of actual cost and schedule performance. The value of a true $(CS)^2$ system was in providing the people who planned and managed the work immediate feedback so that timely corrective action could be taken. Because of entrenched attitudes, developing such a transparent system would require senior management support, which was wholeheartedly provided by Sikorsky's president.

The system developed by Campion and his 10-man team was called the Sikorsky Program Operations Tracking System that became known by its acronym SPOTS. After this system was developed, training was provided to hundreds of users assigned to the UTTAS program to get ready for implementation and validation. During training, major emphasis was placed on the benefits to users of rapidly seeing their performance in time to prevent life-threatening cost or schedule problems. That emphasis seemed to work. During

Kenneth M. Rosen

an early visit by the Army CSCS Review Team to see if Sikorsky was ready to demonstrate SPOTS, the team asked to interview a typical work package manager. Campion elected to have an engineer be interviewed, and he selected Ken Rosen. That selection was hardly a random pick, as Ken was anything but a typical engineer. Rosen was a key contributor to the UTTAS winning effort first in the YUH-60A propulsion system design followed by Black Hawk program engineering management. Rosen later served as vice president for research and engineering at Sikorsky.

As expected, Rosen wowed the Army teams who then proclaimed Sikorsky ready for the official validation process. Army validation was received in February 1973 and complete Tri-Service validation received a month later. SPOTS became the first fully computerized system to be accepted by the government under CSCS requirements on the first attempt. That was a major accomplishment for both the Sikorsky and Army UTTAS teams.

Soon after receiving the Tri-Service validation, Sikorsky was inundated with requests to provide a SPOTS training course to military personnel from all services. One-week training classes were held with Army, Navy, Air Force, as well as DCAA personnel and presentations made by Campion and his team to the Defense Systems Management School at Fort Belvoir and to the Air Force Institute of Technology at Wright-Patterson Air Force Base. All of this training and discussion about SPOTS was aimed at improving the perception that Sikorsky might be the company best able to manage the UTTAS production program.

TEST FAILURES THREATENED FIRST FLIGHT

Before the first UTTAS prototype was cleared to fly, a wide variety of tests needed to be performed to uncover any anomalies that might jeopardize flight safety. These tests, called for in the Airworthiness Qualification Specification, started as aircraft components as test fixtures became available. Soon after laboratory and ground testing began, several early failures surfaced that proved the value and necessity of a thorough preflight test program. Two failures in particular were near heart stoppers, one involving the elastomeric rotor and the other associated with the transmission system. Both could have had potentially catastrophic consequences had they occurred during flight.

The rotor problem, described in Chapter 4, occurred during overstress testing of the entire rotor-head assembly in the hub and shaft structural test facility. While undergoing testing at higher-than-flight levels of load and motions, one of the spherical elastomeric bearings experienced a total collapse caused by fatigue failure of stainless-steel shims within the elastomeric bearing. That failure resulted in outboard movement of the blade attachment spindle to the limit of the test apparatus. Had this failure occurred in flight or on the whirl stand, the consequences could have been catastrophic.

This failure was so severe that it threatened Sikorsky's UTTAS program because the company had no backup design for the elastomeric rotor. Fortunately it was soon determined that the shim failures were caused by the accelerated test conditions coupled with shims made from a stainless-steel alloy having low fatigue strength. By strain gauging certain shims, it was found that the very high amplitude of blade flapping simulated in this test fixture produced shim vibratory bending stresses that were higher than the alloy used initially was capable of withstanding. With the very timely support of the Lord Corporation, who designed and built the elastomeric bearings, an alloy having much greater fatigue strength was substituted, and that completely solved the problem in time for rotor whirl testing and first flight.

The second serious problem occurred on the ground-test vehicle. Of all of the ground tests planned, none was more critical to first flight than the GTV, which was a UTTAS prototype operated on a test pad through the complete power spectrum while restrained by ground anchors. The GTV was the first test where all propulsion, transmission, and rotor systems would operate together on the real airframe and by the real control systems. The Army required operation of the GTV for 50 h before granting clearance to initiate flight operations. That testing was completed in September 1974, and it was

the last of the mandatory preflight tests setting the stage for the Army to conduct safety of flight reviews. One of the most important problems uncovered
on the GTV was the inadequacy of the use of grease lubrication for the
UTTAS tail and intermediate gear boxes. Grease lubrication was proposed
for these two gearboxes to improve ballistic tolerance by greatly lessoning
the likelihood that much grease would drain out of a projectile hole in the
housings. The use of grease was also intended to reduce maintenance by
offering a sealed-for-life assembly. Both of these promised advantages of
grease lubrication appealed to the Army, and all bench testing showed good
performance.

However, aircraft tie-down testing shown in Fig. 98, soon revealed
that there was a flaw with either the grease itself or the design of the internal
gearbox provisions to retain the grease. What was found was that very local
gear tooth overheating could occur without being detected by the gearbox
temperature sensors because of the insulation provided by the grease itself.

This overheating was detected by ground personnel as smoke coming out
of the intermediate gearbox and the GTV was quickly shut down before a fire
erupted. As a result of this experience, an immediate changeover was made to
conventional oil lubrication in time to support the first flight schedule.

The UTTAS test team, who had prepared and negotiated the Airworthiness

Walter A. Lane

Qualification Specification, was led by
Walt Lane. He directed the ground-and
flight-test activities throughout the
UTTAS prototype development program.
Lane later managed all engineering operations at Sikorsky's flight-test facility at
West Palm Beach, Florida. He was
assisted by Andy Lapati who directed all
ground-test activities and by Frank Kreutz
who managed the flight-test program.
This team was able to accomplish all of
the required ground testing in time,
despite the technical problems already
noted. Most importantly, the required
safety-of-flight reviews were successfully
conducted with Army personnel, and the clearance to start flight operations
was achieved on schedule.

Other critical ground testing that had to be completed before the Army
issued clearance to fly are shown in Figs. 99–101. In general, a clean 100-h
ground test was stipulated for the rotor and transmission systems. Laboratory
fatigue testing of many dynamic components was performed to ensure fatigue
life margins before flight operations could begin. Overstress fatigue testing to
the point of component fracture was the preferred approach in order to understand the failure mode and therefore to know where the part needed to be

Fig. 98 UTTAS ground-test vehicle being tested for critical stress and motion, engine, and airframe compatibility and engine stress and vibration. Many test sequences were run on the GTV including shake-down testing, preflight acceptance testing, and a 200-h military qualification test of the drive system. (©Igor I. Sikorsky Historical Archives, Inc.)

strengthened. But there was concern within the company marketing department that fracturing every part that was fatigue tested might raise the customer's anxiety level. However this concern was not felt by the flight standards and UTTAS project technical staffs. They fully appreciated that fatigue test run-outs, which are nonfailures after accumulating high cycles at low stress levels, contribute little to understanding the critical failure mode because the part was not stressed to the point of failure.

Fig. 99 First UTTAS main rotor head and blades on Sikorsky's 8000-hp main rotor whirl stand. Testing began after the elastomeric bearing shim problem was corrected. The required 100-h preflight acceptance testing was completed in August 1974. (©Igor I. Sikorsky Historical Archives, Inc.)

Fig. 100 Cross-beam tail rotor seen on the rotor precession stand to demonstrate stability, performance, and airworthiness. The required 50-h preflight acceptance testing was completed in August 1974. (©Igor I. Sikorsky Historical Archives, Inc.)

Fig. 101 Unlike the more generic main and tail rotor test stands, a unique main transmission test facility was constructed for UTTAS to accommodate its shaft angles and input shaft spacing as well as its mounting system. During preflight acceptance testing, torque levels up to 110% of flight levels were applied, and the 100-h test was completed in August 1974. A month later the 200-h military qualification test was completed. (©Igor I. Sikorsky Historical Archives, Inc.)

Fig. 102   Roll out of the first YUH-60A, S/N 21650, was on 28 June 1974, 22 months after contract award, ready to start preflight systems operation and check out the flight data instrumentation system. (©Igor I. Sikorsky Historical Archives, Inc.)

During most of the basic engineering development phase, the Flight Standards office at AVSCOM stationed an engineer at Sikorsky to review test reports and to monitor test activities. But giving a customer representative freedom to walk the test laboratories with access to all engineering data needed some internal cultural adjustment. As it turned out, his presence was invaluable in helping to communicate test results to AVSCOM and in obtaining timely redirection when necessary. He also helped to expedite Army approval of test plans when late receipt could have delayed start of testing. This key Army engineer at Sikorsky was Jack Kemster, assigned by the Flight Standards Office and pictured in Fig. 145.

Roll out of the first flight aircraft, serial number 21650 shown in Fig. 102, took place right on the schedule set at contract award. That event was a major achievement for the company as well as for the Army UTTAS project office. Clearance to fly was obtained from the Army in mid-October 1974, and the team was primed to begin the flight-test development phase.

At that high point of the program, neither Sikorsky nor the Army could ever have imagined the magnitude of the setbacks that would be experienced shortly after flight operations began. During the first two years of the UTTAS contract, the company's focus was on achieving first flight of the prototype, which it accomplished ahead of schedule and within budget. But its focus during the next year and a half was on coming to grips with major technical problems. As described in Chapter 7, making the UTTAS prototypes fly right became the all-consuming task.

THE DERIVATIVE THAT NEVER WAS

While the prototypes were being designed and built, the opportunity to create the first UTTAS derivative model came about in 1973. Although

Chapter 10 describes a long succession of very successful Black Hawk deriva-tive models, the first attempt to create such a derivative got off on the wrong foot. That misstep happened when Sikorsky tried to create a new armed attack helicopter designed around UTTAS components. The life story of this first potential Black Hawk variant began and ended before the Sikorsky YUH-60A prototype ever flew.

Soon after the AH-56A Cheyenne program was cancelled in 1969, the Army began working to develop a new armed attack helicopter (AAH) but with a more modest speed capability than that required of the AH-56A. Cruise speed was reduced to within the capability of a pure helicopter thereby elimi-nating the need for auxiliary propulsion and wings to unload the rotor. It became apparent, following the Cheyenne termination, that risk containment was a factor behind the Army's restatement of gunship performance require-ments. It was accepted that rotorcraft technology during the early 1970s had clearly not sufficiently matured to bring forth a low-risk compound helicopter that would achieve the goals of the original advanced aerial fire support system.

When the request for proposal for this new AAH was released in 1973 while the UTTAS was being designed, it was clear that its performance and survivability requirements were very close to those of UTTAS. The 145-kn cruise speed, 450 ft/minute rate of climb at 4000 ft 95 deg and endurance of the new armed attack helicopter were all similar to UTTAS. Even the gross weight predicted of the AAH came close to that of the UTTAS.

Because of these similarities, Sikorsky sought to marry the entire UTTAS propulsion system, main and tail rotors, and transmission system to a new airframe tailored to the gunship requirements. The rationale for the approach was that commonality of the expensive lift and propulsion systems across two product lines would bring significant savings in both procurement and operational support costs to both the utility transport and the armed-attack-helicopter programs. This concept seemed so appealing, at least internally, that Sikorsky decided to bid on the AAH and created a proposal team to go forth and bring home another Army program. Figure 103 shows a full scale of Sikorsky's AAH candidate design with its UTTAS lift and propulsion systems.

However, its bid was not successful, and the UTTAS/AAH never saw the light of day, and it has never been resurrected. The Army likely felt that plac-ing its two premier helicopter programs with a single company would incur excessive risk especially because, as noted earlier, Sikorsky was not a familiar Army contractor at that time.

The Army's AAH program ultimately produced the very successful AH-64 Apache helicopter, which elevated Hughes into status as a major helicopter producer along with Bell, Boeing Vertol, and Sikorsky. Most importantly, that program gave the Army a significant increase in war fighting capabilities.

Fig. 103 Sikorsky's armed attack helicopter, proposed to the Army in 1973, was designed with maximum use of UTTAS dynamic components as well its tail empennage. Tandem crew seating and underbody weapon turrets were incorporated. Had this first UTTAS derivative been made and flight tested, raising its rotor would likely have been its first major design improvement. (©Igor I. Sikorsky Historical Archives, Inc.)

It provided a lethal capability against armored vehicles and combat ground forces unmatched at the time by any rotary-wing aircraft. The AH-64 was also designed to an unprecedented level of flight crew protection against high-intensity threats.

Chapter 7

"To Make It Fly Is Everything"

In his foreword to this book, Sergei Sikorsky recalled the words of wisdom given to his father, Igor Sikorsky, by the French aviator, Captain Ferdinand Ferber in 1909: "...To invent a flying machine is nothing; to build it is little; but to make it fly.... Ah, that is everything!" Sixty-five years later, Captain Ferber's perceptive observation reflected the state of the UTTAS program at Sikorsky. Although designing and building the first UTTAS prototypes could be considered more than minor accomplishments, they were indeed achieved without major setbacks. However, when flight operations began, everything changed, unexpectedly and dramatically. To make it fly like the contract specified and as the Army expected became everything. The trial-and-error experiments and final successes of that effort were typical of the art of helicopter design and development but more so.

Soon after first flight, significant technical problems surfaced that were daunting because their causes were not immediately understood. A major concern was that the problems might not be solved in time for the Army's competitive fly off. This concern persisted for nearly a year during the development efforts. The second concern was that if corrected, would the solutions impose penalties in weight, cost or operational capabilities that would undermine Sikorsky's ability to offer a competitive UTTAS production program. The flight development period was the most difficult phase of the entire UTTAS effort made worse by the ever-present competitive pressure on company management and on the UTTAS team.

That period was in stark contrast to the design and build phases leading up to first flight. Engineering and manufacturing work was accomplished on an accelerated schedule as the aircraft's first flight was planned to be launched two months ahead of contract schedule. All major milestones were met, and the company's cost/schedule tracking system showed no issues of concern. The key aircraft systems were performing well during ground testing, and in October 1974 the Army declared the YUH-60A prototype ready to begin flight operations. Health of the program looked good from other perspectives as well. Support for the UTTAS program and for the Army's plan to buy over a thousand production helicopters remained strong within both the Department of Defense and within Congress. Company morale could not have been higher

Fig. 104 First flight of UTTAS Serial Number 21650 took place on October 17, 1974 at Sikorsky's main facility in Stratford, Connecticut 26 months after contract award. The two other prototypes, S/N 21651 and S/N 21652, first flew in January and February 1975. (©Igor I. Sikorsky Historical Archives, Inc.)

at the time of first flight, and it was matched by the positive feelings of Army personnel.

First flight of the YUH-60A, Fig. 104, was a special event because it was the first helicopter designed and built for the Army by Sikorsky in many years and it took place six weeks ahead of contract schedule. Added to that was the satisfaction of beating the Boeing Vertol YUH-61A to first flight by about four weeks. The program's competitive environment tended to amplify the smallest of achievements. It also greatly amplified the concerns about the problems soon to be encountered.

The first two flights of the YUH-60A were made within the company's flight field in Stratford, Connecticut. They were made by veteran Sikorsky pilots Dick Wright and John Dixson pictured in Fig. 105. These initial flights concentrated on ground taxi work followed by evaluations of hover and low-speed control harmony and response. All telemetry data were very positive as

Fig. 105 Piloting the first YUH-60A flight were Sikorsky chief pilot, Dick Wright, left, and John Dixson, UTTAS chief test pilot, both of whom conducted critical flight-envelope expansions and demonstrations throughout the flight-test and development program. (©Igor I. Sikorsky Historical Archives, Inc.)

were pilots' comments about the aircraft. The consensus was that the UTTAS flight development program was off to an excellent start. Those early upbeat indications from those first two flights were good news but not accurate omens for the future.

Several days after the first flight, the pilots were authorized to begin "out-of-the-yard" flying to start expanding the flight envelope. During that first up-and-away flight, the YUH-60A gave strong indications that helicopter engineering was still largely an art and not yet a science. In that single flight, Dixson and Wright encountered four serious and completely unexpected problems.

By far the most worrisome were the extremely uncomfortable vibration levels in the cockpit, much higher than predicted and much higher than specification requirements. The second major surprise was that the power needed for high-speed flight was significantly higher than calculated levels, which cast doubt on the aircraft's ability to reach design cruise speed or endurance. The pilots also reported the presence of a bothersome level of side-to-side cockpit vibration, described as tail shake that was judged to be unacceptable. To add to the bad news, the pilots found that the YUH-60A exhibited a very high nose-up attitude during deceleration to a landing. This was a safety-of-flight concern because visibility of the landing zone was lost during deceleration for a landing. These disappointments coming out of only an hour of flying would dominate the flight development effort for nearly a year and a half. They would also create major concerns about Sikorsky's competitive standing against the BV YUH-61A pictured in Fig. 106.

Igor Sikorsky, in a lecture to a class of engineering students, once said: "In the course of your work you will from time to time encounter the situation where the facts and the theory do not coincide. In such circumstances, young gentlemen, it is my earnest advice to respect the facts." Sikorsky's profound advice could appropriately have been directed to the UTTAS design team, who learned first hand how large the gap between prediction and reality could be. Respecting the facts and finding solutions became the focus of

Fig. 106 Boeing Vertol's YUH-61A first flew about a month after the Sikorsky YUH-60A at Grumman's flight test facility in Calverton, Long Island, New York. (Boeing Vertol photo)

engineering and management attention right up to March 1976 when the Army accepted the prototypes for competitive testing.

As the causes of these major problems gradually began to be understood, design changes were made and new hardware installed, but many redesigns were not successful. Some design changes came from experimentation, some from wind-tunnel testing and some from intuitive guesses. Each successful change gradually brought the aircraft closer to the specification. Through these changes, the UTTAS prototype was transformed into its production design that became the UH-60A Black Hawk.

In early 1976, nearly a year and a half after the first UTTAS flight, the last of the design changes was test flown on one of the prototypes. All three YUH-60A prototypes were then modified to the same new configuration. During this development period, the Army neither encouraged nor prohibited design changes because both contractors retained configuration management responsibility. Army personnel were surprised at the extent of some of the changes but never revealed if Boeing Vertol needed or planned to make changes as significant as those made by Sikorsky. The technical story of how each critical problem was resolved is described next.

MAJOR PROBLEM—VIBRATION

The Army's vibration specification was 0.05 g at the crew stations, which was approximately one-quarter of the levels typically experienced in Vietnam-era helicopters. This goal was acknowledged to be aggressive, but its achievement was judged to be worth the benefits to crew comfort and system reliability. Sikorsky's approach to meet the 0.05-g level was based on using its well-proven bifilar vibration absorber, shown in Fig. 107, mounted on the main rotor head right at the source of the vibratory forces.

Fig. 107 Shown is the initial self-tuning bifilar absorber that mounts on top of the UTTAS rotor head. In-plane oscillation of the four weights produce forces that try to cancel in-plane unbalanced forces generated by the rotor blades. (©Igor I. Sikorsky Historical Archives, Inc.)

The bifilar absorber had seen extensive use on Sikorsky S-61 commercial and military models, and its benefits were well documented. In the UTTAS design phase, Sikorsky felt that the vibration levels could be achieved with just the bifilar absorber, given that the natural frequencies of the airframe vibration modes would end up adequately separated from rotor excitation frequencies. The bifilar was therefore the only vibration control hardware used throughout Sikorsky's UTTAS design phase up to first flight. But that approach was to soon change.

The loads and vibration levels presented in this chapter were measured on the UTTAS prototypes during the 1976 time period. The final values achieved might not be representative of production Black Hawk helicopters as a result of continuous improvements. Chapter 10 discusses the most significant of such improvements which is the advanced active vibration control system installed in newer H-60 derivative models.

The first realization that vibration would be a very significant problem surfaced in the third flight. Both pilots experienced severe four-per-revolution (4P) vibrations levels that were an order of magnitude higher than the design specification. The levels were particularly severe in the vertical direction but also exceeded specification in the lateral direction. Figure 108 shows the accelerations measured against airspeed illustrating the magnitude of this problem.

The severity of cockpit vibration was a profound shock, and the challenge that faced the team is clear from the data in Fig. 108. Resolution of this problem required over a year, but in the end an acceptable vibration environment was achieved in time for the prototypes to begin the Army's competitive testing. It was achieved at a weight penalty greater than planned, but fortunately the aircraft's excellent performance margins permitted that penalty to be absorbed. The final vibration solution during the UTTAS BED phase

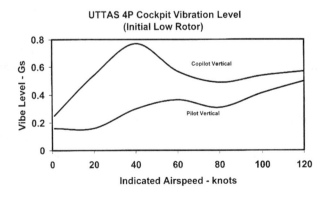

Fig. 108   Initial cockpit vibration levels at the time of first UTTAS flights at the pilot and copilot locations were an order of magnitude over specification limits.

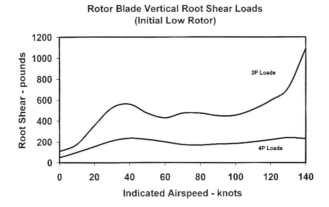

Fig. 109   Very high levels of 3P blade vertical shear loads were measured in early UTTAS flight testing with the low rotor before design changes were made.

consisted of the raised rotor, an enlarged bifilar absorber, the installation of a 4P fixed system absorber, and stiffening of the cockpit floor beams. Each of these design improvements was incrementally added when test data confirmed its effectiveness. Other potential improvements did not show sufficient benefit to justify their weight and so were discarded.

The lengthy effort to understand this problem began with flight measurement of the vibratory loading applied by the blades to the rotor head, referred to as root shears. What was found was that the blade-root vertical shear loading at a frequency of 3P was far greater than the vertical shear loading at 4P across the entire flight speed range. The magnitude of the 3P vertical loading is shown in Fig. 109, where the 3P shear loads are seen to be several multiples of the 4P loading. Three-per-rev content was expected to be present because rotor blades typically have a first flatwise-bending natural frequency near 3P; however, the magnitudes measured on the UTTAS were far larger than expected. There were other factors causing this high blade 3P response, but the causes were not immediately understood.

At the same time that rotor flight loads data were being acquired, data from laboratory structural testing of the UTTAS airframe began to explain why the vibration problem was so severe.

The shake testing, shown in Fig. 110, was performed on the UTTAS Static Test Article whose structure was identical to that of the flight-test aircraft. Dummy weights were installed to replicate high-mass components such as engines, gearboxes, and rotors. The entire airframe assembly was then suspended by shock cords and subjected to vibratory forces representing main rotor excitations.

What was found through this shake testing was that the natural frequencies of certain airframe bending modes were much closer than planned to the

Fig. 110 UTTAS Static Test Article was suspended, by a shock cord system while excitations were applied throughout the range of rotor frequencies. Response was measured at various cockpit and cabin locations. (©Igor I. Sikorsky Historical Archives, Inc.)

rotor 4P primary excitation frequency. This was especially true for principal frequencies involving motion of the main rotor transmission assembly. The relative flexibility of the fuselage center section to which the transmission is attached almost completely influenced the transmission modal frequencies. This area of airframe structure turned out to be more flexible than desired because of the structural cutouts for the large doors on either side of the cabin directly below the transmission. In addition to these cutouts, the relatively low depth of the cabin roof structure, influenced by the compactness needed for air transport, further contributed to a more flexible fuselage than was expected. Shake tests of the airframe, shown in Fig. 110, confirmed that all three principal transmission modes (vertical, pitch, and roll) were very close to 4P.

Figures 111 and 112 illustrate the proximity of the transmission pitch and roll modes of the original UTTAS configuration at the time of first flight.

The effect of these modes near 4P was especially pronounced because of the high measured 3P vertical shears shown earlier in Fig. 109. Such 3P vertical forces in the rotating system are felt as 4P rolling and pitching moments in the fixed system in four-bladed rotors. This was especially troublesome for the YUH-60A because of the close proximity of the key airframe modes. That proximity could have been avoided during the airframe structural design period had the analytical predictions been both available in time and acted upon in time. That was a lost engineering opportunity to detune the airframe through structural redesign. But in the end, significant detuning of the airframe was achieved as a result of an unplanned design change. That change was raising the rotational plane of the main rotor, which is discussed next.

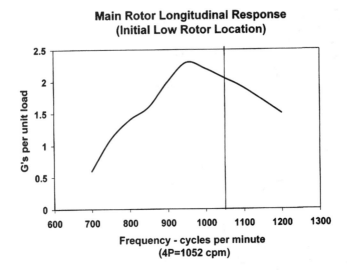

Fig. 111   Main rotor longitudinal response in *gs* per 1000 lb with the original low rotor illustrating proximity of pitch mode to the 4-per-rev excitation frequency.

While the airframe dynamics were being studied, design changes were made to the 4P bifilar absorber to try to increase its effectiveness. The most effective change made was to double the length of each arm of the bifilar absorber in order to double the forces that it could produce. That change was effective, but it alone was not enough to produce a smooth cockpit/cabin environment. As the search for vibration solutions continued, concurrent examination of the roll played by the low rotor position began to point to another possible root cause of the problem.

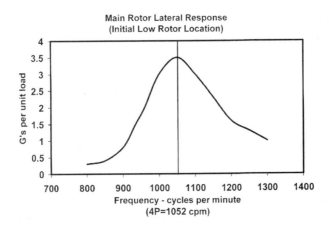

Fig. 112   Main rotor lateral response with the original low rotor showing the transmission roll mode frequency right at 4P, which was the worst possible placement.

Effect of Rotor Location

The idea of raising the UTTAS main rotor to correct the vibration levels was not advanced immediately when this problem first surfaced. In fact, the analytical efforts that led to the raised rotor solution were directed not at the vibration problem but at the problem of higher-than-predicted forward flight power that was also revealed in early UTTAS flights. It was thought that the low rotor position might create interference flow conditions that could increase power in forward flight. As it happened, the technical findings that led to raising the rotor were somewhat unexpected but of enormous value in helping to understand the relationship between rotor location and the high vibratory blade-root shears mentioned earlier.

These aerodynamic and vibration investigations were unconnected until the point was reached where analysis found that the fuselage turbulent flowfield contained strong 3P coefficients that were totally unexpected. The breakthrough came when this flowfield understanding was associated with the high 3P blade vertical shear forces measured at the main rotor. Using newly developed computer codes, analysis began to show that the predicted fuselage body flows could indeed cause high vibrations, and that raising the rotor could lessen them considerably. At that point the idea of raising the rotor to address two problems was put forward by Sikorsky aerodynamicists, principally Bob Moffitt, who first advanced an explanation of the high 3P excitation relative to rotor position. Of crucial help in arriving at this explanation was the work of Tom Sheehy in developing computer codes to predict fuselage airflow fields and in the work of John Marshal in developing blade dynamic codes.

The thought of raising the rotor, which seemed like a wild idea at first, began to gather momentum among company senior technical managers, aided by the insight of Henry (Hank) Velkoff from Ohio State University, who was an aerodynamic consultant to Sikorsky. But concern was legitimately raised because a higher rotor location could seriously compromise air transport, which clearly was a high-priority Army requirement.

The most serious consideration from the marketing viewpoint was how the company's competitive position would be impacted if Sikorsky raised the rotor while Boeing Vertol did not. The excellent air transport capability with the low rotor, emphasized in the company's UTTAS proposal and well received by the Army, would likely be seriously compromised. A raised rotor could possibly require removal of the blades, rotor head, and main gearbox to fit inside the C-130 transport. Removal of these major components would require far more manpower and elapsed time than permitted by the Army's specification. Raising the rotor with these consequences was a difficult decision because it was known from visual sightings that the Boeing Vertol prototypes were flying with their original low rotor configurations. In addition, there was no guarantee that raising the rotor would significantly alleviate the vibration problem. However it was certain that raising the rotor would certainly increase both aircraft weight and drag. The decision to experiment with a raised rotor was especially agonizing but had to be made as there were no vibration solutions with any promise of success.

What helped resolve the company's concern and pave the way for raising the rotor was the creativity of two Sikorsky rotor designers who found a way to solve the potential air transport problem posed by the raised rotor. Donald Ferris, holder of 42 patents, and Robert Rybicki, holder of 18 patents, together invented a two-position rotor system that would still meet the Army's air transport requirements. Their ingenious and elegant design solution used a removable new part, called the rotor shaft extender. This extender locates the rotor plane 15 in. higher during flight, but it permits the rotor to be lowered for air transport. In preparing the aircraft for air transport, the extender is removed and stored in the cabin. It is reinstalled when the aircraft is unloaded and made ready to fly. This design innovation permits the aircraft to be quickly prepared for air transport within the specified 1.5-h elapsed time, but it requires approximately 13 man-hours for reassembly as demonstrated by the Army instead of the specified 5 man-hours.

With this novel solution to the air transport rotor height constraint, Sikorsky president Gerry Tobias with the recommendation of Bill Paul, vice president of engineering, made the decision to proceed with experimental hardware to raise the rotor on one of the prototypes as quickly as possible. That decision was also approved by Harry Gray, UAC chief executive officer. Analysis indicated that raising the rotor in the neighborhood of 15 in. would significantly reduce the 3P excitations. However, this experiment needed Army approval because it was such a major departure from the UTTAS contract configuration, and it potentially affected weight and performance.

Within days of Sikorsky's decision to fly the raised rotor, Brigadier General Jerry Laurer, the UTTAS project manager, was briefed by the author to get Army approval for this flight evaluation. His reaction to the raised rotor idea was one of surprise and perhaps some shock about the possible impact on air transport, but he remained as neutral and as noncommittal as possible: "it's your design and you should know what the Army feels is important."

General Lauer's reaction to this design change was typical of the Army's reaction to all contractor design changes. The Army's position on configuration management during the development phase was to give freedom to the contractors to make their own critical design decisions that ultimately could spell victory or defeat in the UTTAS competition. The Army wanted no part of that decision process. Consequently, without commenting on the wisdom or absurdity of raising the rotor, the Army Flight Standards Division, led by Charlie Crawford, studied Sikorsky's design approach and established the preflight fatigue test and functional requirements to ensure flight safety.

Sikorsky quickly constructed an extension of the rotor shaft using existing titanium forgings left over from another program. The fatigue strength of the

Fig. 113   Raised main rotor with two extenders bolted together for early flight evaluation on one of the three prototypes. The bulge seen midway up the rotor shaft is the bolted connection. Note that the UTTAS at that point had the stabilator installed, which first flew two months earlier. (©Igor I. Sikorsky Historical Archives, Inc.)

experimental bolted assemble was confirmed by subjecting the hardware to the million overstress fatigue cycles stipulated by the Army as one of the preflight requirements. The experimental shaft extension consisted of two flanged shafts machined from existing hand forgings and bolted together to make up the 15-in. rotor height increase. The urgency of this experiment made it opportune to use material on hand rather than delay the test until new forgings of the correct length could be obtained. Betting on success, new one-piece forgings to retrofit the three flying prototypes and the ground-test vehicle were immediately ordered.

First flight of the raised rotor with the experimental extenders, Fig. 113, took place on 17 May, 1975 just minutes after the Army cleared this installation to fly. Shortly into this flight, the pilots reported a significant reduction in 4P vibration levels confirming predictions.

The magnitude of the vibration reductions was most encouraging, but the levels achieved were not yet down to specification requirements. However at

Fig. 114   Production Black Hawk raised rotor extender in its normal position. This part is removed, and the four control push-rods are disconnected to lower the rotor for air transport. The extender is stored in the cabin during air transport while the folded blades and lowered main rotor head remain on the aircraft. (©Igor I. Sikorsky Historical Archives, Inc.)

Fig. 115 Airflow deflected up into the rotor caused large blade angle-of-attack changes that amplified the 3P blade-root shear loads.

that point the raised rotor became the most important part of the overall vibration improvement package. As a result, Sikorsky made the decision to convert all three prototypes to the raised rotor configuration but with hardware designed to the planned production standard shown in Fig. 114. The initial concerns about not achieving air transport requirements with a raised rotor were resolved by the clever design solution described earlier.

The reasons that the low rotor produced such an unacceptable vibration situation are related to the effects of the upward airflow from the cockpit area into the rotor disc [22] and to the natural frequencies of the transmission/airframe bending modes. The raised rotor was the key to the initial vibration reduction effort because it reduced rotor excitations as well as detuning the transmission roll and pitch modes. Figure 115 illustrates the freestream airflow diverted up into the rotor by the cockpit and upper fuselage.

This local inflow significantly altered the local blade angles of attack particularly over the nose. Analysis indicated that the angle at attack changed by approximately 6 degrees at 80 knots flight speed at about 30% blade radius station. Figure 116 shows the change in blade angle of attack caused by the fuselage.

The fuselage influence on blade angle of attack just shown is expanded in Fig. 117, which illustrates how strongly the UTTAS airframe affected the rotor angles of attack at various azimuth positions. The result was that these interference effects between the rotor disc and airframe caused an amplification of 3P vertical shears at the rotor head.

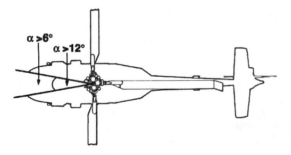

Fig. 116 Rotor-blade angle of attack changes caused by upwash effects on the rotor are noted in two zones over the UTTAS cockpit with the rotor in its original low position.

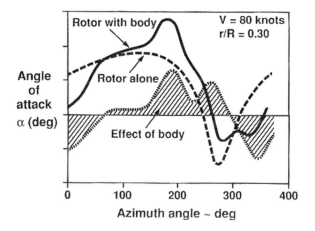

Fig. 117 Initial low rotor position resulted in substantial effect of the UTTAS fuselage on rotor-blade angle-of-attack distribution.

Analyses showed that the 3P vertical shears could be reduced if the distance from the rotor to the overhead canopy could be increased. By reducing the 3P vertical root shears, the applied 4P pitch and roll excitations of the airframe would in turn be reduced, and this rationale led to the decision to flight test a raised rotor.

Figure 118 shows the measured reduction in 3P vertical loads applied to the rotor by the blades as a function of airspeed for the original low and raised rotor locations.

The large reduction in 3P loads applied by the blades to the rotor head significantly reduced the 4P moments felt in the stationary system, that is, at the main transmission and airframe. In addition to the lower excitation, the

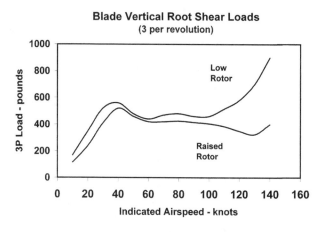

Fig. 118 Raised rotor resulted in a dramatic reduction of vertical root shear loads that in turn greatly reduced airframe 4P excitation.

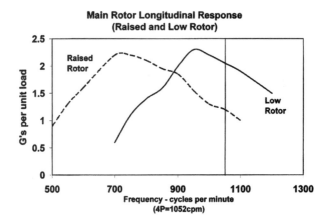

Fig. 119   Raised rotor greatly reduced longitudinal response at the critical 4P frequency by moving the transmission pitch mode away from 4P.

airframe response was further reduced because the raised rotor moved the transmission pitch and roll vibration modes away from the 4P-excitation frequency.

Prior to raising the rotor, several attempts were made to change airframe tuning by installing kits to stiffen the cabin structure in the hope of moving the transmission modes above 4P. But because of the large door cutouts and minimal depth of the overhead structure discussed earlier, the stiffening kits did not produce significant increases to the transmission primary modal frequencies. When the raised rotor was installed, it was found to lower these frequencies, thereby achieving greater separation from rotor excitation frequencies so that no further structural experiments were conducted except for the local cockpit stiffening described next.

The extent to which the shaft extension had a softening effect on natural frequencies in both the critical modes was a most welcome surprise. Figures 119 and 120 show the dramatic effect of the raised rotor structural components on the key airframe modes. The reduction in response at the 4P frequency was substantial and together with the reduction in 3P vertical shears shown in Fig. 118 explained the large vibration reduction attributed to the raised rotor.

FIXED SYSTEM ABSORBERS AND COCKPIT STIFFENING

Although raising the rotor made a significant improvement, vibration levels were not yet down to specification. The cabin overhead structure still showed excessive response in spite of the greater spread between 4P and the transmission pitch mode natural frequency from the added flexibility of the raised rotor. With these data, Bill Girvan, a dynamics engineer responsible for

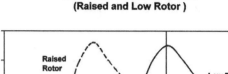

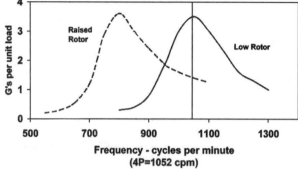

Fig. 120   Lateral rotor response was also significantly lowered by increasing separation of the transmission roll mode from 4P.

doubling the effectiveness of the bifilar, suggested installation of simple spring-mass absorbers to reduce the still excessive airframe response. Various airframe locations were evaluated including two 4P vertical absorbers in the cabin overhead area, one aft of the main transmission and one forward of it. In addition to the remaining response of the cabin overhead structure, cockpit floor motion was still creating a 4P problem at the crew stations. Girvan experimented with adding a cockpit nose absorber plus moving cockpit structural response further away from 4P by stiffening the cockpit floor beams.

The UTTAS cockpit structure was cantilevered from the cabin by the four longitudinal keel beams that run from the aft cabin bulkhead forward to the cockpit nose intended to prevent plowing in a crash. However, these cantilevered beams tended to make the cockpit respond somewhat as a springboard excited by the transmission 4P pitch mode, and that response produced unacceptable cockpit vertical vibrations. Stiffening these beams in the cockpit-to-cabin transition by bonding graphite laminates to the beam caps was effective in detuning the springboard effect. Figure 121 shows both the overhead 4P absorbers and the area of the cockpit keel beams stiffened by the graphite laminates.

Response was measured with the stiffened cockpit beams in two absorber configurations: first with a nose absorber but without the two cabin overhead absorbers and second without the nose absorber but with two cabin absorbers. Figure 122 shows the results of these experiments from which the decision was made to use only the cabin overhead units.

The cabin overhead absorbers plus the cockpit stiffening brought about further significant reductions in cockpit vertical vibration at the crew stations. Figure 123 shows the combined effects of these changes. Further testing determined that the aft cabin overhead absorber was no longer producing

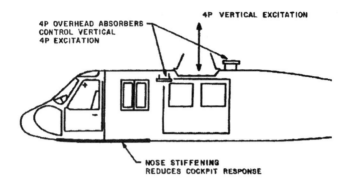

Fig. 121 Vibration absorbers plus airframe nose stiffening became part of the vibration control solution.

benefits worth its weight, and it was removed from the vibration package for the production UH-60A Black Hawk and copilot locations. It was also determined that the benefits of the graphite stiffening kit could be achieved at less cost, but at a slight weight penalty, by an appropriate increase in thickness of the aluminum keel beam caps.

At that point in early 1976, within a few weeks of the scheduled delivery of the prototypes to the Army, the vibration reduction package was finalized. Cockpit vibration level was reduced by almost an order of magnitude down

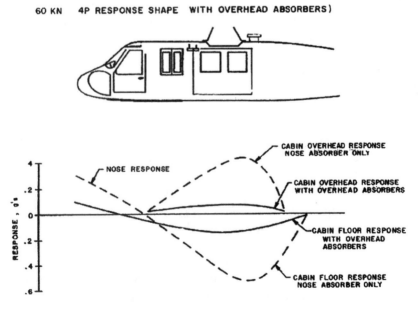

Fig. 122 Installation of two overhead 4-per-rev absorbers resulted in significant reduction in cabin vibration levels.

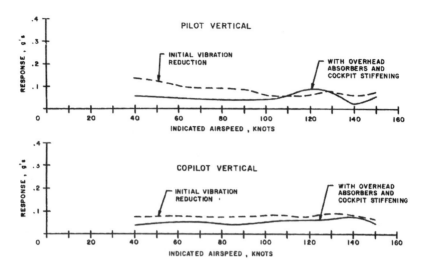

Fig. 123   Combined effects of the raised rotor, 4P absorbers, and airframe nose-stiffening reduced cockpit levels to near 0.05 g.

to near the original specification of 0.05-g. However, in spite of a very aggressive vibration reduction program it became apparent that the 0.05-g goal could not be achieved across the speed range at acceptable weight penalties. What was achieved was a large decrease in vibration down to an average of 0.1-g or less, which was judged by Army pilots to be acceptable. At this level, vibration was less than half of what it was in helicopters of that era. Given the UTTAS program cost and schedule constraints, and limited by the vibration control technology available at the time, further improvement effort was not warranted, and the level of 0.1-g became the requirement in the UH-60A Black Hawk production specification.

The final package of improvements, consisting of the raised rotor, enlarged bifilar, one cabin overhead absorber, and local cockpit stiffening, was incorporated in the UH-60A starting with the first production unit. Reducing vibration levels down to near the original Army specification was an achievement that helped make the difference between winning and losing the production competition. This vibration solution was further improved upon during the maturity phase when additional refinements to the vibration control package, described in Chapter 9, were developed.

The next major change to the Black Hawk vibration control system would come 25 years later using Sikorsky's active vibration control system (AVCS). The all-new AVCS was developed by Sikorsky for its S-92 helicopter and later made part of the Army UH-60M model described in Chapter 10. The application of new technology resulted in further reductions in vibration levels at a lower total weight penalty.

"PIN THE TAIL ON" AND GETTING IT RIGHT

It took many experimental flights with different configurations before Igor Sikorsky found the right tail design of his VS-300 helicopter in 1939. Since then, design of the vertical and horizontal tail surfaces of helicopters have historically been the last parts of the configuration to be finalized. The UTTAS program was found to be no exception to that historical experience. It continued to reveal the lack of full understanding of main rotor wake characteristics and its effect on tail surfaces as well as on the tail rotor. In the case of UTTAS, a lengthy experimental process led to changing the initial fixed horizontal tail to a variable incidence fly-by-wire stabilator. Although it added mechanical and electronic complexity, the stabilator proved to offer far more handling qualities benefits than were initially expected, and the stabilator in large measure became a major contributor to the UH-60 excellent flying qualities.

Development of the UTTAS tail configuration started early in the flight development phase. During the approach to landing from their first flight out of the company flight field, Sikorsky UTTAS test pilots, Dick Wright and John Dixson, encountered high nose-up attitudes that took away visibility over the cockpit nose. This was later found to be more objectionable during rapid deceleration and aborted takeoff maneuvers, clearly making it a safety concern. In addition, the pilots had difficulty transitioning from hover to forward flight when the aircraft center-of-gravity was positioned in the full aft location.

The cause was quickly identified to be main rotor wake impingement on the horizontal stabilizer, and the effect was magnified by the stabilizer's large size. The prototype's initial stabilizer had unusual proportions particularly in that its area of 60 ft^2 was quite large relative to helicopters of similar size. Its large area was intended to provide good stability characteristics in forward flight in view of the aircraft's aft center-of-gravity location. This aft c.g. location, discussed in Chapter 3, was intentional. Its purpose was to help meet air transport requirements by using the canted tail-rotor's lift component to allow the c.g. to be aft of the main rotor, thereby shortening the distance between the aircraft nose and rotor axis. The other unusual feature was the stabilizer's significant aft plan-form sweep shown in Fig. 124 designed to try to avoid this rotor downwash impingement.

A swept tail was expected to result in a more gradual immersion into the rotor wake and therefore produce an acceptable body attitude situation. But the facts again proved otherwise, and a lengthy search for the "right" horizontal tail began.

Within days after finding this problem, a flight with the stabilizer taken off the aircraft confirmed the suspected cause, and a program was launched to determine whether the stabilizer's area or its location or both were responsible. Figure 125 depicts the tail download that caused the nose-up attitude condition.

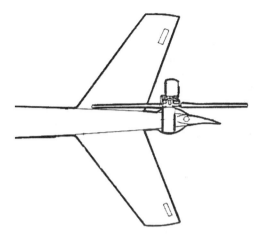

Fig. 124   Initial UTTAS large-area stabilizer swept aft in an unsuccessful attempt to soften main rotor downwash impingement.

Several weeks after the flight without a stabilizer, a smaller-area stabilizer made up from two production S-61 horizontal tails installed 12 in. further aft, shown in Fig. 126, was flown on 23 November, 1974, but minimal improvement was noted. Total stabilizer area was still too large and the aft location did not avoid main rotor wake.

To evaluate the influence of horizontal tail location, an experiment was conducted with widely separated tail sections. The "Z" tail as it was called, shown in Fig. 127, was flown first on 11 February, 1975. Improvement was noted, but the nose-up attitude was still not acceptable to the pilots. Immediately following the "Z" tail experiment, a flight was made, still on February 11, with the lower half of that tail configuration removed as shown in Fig. 128. This high tail, now half the area of the original stabilizer, showed very significant improvement in the nose-up attitude condition; however, the

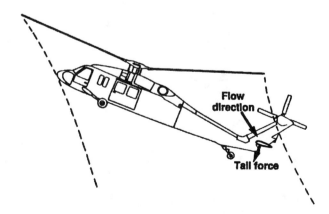

Fig. 125   Rotor downwash on the fixed stabilizer caused large nose-up moments and unacceptably high aircraft attitudes particularly during quick-stop maneuvers.

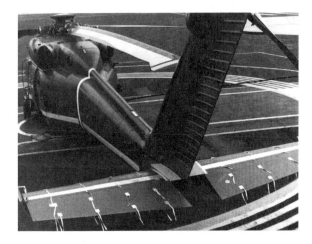

Fig. 126 Two small-area
S-61 stabilizers were installed and test flown with little
benefit to the nose-up
attitude problem. Tufts were
attached to the airframe to
visualize flow behavior.
(©Igor I. Sikorsky Historical
Archives, Inc.)

Fig. 127 "Z" tail configuration helped reduce the
nose-up problem indicating
that the lower stabilizer area
was controlling attitude.
(©Igor I. Sikorsky Historical
Archives, Inc.)

Fig. 128 Lower half of the
Z tail was removed, resulting
in an improvement but at
the expense of forward-flight
stability. (©Igor I. Sikorsky
Historical Archives, Inc.)

relatively small area did not provide adequate forward-flight stability characteristics.

While these tail experiments were being conducted, an unexpected helicopter visited the Sikorsky flight field in Stratford, Connecticut. That helicopter was one of the Boeing Vertol YUH-61A prototype aircraft. It had flown from its test facility at Calverton, New York, across Long Island Sound to pay the Sikorsky UTTAS team a special visit. After contacting the control tower, the Boeing Vertol machine made a low pass over the flight field, dropped a small package and flew away. In a nicely wrapped package was a child's coloring book entitled "Pin the Tail on the Donkey." The Boeing Vertol team's coloring book was an appropriate comment on Sikorsky's trial-and-error process at finding the right tail. Later, after a solution was finally found, Chief UTTAS Test Pilot John Dixson happened to fly a YUH-60A over the Boeing Vertol Calverton facility. In the spirit of rivalry, Dixson took the opportunity to drop a small package as a token of good will. But its contents were not as elegant as the Boeing Vertol gift package. They could be collected anywhere, especially in barnyards.

The last of the fixed tail experiments took place on March 10 with flight of the large anhedral tail shown in Fig. 129. This tail, supported by a strut because of its size, flew better, but longitudinal stability was not entirely acceptable.

During the four months of this tail experimentation, design of a variable incidence stabilizer was initiated as a stand-by configuration in the event that a fixed-tail solution could not be found. This variable-incidence horizontal tail, referred to as the stabilator, was initially intended to solve only the pitch attitude problem by automatically changing its incidence during low-speed flight to minimize the rotor downwash effects. It was also designed with an area of 40 ft^2, down from the original area of 60 ft^2, yet it provided superior longitudinal stability characteristics. The stabilator design evolved

Fig. 129 Large-area anhedral stabilizer supported by a strut did not fully restore stability. (©Igor I. Sikorsky Historical Archives, Inc.)

under the leadership of Lou Cotton, with electronics design help from Ray Johnson and Dave Verzella and with airframe design help from John Chapkovich. The stabilator's benefits became better understood as its control system design was created. In particular, its ability to generate forces at the tail independent of flight speed was used to fine tune handling qualities throughout the entire flight envelope. In addition, its ability to trim attitude helped to increase flight speed capability. In the final analysis, the stabilator improved flying qualities in ways that could not have been achieved with the original fixed stabilizer even if the fixed stabilizer had functioned as planned.

First flight of the stabilator, shown in Fig. 130, was on 13 March, 1975 nearly five months after the UTTAS first flight, and was a success in all respects. It immediately became the baseline design and was retrofitted on all three prototypes with electronic fine tuning to capture all of its potential flying qualities and cruise speed benefits.

The stabilator was designed as a first-generation fly-by-wire system with manual override. There are no mechanical control connections to the cockpit. Two electric jackscrew actuators acting in series and controlled by two separate sets of electronics set the stabilator incidence. The two actuators are mounted on the tail pylon structure and together position the stabilator as high as 40 deg nose up for hover and low-speed flight and as low as –8 deg nose down for certain cruise and maneuvering flight conditions. In addition, the –8 deg incidence allows good control margins at full forward c.g. during high-speed autorotations.

The large nose-up incidence during low-speed and hover flight completely solved the aircraft attitude problem by greatly reducing rotor downwash force as illustrated in Fig. 131.

The schedule of stabilator incidence as a function of indicated airspeed is shown in Fig. 132, which also shows the coupling of collective stick position on stabilator incidence [23].

Fig. 130 First flight of the fully controllable stabilator was successful in correcting nose-up attitude and in improving stability. (©Igor I. Sikorsky Historical Archives, Inc.)

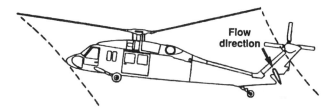

Fig. 131   Stabilator nose-up incidence of approximately 40 deg during low-speed flight almost completely eliminated the main-rotor downwash effect.

The stabilator's variable incidence offered other handling quality enhancement opportunities once the basic sensor/computer/actuator redundant equipment was installed. Collective pitch coupling to stabilator incidence was used to reduce nose-up attitudes during transition to hover and improved fuselage attitudes as well as pilot visibility during low speed flight. Figure 133 shows the attitude variation with various fixed tail settings and with the critical aft c.g. condition.

In addition to airspeed and collective stick position, two additional inputs were used to control stabilator incidence. The third input is aircraft pitch rate that helps decouple collective-to-aircraft pitch motions common to single-rotor helicopters. Pitch-rate coupling further improves aircraft pitch damping in cruise flight as well as providing positive maneuvering stability in forward flight. The fourth input to stabilator incidence is aircraft lateral

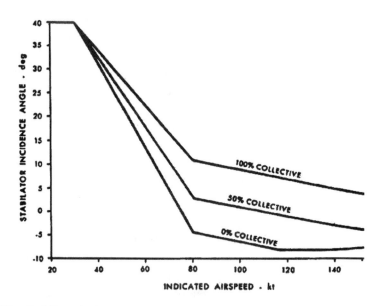

Fig. 132   Stabilator incidence schedule is shown as functions of indicated airspeed and collective stick position.

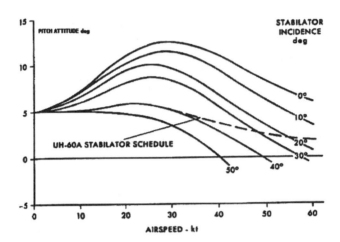

Fig. 133   Aircraft level flight pitch attitude vs airspeed.

acceleration. That input reduces aircraft pitch disturbances caused by gusts on the tail rotor, which create pitching moments because of the tail-rotor's cant angle.

All components that control the stabilator constitute a dual fail-safe configuration with two independent subsystems consisting of electronics, actuators, sensors, fault monitors, power supply, and wiring. In the event of an automatic shutdown resulting from disagreement between the two systems above a set value, the pilots can manually control stabilator position by slew switches in the cockpit control panel in addition to a slew switch mounted on each cyclic stick. These switches bypass all electronics and connect 26-V power directly to the actuators.

Getting to the right tail design was a long process relying heavily on flight-test evaluations of alternative tail configurations. It was a frustrating process as the expression on John Dixson's face in Fig. 134 shows. But finally a design was found that has endured essentially without change throughout all of the various Black Hawk H-60 derivatives built to date. The stabilator solution with all of the flying quality enhancements that it provided was the result of the lengthy effort to pin the UTTAS tail on right.

ACHIEVING THE "UTTAS MANEUVER"

Prior to development of Sikorsky's improved rotor blade for the CH-53D that introduced cambered airfoils, essentially all Sikorsky metal rotor blades used the NASA 0012 airfoil. The symmetrical 0012 airfoil had been selected because of its low pitching moments that helped minimize control system loads because earlier blade spar materials lacked the torsional stiffness of current spars. In addition, low pitching moments were desirable when flight

Fig. 134 UTTAS chief test pilot, John Dixson, debriefing Sikorsky president Gerry Tobias, center, and the author after one of the many stabilizer evaluation flights. (©Igor I. Sikorsky Historical Archives, Inc.)

control systems were manual prior to the advent of irreversible hydraulic servos. However, new-generation helicopters in the UTTAS time frame needed better high-speed performance, where lift capability and drag divergence at high Mach numbers become prime considerations as well as potential limitations. Improved maneuver capability also became more important in combat operations as a result of aggressive nap-of-the-Earth flight techniques. Advanced airfoils were clearly needed in order to achieve new performance and maneuverability requirements.

During the late 1960s, airfoil research by Sikorsky in conjunction with the United Aircraft Research Laboratories (UARL) developed a new cambered high-lift airfoil with 9 1/2% thickness. Its characteristics were well matched to projected helicopter performance requirements. This airfoil, designated as the SC1095, showed a 10 to 20% increase in maximum lift coefficient and a 4 to 7% increase in drag-divergence Mach-number boundaries compared with the earlier 0012 airfoil. The new airfoil also produced very low pitching moments for a cambered airfoil that added to its attractiveness. The SC1095 airfoil was selected for the CH-53D improved rotor blade and flight tests confirmed significant performance improvements for that aircraft. Titanium-spar blades with this airfoil first flew in September 1971, leading to gross weights to 38,000 lb and speeds to 180 kn. As a result, the SC1095 airfoil was selected for the UTTAS main and tail rotor blades because its demonstrated capabilities were well matched to UTTAS performance requirements.

Both main and tail rotors performed well with the SC1095 airfoil. However when the flight envelope was sufficiently expanded to attempt to achieve the "UTTAS maneuver," the facts again seemed to contradict theory. This particular maneuver was a nap-of-the-Earth obstacle avoidance flight path that required pulling at least 1.75 g to clear an obstacle and holding that load factor for 3 s followed by a push over to 0.25 g to return to the prior altitude.

Its purpose was to minimize exposure to ground fire during combat nap-of-the-Earth flight. When Sikorsky pilots first tried to perform this maneuver at simulated hot and high ambient conditions, they were unable to hold the 1.75-g load factor for the specified 3 s.

The first reaction to this shortfall was that rotor solidity might have been too low, which implied increasing blade chord in order to generate the higher lift needed. Increasing chord would have had major impact on blade tooling, blade weight, and perhaps rotor head configuration. But fortunately, after an intense study by a team of senior Sikorsky aerodynamicists, the cause of the lift shortfall was found, and a clever design solution was developed. Within days after it was conceived, this design solution was added to a set of UTTAS blades and quickly flown to reevaluate the 1.75-g pull-and-hold maneuver. The modification described next fully corrected the problem and represented another in a series of "elegant" solutions made possible by creativity heightened by the survival instinct during an intense competition.

The UTTAS rotor's initial insufficient transient lift problem was caused by two unconnected factors. The first was related to the method used to measure characteristics of the new SC1095 airfoil in the UARL wind tunnel. Unknown at the time was that the two-dimensional insert used to measure airfoil lift coefficients was generating data that were in fact optimistic. Later, after the load factor shortfall was found in flight testing, a new tunnel spanning airfoil rig revealed lower, but correct, maximum lift coefficients for this airfoil. The second factor was related to the methods used at the time to analyze rotor performance.

During the UTTAS era, Sikorsky aerodynamicists used what is referred to as a "constant inflow" model that did not accurately predict the stall region of the blade when operating at very high lift. Since that period, the more accurate "variable inflow" vortex-wake-based rotor model showed that a rotor blade initially stalls inboard of the tip at approximately 85% span. This knowledge allowed rotor-blade designers to use a high-lift airfoil inboard of this tip stall region but then terminate that airfoil shape at a spanwise location before it is forced to operate where advancing side compressibility would become a problem. Had that been understood at the time the UTTAS blade was designed, a different airfoil would have been used in the outboard portion of the blade. As it turned out, this solution was arrived at independently through the collective intellect of a team of very capable aerodynamicists.

In addition to these computational shortfalls, a further issue affecting rotor maneuver performance was that of airframe parasite drag. During early flight testing, the forward-flight power required was greater than predicted because airframe drag was higher than that measured by early wind-tunnel testing. The higher propulsive force required from the rotor, because of the drag increase, exacerbated the airfoil lift problem during the pull-up maneuvers at higher speeds. As discussed next in this chapter, a concerted attack on the drag issue substantially reduced the drag effect on maneuverability; however, the major contributing factor to solving the load factor problem was the airfoil refinement described next.

When the maneuver problem surfaced, a team was formed to search for potential solutions short of resizing the main rotor blade. That team consisted of Sikorsky engineers Evan Fradenburgh, Dave Clark, Robert Moffitt, Bob Flemming, Gary DeSimone, and a Sikorsky consultant Henry "Hank" Velkoff, who was an aerospace professor at Ohio State University. By examining early results of the new variable inflow model applied to a high twist blade, the team realized that a higher-lift airfoil could be used to advantage in a certain area of the blade while the SC1095 could be used to advantage in other areas of the blade. The team in effect designed a "drooped snoot" addition to the SC1095 that had the promise of producing the higher lift coefficient needed to meet the maneuver requirement.

The basic shape of this add-on leading-edge droop was patterned after the NACA 23012 airfoil and scarfed on to the leading edge of the SC1095 airfoil. This new airfoil, called the SC-1094 R8, was quickly added to an existing set of UTTAS blades using balsa wood and fiberglass. These modified blades were flight tested in advance of any experimental data on this new airfoil, and their first flight confirmed the team's prediction. At that point the "drooped snoot" became the production airfoil in the region shown in Fig. 135.

Maneuver capability with the R8 airfoil is shown in Fig. 136. The pull-up load factor with the R8 met Army requirements of holding 1.75 g for 3 s while the push-over achieved 0 g, which is better than the 0.25-g requirement. With this improved design, the Army's objective of minimizing the aircraft's exposure to ground fire during low-level flying was achieved.

Both the aerodynamic and structural design envelopes achieved for the UTTAS in its final configuration are shown in Fig. 137 up to limit dive speed.

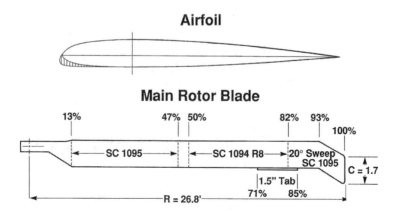

Fig. 135   Black Hawk main rotor-blade airfoil spanwise variation and blade dimensional geometry.

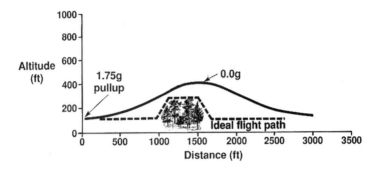

Fig. 136   Nap-of-the-Earth UTTAS maneuver required the 1.75-*g* pull-up to be held for 3 s.

The fully articulated rotor with the right amount of hinge offset together with the right blade aerodynamic design achieved a major improvement in load factor capability.

The structural design and aerodynamic configuration of the main rotor blades developed during the UTTAS program remained the Black Hawk production standard for over 25 years. Advanced composite materials and newly developed airfoils, tip geometry, and planform were introduced in UH-60M model in the 2001 time period. Chapter 10 discusses these rotor-blade changes and how they further improved aircraft performance.

RECOVERING THE SPEED SHORTFALL

Early flight testing pointed to a significant shortfall in UTTAS forward-flight speed of approximately 20 kn. Airframe drag was found to be much

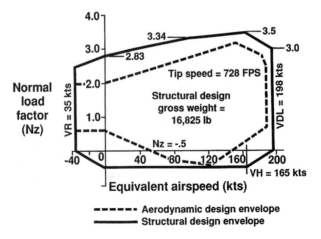

Fig. 137   Aerodynamic and structural envelopes demonstrated during the UTTAS qualification testing were as shown.

above the predicted value and was the prime reason for the large power increase with speed. Resolution of the speed shortfall required both wind-tunnel and in-flight experimentation. In addition to the performance problem, high levels of tail excitation were reported by the pilots. They described it to be much worse than the tail shake typically encountered by many helicopters in certain flight conditions.

Fortunately both the speed and tail shake problems were related to the airframe configuration, and, as it turned out, major reshaping of the aft portion of the main rotor pylon intended to reduce drag also greatly reduced tail excitation. The rotor pylon reshaping provided a smoother path for the airstream above and below the engine exhaust area so as to reduce flow separation and turbulence. Buffeting at the tail rotor and at the large tail surfaces, caused by flow separation at the pylon, was especially severe at high angles of attack during descending flight.

As mentioned earlier, Sikorsky exploited the ability of the new stabilator to generate forces at the tail independent of fuselage attitude. This made good use of the computers, actuators, and sensors that were already part of the configuration needed to solve the nose-up attitude problem. The stabilator turned out to be another knob to turn in searching for solutions to this speed problem and it was used to set optimum fuselage attitude in forward flight so as to minimize parasite drag. However, many more airframe design refinements were necessary to fully recover the speed shortfall.

This performance problem was particularly vexing as the pilots reported that at 125 kn or so the aircraft seemed to encounter an invisible brick wall, and telemetry data confirmed a greater-than-expected increase in power required. The aerodynamic designs of both the rotor blades and the airframe were initially suspect, but the airframe was later determined to be the cause and focus was directed toward drag reduction. Raising the main rotor to help solve the vibration problem did adversely affect forward-flight power but not to a great extent.

The initial UTTAS design had been wind-tunnel tested at 1/10 scale during early studies and again prior to proposal preparation. Parasite drag was estimated to be just over 22 ft^2 including momentum losses and drag created by antennas, leakage, and miscellaneous effects. This resulted in a predicted cruise speed of 150 kn at mission gross weight of 15,500 lb and at 4000 ft 95 deg. During proposal review, the Army estimated drag to be somewhat higher at 23 ft^2 and reducing cruise speed to be 148 kn. In addition, gross weight had grown to 15,850 lb at contract award in August 1972.

Because of the weight escalation, Sikorsky elected to increase rotor diameter by 4 in. to 53 ft 4 in. order to maintain vertical climb performance at 550 ft/min. Later during flight testing, an additional increase of 4 in. was made by lengthening the blade-tip cap to end up with a rotor diameter of 53 ft 8 in., which has remained unchanged throughout production of all H-60

(S-70) models. That last diameter increase was made to offset the growth in empty weight primarily caused by all of the design improvements described in this chapter.

While the UTTAS detail design was underway during 1973, Sikorsky built a quarter-scale wind-tunnel model to evaluate airframe aerodynamics and stability characteristics. Data from that testing in the UTC large subsonic wind tunnel confirmed the Army's estimate of 23 ft². During this testing, the pronounced effect of body attitude on parasite drag became apparent. In particular, the landing-gear stub wings showed very adverse lift-and-drag effects and became opportunities for drag reduction. In addition to changing the stub wing incidence, an extensive list of other drag clean-up items, which also included a reshaping of the main rotor pylon, was developed. By that time construction of the UTTAS prototypes was well along, and it was decided to avoid making major design changes. However, soon after flight testing uncovered the power problem that list became a statement of work for performance recovery.

The speed shortfall was overwhelming to say the least. Whereas a speed in the high 150-kn range was predicted, actual speed in only the high 120-kn range was possible. Based on actual performance, total drag was calculated to be approximately 32 ft² including external instrumentation slip rings. Discounting instrumentation drag, parasite drag appeared to be over 28 ft², significantly above all prior predictions. With that drag, the UTTAS speed shortfall was in the neighborhood of 20 kn. A greater-than-expected nose-down attitude in forward flight with the original fixed stabilizer contributed to the drag problem. The low main rotor position was thought to further exacerbate the problem because of the strong upflow from the cockpit area into the main rotor. Although possibly part of the drag problem, this upflow was found to be much more responsible for the vibration problem discussed earlier. When the raised rotor was tested in May 1975, measurements indicated that the impact on rotor performance was minimal, but the shaft extender hardware did add about 1 ft² of drag. That increase had to be offset during the drag-reduction effort.

Several wind-tunnel test entries were made in 1975 with the quarter-scale model to focus on reshaping the rotor pylon, reducing momentum losses, and optimizing the stub wing incidence, and other opportunities found during earlier testing. Most of this effort centered on reshaping the main rotor pylon in the area between the engine exhausts and above the fuselage aft transition.

Figure 138 shows the extent of the rotor pylon reshaping developed in the wind tunnel, which contributed to a large increment of the drag reduction and to all of the tail shake elimination. The initial and final pylon shapes are shown in Figs. 139 and 140.

a)   b)

Fig. 138   Wind-tunnel models of a) the original UTTAS main-rotor pylon and b) the production Black Hawk configuration. (©Igor I. Sikorsky Historical Archives, Inc.)

The final shaping of the main-rotor pylon was not unlike that of Sikorsky's S-61 series, which at the time was referred to as the "horse collar" design.

The final pylon reshaping is shown in Fig. 140 along with the raised rotor and the aerodynamic effects of the flow separator are depicted in Fig. 141.

The main-rotor pylon reshaping made the most dramatic improvement; however, many other design changes contributed to solving the performance shortfall, including the following: 1) increasing the landing gear stub wing incidence from 0 to 7 deg for the prototypes and to 14 deg for production UH-60s; 2) reshaping the tail-wheel drag beam from a flat to a circular structure; 3) adding fairings to window and door tracks, reshaping the FM homing antennas, reducing the cockpit footstep size, contouring the bifilar weights, and reshaping the tail gearbox fairing; 4) reducing entrance areas for cooling of the electronics bay, hydraulics and flight controls compartment, and changing gearbox cooling scoops to screened openings; 5) adding a rounded lip to the large main-rotor pylon upper opening to redirect air leaving the pylon area; 6) adding a fairing over the oil cooler blower exhaust to redirect outlet flow to an aft direction; and 7) adding spring-actuated covers to the maintenance access steps and covers to the refuel ports in the fuselage transition area.

Fig. 139 Original pylon shape initially built into the three YUH-60A prototypes. This early UTTAS configuration still had the low main rotor. (©Igor I. Sikorsky Historical Archives, Inc.)

Fig. 140 Final Black Hawk main-rotor pylon flow separator geometry developed in wind-tunnel testing. (©Igor I. Sikorsky Historical Archives, Inc.)

Another change that helped recover cruise speed was an increase in engine power available. By operating at a slightly higher rotational speed, the T700-GE-700 produced an extra 23 hp each. That gain was quickly exploited by making a small increase in the gear ratio of the main gearbox high-speed module. The gain in speed was about 1 kn.

The combined effect of these design changes reduced the parasite drag down to 26 ft² plus they effectively eliminated tail shake. Especially helpful in leading this effort were Bob Flemming, Dean Cooper, and Jim Rorke. Dave Clark provided close technical support, and Evan Fradenburgh made important contributions to the flow separator design and to other improvements.

FLOW SEPARATOR EFFECTS
Aft pylon *without* flow separator

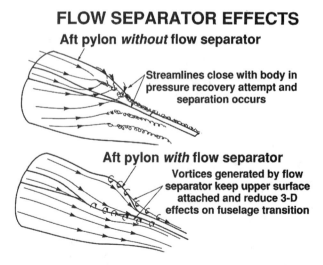

Streamlines close with body in pressure recovery attempt and separation occurs

Aft pylon *with* flow separator
Vortices generated by flow separator keep upper surface attached and reduce 3-D effects on fuselage transition

Fig. 141 Airflow patterns before and after redesign of the main-rotor pylon. The flow separator significantly reduced both tail-rotor excitation and airframe parasite drag.

All design changes were incorporated in Sikorsky's three prototypes in time for Army's fly-off evaluation. In its refined aerodynamic configuration, the YUH-60A mission cruise speed at the specified hot and high conditions was 147 kn. That was approximately 20 kn better than the initial "brick wall" experience encountered a year earlier.

The Army's speed assessment of Sikorsky's proposal in September 1972 was 148 kn. In January 1977, the Army assessed the speed of Sikorsky's production design to be 147 kn. That evaluation confirmed that the large initial cruise speed shortfall was driven to almost zero by the changes made to the prototype configuration.

READY FOR ARMY EVALUATION

The three-view drawing, Fig. 142, shows the most obvious design changes that transformed the prototype YUH-60A into the production UH-60A Black Hawk. The significant design changes that can be seen include the raised rotor, stabilator, reduced vertical fin area, recontoured main-rotor pylon, and reshaped forward sliding fairing.

The decision to correct all major problems and to retrofit the prototypes before delivering them to the Army was a key Sikorsky strategy that played a critical role in the production award. Gerry Tobias, the new Sikorsky president named at the end of 1973, was convinced that the company should not postpone correction of major problems to the production phase, but instead it should do whatever it would take to correct the problems during the development phase. This led to almost around-the-clock work by engineers and manufacturing people to design build and test experimental hardware until solutions were demonstrated.

The senior management of United Technologies Corporation, formerly named United Aircraft Corporation, continued their close oversight of the

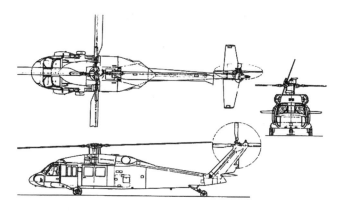

Fig. 142   This illustrates some of the key configuration changes that corrected the major problems and that became part of the Black Hawk configuration.

Fig. 143   United Technologies Corporation CEO Harry Gray flying in the company-owned S-70 with experimental markings in March 1976. (©Igor I. Sikorsky Historical Archives, Inc.)

UTTAS program during the difficult flight development period. Its CEO Harry Gray in particular wanted to experience the improvements in vibration, flying qualities, and performance. He got the opportunity to do this with the company owned S-70. That aircraft was reconfigured to match the three YUH-60A prototypes about to be delivered to the Army for the start of the Army's fly-off competitive testing.

Gray, seen in Fig. 143, was impressed, as were all government personnel who flew in the S-70 during tours, with the aircraft's exhilarating flight performance especially after performing a split-S maneuver with Chief UTTAS pilot, John Dixson.

The YUH-60A was improved to the extent that it about equaled its paper design of three years earlier in nearly all respects. Sikorsky was able to meet its contract commitment, and the YUH-60A was ready to fly off against the Boeing Vertol YUH-61A for the ultimate prize of the production award. Chapter 8 describes that evaluation.

ARMY FLY-OFF

The intense UTTAS development to get the YUH-60A to fly right was aimed at convincing the Army that the Sikorsky prototype met its design requirements and was ready for production. The thoroughness of the Army's fly-off test program would determine whether or not that goal was achieved. It would also reveal how the Sikorsky YUH-60A stacked up against the Boeing Vertol YUH-61A.

Award of the prototype programs to both companies in 1972 was based on Army evaluation of paper proposal aircraft. But in 1976, the Army would select the sole-source production winner on the basis of an eight-month real aircraft competitive evaluation. All of the design and flight development work from August 1972 to December 1975 was aimed at making the prototypes as good as they could be in anticipation of that evaluation.

The Army fly-off was referred to as the government competitive test (GCT) phase. During the preceding year, Army personnel were trained, and many government test sites were readied for GCT, so that its postponement to give the contractors more development time was not an option. The Army's plan was to finish its evaluation by the fourth quarter of 1976 in time to select the winner of the UTTAS production award by the end of that year.

Once the prototypes were delivered for Army testing, there was essentially no opportunity for further significant design improvement. After delivery for GCT, the Army would assume responsibility for configuration management. During GCT, only design changes directed by the Army or those required by safety-of-flight considerations would be permitted. This provided more incentive for the contractors to fine tune their prototypes as best they could before delivery to the Army. More time would have been desired for additional tweaking of the prototypes; however, it appeared that the Army was pulling harder to receive the prototypes than the contractors were pushing to deliver them.

Before the prototypes could be accepted, the Army scheduled a preliminary evaluation (APE) in order to determine that the aircraft could be operated safely by typical Army pilots throughout the range of planned testing. The APE began at each contractor's facility in November 1975 in anticipation of the start of formal Army testing planned for January 1976. But on November 11, 1975, one of the Boeing Vertol prototypes made a crash landing in a heavily wooded area near their Calverton, New York, flight-test facility. The pilots were fortunate to be able to walk away because of good crashworthiness design; however, the aircraft's fuselage was ruptured in the tailcone area [24]. That event created a serious problem with the timing and scope of the GCT fly-off because the immediate assessment was that Boeing Vertol appeared able to deliver only two prototypes. Even if that course were to be followed, an additional problem was that the crash occurred before sufficient flight-test data, specifically in structural demonstration, were acquired to clear the Boeing Vertol prototype for Army acceptance. As a result, there was no question that the start of GCT had to be delayed past January 1976.

Several options were considered by the Army to start GCT later than planned but still in time to support a final selection of the winner by the end of 1976. The first option was to accept the company-owned prototypes into the Army evaluation to make up for the damaged BV aircraft. Earlier in the program both companies elected to build internally funded demonstrators, in effect making four prototypes available to each.

The Army permitted use of the government-funded tooling and engineering data for this purpose. Sikorsky's motivation for building its own S-70, which is the company's designation for its UTTAS design, was to use it as an additional flight test vehicle to explore alternate solutions and design improvements using internal research and development (IR&D) funding. In addition, the company used that aircraft for demonstration flights to prospective customers and government personnel. The S-70 seen in Fig. 144 proved to be very useful in helping to evaluate different vibration solutions.

The option of inducting the Boeing Vertol-owned aircraft into the fly-off evaluation was evaluated, but doing so would require congressional approval, and the Army was reluctant to pursue that course. While this deliberation was taking place, Boeing Vertol concluded that its crashed prototype could be repaired and be made available for testing by March. The Army then rescheduled acceptance of the Boeing Vertol and Sikorsky prototypes from January to March 1976, still hoping to make the production selection by year's end. That was good news because more time suddenly became available to continue design refinement by both companies. Sikorsky used that time to fine tune vibration reduction as well as to correct shortcomings found by Army pilots during APE flying. From the financial point of view, that extra time was regarded as two more months of bleeding as a result of unbudgeted work.

ARMY TAKES DELIVERY

In mid-March, the prototypes were accepted by the Army and preparations made to air transport two aircraft from each company to Fort Benning, Georgia, and one to Edwards Air Force Base in California. Delivery of the

Fig. 144   First company-owned S-70 built in the same configuration as the three YUH-60A prototypes was used for IR&D work as well as customer demonstrations. Its rotor was later raised and other modifications made to equal the final UTTAS design. (©Igor I. Sikorsky Historical Archives, Inc.)

prototypes was a major event that marked the beginning of the most crucial phase of this competitive program. Several Army and Sikorsky participants involved in the Army acceptance process are seen in Fig. 145.

The visit to Fort Benning by the UTTAS prototypes was only for several days to begin the formal government competitive test program with static displays and flight demonstrations by company pilots. This event at Fort Benning in March 1976 was the first time the competing aircraft and their program management teams were brought together. Walk-around inspections revealed some new insight into what had been known about the competitor's aircraft, but cordial discussions with the competitor's people added little more. Figure 146 pictures the YUH-60A and YUH-61A in a flyby past the reviewing stand.

The chief UTTAS pilots of both teams, John Dixson from Sikorsky and Frank Duke from Boeing Vertol, flew the demonstration flights that were on the tame side. Both would have liked to show the maneuver and performance capabilities demonstrated during envelope expansion testing. But the demonstration flight cards conformed to Army ground rules. After Boeing completed its demonstration, Dixson mentioned that he would "like to take the gloves off" when it was Sikorsky's turn to fly, but he was encouraged to follow the flight card, which he did.

Fig. 145   Colonel "Bud" Patnode signing the DD-250 form accepting the three YUH-60A prototypes. Standing at the far left is Don Baerveldt from the Army UTTAS program office and behind him is Joe Konner Sikorsky configuration manager. Standing in the foreground is Ray Leoni, deputy UTTAS program manager and author; behind him is Bob Wolfe representing the Army's Flight Standards Office; behind Col. Patnode is Ken Horsey, UTTAS vice president and program manager, and next is Karl Mittag chief of the Army's acceptance pilots. Second from the right is Jack Kemster, the flight standards' on-site observer, who is followed by Charlie Martin Sikorsky UTTAS contract manager. Bob Wolfe was assigned to head the Army's technical evaluation of the production proposals. (©Igor I. Sikorsky Historical Archives, Inc.)

The prototypes were then flown from Fort Benning to Fort Rucker, Alabama, for the start of development testing (DT) that included training of Army pilots and maintenance personnel. Test duration at Fort Rucker was approximately three months to evaluate how well the prototypes met their specification in areas not having to do with flight performance. Extensive testing was done to simulate aircraft system failures and the capability of

Fig. 146   Boeing Vertol and Sikorsky UTTAS prototypes flying together at Fort Benning to formally start the Army competitive fly-off. (©Igor I. Sikorsky Historical Archives, Inc.)

backup systems to provide safe operation. Maintenance demonstrations were performed to evaluate predicted man-hours and elapsed times to change engines, major dynamic components, as well as preparation of the prototypes for air transport. External loads were carried and jettisoned to validate safe operation of release mechanisms and safe environment for crew members operating these mechanisms.

When the Army testing was completed at Fort Rucker, the two prototypes from each company were flown to Fort Campbell, Kentucky, for the start of the operational testing (OT) phase. The purpose of that phase was to evaluate how well the aircraft could perform the intended combat assault missions by flying simulated missions in as realistic conditions as could be found. During their three-month stay at Fort Campbell, the aircraft were kept outdoors exposed to weather. All Army personnel lived and serviced the prototypes from tents at an operating base called Bastogne DZ at Fort Campbell. Simulated assault missions were flown in whatever weather conditions prevailed and at night with full 11-man rifle squads.

During all of its flying, the Army recorded every maintenance action, every component failure, and every mission abort experienced on the prototypes. This detailed record keeping was performed by a dedicated Army team with on-site observation by contractor personnel. Every month the Army convened a contractor data review meeting and permitted the contractors to challenge the inclusions of certain data. For example if a component replacement was recorded as a failure when evidence pointed to a maintenance error by an Army mechanic, that data entry would be reversed, which in effect lowered the observed failure rate. The purpose of those challenge reviews was to weed out reliability and maintainability data that did not accurately reflect inherent aircraft capability. Data thrown out included maintenance and handbook errors, installation of older parts where newly designed ones were available, operating procedure errors, and several other categories causing maintenance actions that did not reflect true aircraft needs.

When the eight-month GCT testing and data recording was finished, the Army had an accurate and unassailable assessment of reliability, availability, and maintainability that served it well during production proposal negotiations.

INDICATION OF COMPETITIVE ADVANTAGE

The first tangible evidence that the Sikorsky prototypes might have a performance advantage over the Boeing Vertol machines came from a pilot's report during operational testing at Fort Campbell in May 1976. That particular Army testing was intended to demonstrate that the UTTAS prototypes were capable of lifting an external load of 7000 lb with their cargo hooks. That was the external load required by the Army's specification and represented the weights of certain vehicles and weapons intended to be transported as external loads attached to the aircraft cargo hook. The demonstration was to be conducted with a two-man flight crew plus a crew chief and mechanic in the cabin. The fuel load carried aboard the prototypes was whatever could be lifted along with the 7000-lb load plus the four-man crew. The ambient condition on the day of the testing was a temperature of 80°F and essentially at sea-level altitude.

Sikorsky pilot Dick Faull reported that the YUH-60A was able to pick up the 7000-lb weight with "no sweat" and with four men aboard plus a total of 1500-lb of fuel in the aircraft tanks. That amount of fuel represented about three-quarters full tanks. At no time during this demonstration did the pilot come close to pulling engine-topping power, which meant that additional lift capability was available from the aircraft. A contractor pilot was asked to fly alongside the Army copilot because that test was the first external load operation to be conducted.

Right after that demonstration, the Boeing Vertol YUH-61A made the same attempt while carrying a four-man crew plus a reported fuel load of only 1000 lb. Observers indicated that while attempting to lift the 7000-lb load, the pilots had to pull engine-topping power but could still not lift the load. The pilots aborted their attempt when the main rotor rotational speed began to droop excessively. Later, on subsequent attempts the YUH-61A was able to lift 5300 lb and fly around the pattern, but reports circulated that the Boeing Vertol personnel on site were not happy about the whole experience after witnessing the YUH-60A performance.

Sikorsky regarded the results of this side-by-side testing as the first confirmation that its focus on achieving as high a lift efficiency as possible was paying off. Chapter 3 described the design techniques used to maximize overall lift efficiency through rotor-blade aerodynamic design that produced the highest rotor figure of merit ever achieved by Sikorsky. To this high rotor efficiency was added the benefits of the canted tail rotor as well as an efficient three-stage main transmission. In addition, design of Sikorsky's engine inlet and exhaust may have contributed to better performance. It was surmised that the YUH-60A experienced less inlet temperature rise than its competitor from exhaust gases being drawn into the inlet during certain flight conditions.

All of this meant that the YUH-60A had a significantly greater total lift capability using the same installed engine power as in the YUH-61A. Even though the empty weight of the Sikorsky prototype was greater and its rotor diameter larger than its competitor, it was clearly able to provide a greater useful load. Because of lift efficiency, its maximum gross weight was proportionally greater than its empty weight resulting in a larger useful load capability. "Useful load" is the term used to quantify what the aircraft can lift above its own bare weight. In the final analysis useful load is what the customer buys, especially in a transport helicopter.

POTENTIAL TRAGEDY BECOMES A VICTORY

During one of many night missions at Fort Campbell, an accident occurred while a Sikorsky YUH-60A was carrying a full complement of Army troops and aircrew that could have had tragic consequences. At 11:15 on the night of 9 August, 1976, this aircraft was forced to make an emergency landing in a heavily wooded area of Fort Campbell with 14 Army personnel onboard. Figure 147 taken by the Army early on August 10 shows the Sikorsky UTTAS down in a dense pine forest. Its blades appeared intact after cutting through the trees like a rotary lawn mower.

At first light the next morning, an Army team began inspecting the aircraft looking for clues to the vibration problem reported by the pilots that prompted the emergency landing. Figure 148 shows the forward fairing slid to its open position and also shows distress to the main rotor blade pointing to the right in the three o'clock position.

Fig. 147 Fully loaded YUH-60A goes down in a pine forest at night. This photo was taken by the Army early the next morning. During the night emergency landing in a heavy mist, the pilots saw the tree tops and thought they were descending into a cornfield. The circular swath of chopped trees is apparent. (U.S. Army photo)

Fig. 148   After bringing out the 14 troops and crew, Army personnel had begun clearing stumps and inspecting the aircraft. One rotor blade had lost its surface skin, which caused the vibration leading to attempting a precautionary landing. (U.S. Army photo)

The company's on-site service representative immediately called the company, and arrangements were made during the night to fly a team of engineers directly to Fort Campbell with permission to land on the Army airfield. Shortly after noon on August 10, the Sikorsky team was led through the woods to the crash site area where the aircraft could only be seen from just a few feet away because of the density of trees and undergrowth.

Figure 149 was taken as the team approached the aircraft and first impression added to the concern about personnel injuries and the condition of the aircraft. Only after reaching the crash site was the Sikorsky team told that the occupants did not sustain serious injuries. Fortunately the only injury, which

Fig. 149   First glimpse of the aircraft as it was approached through the woods by the Sikorsky and Army team. (©Igor I. Sikorsky Historical Archives, Inc.)

was considered minor, was to one of the soldiers when he jumped out of the cargo door and bumped his head against an adjacent tree stump just cut down to rotor height by the rotor blades.

Army personnel were starting to saw down to the ground over 40 trees severed by the YUH-60A rotor blades many as large as 5 in. in diameter.

Figures 150 and 151 show the main and tail-rotor blades and general terrain conditions at the site.

The inspection team consisted of about a dozen Army and Sikorsky engineers some of whom are pictured in Figs. 152 and 153.

Close inspection by Army and Sikorsky personnel found that the only visible damage was to the four main and four tail-rotor blades other than nicks and dents to the airframe that were of no structural concern. All gearboxes and engines turned freely, and all flight controls responded properly. There was no evidence of fuel leakage or any distress noted on flight-critical systems. The decision by Col. Ron Perry, Army Test Board manager at Fort Campbell and supported by the Sikorsky team, was that only the main- and tail-rotor blades needed to be replaced.

By the end of the day, two Army mechanics replaced the rotor blades using the portable maintenance crane shown in Fig. 154 while the site was being cleared to permit safe ground run-up.

The cause of this mishap was quickly determined to be a faulty adhesive bond of the fiberglass skin in the tip region of one main rotor blade. During flight, a corner of the skin began to peel back because of the high air loads. That produced a strong 1-per-rev vibration felt throughout the aircraft

Fig. 150   Fiberglass skin torn off one blade during a night flight caused severe vibrations leading to a well-executed emergency landing by Army pilots under full control. (©Igor I. Sikorsky Historical Archives, Inc.)

Fig. 151   Repetitive slash marks were found on one tree made by the tail rotor confirming that the descent was vertical with zero forward speed. Note that this aircraft is serial number 21650, which was the first UTTAS prototype to fly, and it continued flight operations subsequent to this tree encounter. (©Igor I. Sikorsky Historical Archives, Inc.)

that steadily worsened. Figure 150 shows the area where a portion of the blade outer skin came loose. There were no problem indications on the caution advisory panel or from the engine instruments, but the 1P vibration was so pronounced that the pilot, CW2 Charlie Lovell, decided to make an

Fig. 152   Investigators at the accident site included Nelson Itterly, left, from the Army UTTAS Project Office; Bob Zincone, Sikorsky director of engineering; and Daniel Schrage, right, from the Army's Flight Standards Office. (©Igor I. Sikorsky Historical Archives, Inc.)

Fig. 153 Sikorsky UTTAS program manager and author relieved by the absence of serious injury to the 14 Army occupants and the unbelievably good condition of the aircraft. Although not a real test of crashworthiness, this event impressed observers and especially Army crewmen with the robustness of the YUH-60A. (©Igor I. Sikorsky Historical Archives, Inc.)

immediate landing. Because of total darkness with a ground mist, the aircraft's landing lights made the tops of the tall pine trees protruding through the mist appear to be a cornfield. It looked like a perfect place for an emergency landing.

Fig. 154 Army mechanics changing blades with the portable maintenance crane that was part of the UTTAS logistics support package. (©Igor I. Sikorsky Historical Archives, Inc.)

CW2 Lovell descended vertically under full control right through the pine forest to touchdown. His excellent landing under very stressful conditions, essentially with zero lateral and low vertical velocity, prevented occupant injury or serious aircraft damage. Although not a test of the aircraft's energy-absorbing features described in Chapter 5, the mishap was a test of spar strength of the main and tail blades as well as the attachment strengths of gearboxes and airframe. In that test the losers were the pine trees as none of the titanium spars of the main rotor or composite spars of the tail rotor were fractured and no cracks were found in any component. None of the main rotor titanium spars lost any internal pressure, indicating that there were no spar cracks, and blade distress was mostly cosmetic even after cutting down so many trees multiple times during the descent.

Watching A/C 21650 take off on day three after the emergency landing brought a great feeling of pride to the Sikorsky team. The Army team on site cheered just as loudly when the YUH-60A took off safely for its flight back to base. Figures 155 and 156 are pictures taken by Sikorsky at takeoff and by the Army at arrival.

Reaction to this mishap by Army personnel assigned to the Sikorsky prototypes was very positive in terms of their confidence in the robust construction of the aircraft and its rotors. The Army's then project manager of the UTTAS program, Major General Jerry B. Lauer, expressed that feeling most clearly in his letter of 23 August 1976 to Sikorsky president Gerry Tobias:

> While this was an unfortunate incident, much can be learned from it. Having personally visited the crash site, I must say it was an excellent demonstration of the ruggedness of your aircraft to have it flown back to the test site following the replacement of only the main and tail rotor blades. This speaks extremely well of its structural integrity.

Fig. 155   YUH-60A S/N 21650, nicknamed "Phoenix," lifts off from the cleared site two days after the incident. The only components replaced were the four main blades and both tail-rotor paddles. (©Igor I. Sikorsky Historical Archives, Inc.)

Fig. 156   Aircraft 21650 landing at its base accompanied by a UH-1 flying as chase aircraft. Just before landing, and reflecting the spirit of the competition between the rival contractor camps, CW4 Dick Seefeldt and CW2 Larry Woodrum flying 21650 performed a high-speed pass directly over the Boeing Vertol support trailer and its occupants. (U.S. Army photo)

There was no doubt that for the Sikorsky UTTAS program the flight of the Phoenix was a flight from potential disaster to a cause for celebration by the Army and Sikorsky.

PERFORMANCE AND CLIMATIC TESTING

While development testing (DT) and operational testing (OT) were underway at Forts Rucker and Campbell, other competitive evaluation work was underway or soon to start by the Army. Shortly after DT and OT testing began with two flying prototypes, the third UTTAS from Boeing Vertol and from Sikorsky was airlifted to Edwards Air Force Base in California. Both test aircraft were fully instrumented to acquire and transmit data relative to flight performance, stability, and control as well as structural and propulsion information.

The Army's test facility at Edwards Air Force Base was called the Army Engineering Flight Activity (AEFA) and at the time of UTTAS testing was commanded by Lt. Col Denny Boyle. In addition to the Edwards facility, other sites were used for specialized performance testing, including at Bishop, California, where altitude evaluation was performed. The enormous amount of flight data including tethered flight was used by the contractors to fine tune their UTTAS designs and by the Army during the production proposal evaluation period in the last quarter of 1976. One of the key design changes made by Sikorsky as a result of Army flight data was to increase main rotor diameter by 4 in. This was easily accomplished by lengthening the blade-tip caps by 2 in. That change helped recover performance degradation caused by an accumulation of small weight increases.

During this flight-test period, the ground-test vehicle (GTV) had completed its planned tie-down testing and was being prepared for its next assignment. The GTV was built as part of the UTTAS prototype program to operationally

**Fig. 157   This photo was taken while the climatic hangar was refrigerated down to
−65°F. (©Igor I. Sikorsky Historical Archives, Inc.)**

test engines, transmissions, and rotor systems to ensure safety prior to first
flight. But its formal purpose was to qualify the UTTAS propulsion system to
military standards. The GTV was also the right aircraft system for the Army
to evaluate UTTAS operational capabilities at the extremes of design environmental conditions. That evaluation was planned for the climatic hangar at
Eglin Air Force Base, Florida. Climatic hangar testing spanned the temperature range from −65 to +125°F.

Climatic testing at Eglin took place from September to November 1976
with typically a week of full aircraft operation first at successively decreasing
temperatures until −65°F was reached then increasing temperatures to +125°F.
This testing resulted in modifications to certain operating procedures as well
as improvements to certain subsystems. Figure 157 shows the Sikorsky test
team in the climatic hangar with the GTV.

Evaluating the capability of the UTTAS prototypes to operate from naval
vessels equipped with landing pads was another Army task during the GVT
test period. Several Navy helicopter pilots were trained to fly the prototypes,
and they were active participants during early UTTAS design reviews and
during preflight acceptance testing. Many landings and takeoffs were
successfully performed from the fast frigate pictured in Fig. 158.

The U.S. Navy's Seahawk program, described in Chapter 10 and initiated
soon after Sikorsky won the UTTAS production award, was the first of many
ship-based Black Hawk derivative models.

ICING FLIGHT TESTING

The requirement for UTTAS to operate during moderate icing conditions
was specified in the Army's RFP and in the development contracts. Early in
the UTTAS BED phase, Sikorsky felt that its YUH-60A would be able to

Fig. 158   One of Sikorsky UTTAS prototypes about to make its first landing aboard the USS Paul Fast Frigate 1080. (©Igor I. Sikorsky Historical Archives, Inc.)

avoid the need for special heating equipment to keep the main- and tail-rotor blades free from significant ice accretion during the most critical conditions of liquid water content and temperature. It was thought that kinetic heating of the blades during icing condition would be sufficient to allow safe flight. That had been the case with the much larger Sikorsky CH-53D transport helicopter that was cleared to fly in icing conditions without the need for special blade heating equipment.

Because of the program's highly competitive nature and rather than chance coming in second to Boeing Vertol during the Army icing evaluation, Sikorsky management decided to fund a rotor deicing system for both the main and tail rotors just in case its first assessment was incorrect. A small team was assembled led by a young engineer, George Sipprell, who reported to Ken Rosen, to analyze, design, and construct a rotor de-ice system. Time was of the essence as the decision to install a rotor de-ice system was not made until well after first flight.

The design incorporated electrically pulsed blade elements to periodically melt the bond between the accreted ice and the blade. Any accreted ice would be slung away by centrifugal force. The system controller continuously established the on and off times of the heating elements. It did this based on aircraft sensors that fed data on liquid water content and on ambient temperature. Sipprell's team essentially lived in the shop, as an experimental system was clobbered together using control and slip ring components from other programs. The Goodyear Company provided the electrothermal blankets that were embedded in the blade outer composite skins. The main- and tail-rotor systems seemed to function properly on the ground, but their effectiveness in flight under actual icing conditions could not be verified before the Army flight evaluation at Fort Greely in Alaska.

After completing performance testing at Edwards Air Force Base, one of the three instrumented prototypes, S/N 21651, was brought to Alaska for the icing flight evaluation. At that site the rotor de-ice system was installed in preparation for flight behind an Army CH-47 transport helicopter. The CH-47 was specially configured to evaluate ice accretion on a test helicopter that was flying close behind in simulated natural icing conditions. It was equipped with large internal water tanks, and it trailed external spray rigs to disburse droplets of yellow-colored water vapor onto the helicopter being tested. The ice accretion was filmed by a chase aircraft and was discernable by its yellow color. That testing helped establish those critical areas of UTTAS that needed protection to fly safely in moderate icing conditions.

The most important finding of that testing was that the YUH-60A definitely needed the rotor de-ice system to safely fly in moderate icing conditions. During one flight behind the tanker, the flight crew intentionally turned off the de-ice system to simulate nonheated main and tail rotors. What happened rather quickly was a rapid rise in engine power to maintain speed and altitude as ice accreted on the blades. The ice accretion seriously altered blade airfoil shape and performance. The Alaska testing clearly confirmed that the de-ice system functioned as designed and was needed as an essential part of the UTTAS overall ice protection system. Refinements that were added as a result of this Army testing included electric heating of the rotor blade droop stops.

Figure 159 shows the YUH-60A shortly after flight behind the CH-47 tanker with ice accretion in cockpit areas.

Fig. 159 This photo taken immediately after flying behind the tanker shows clear windshields and engine inlets as well as rotor blades. The white appearing ice was actually yellow from the CH-47 tanker. (©Igor I. Sikorsky Historical Archives, Inc.)

READY FOR THE FINAL SELECTION

While the Army's fly-off evaluation was underway, the two companies submitted their production proposals in accordance with the Army's Letter of Instruction released in early 1976. Now having gathered operational, performance, and reliability data during hundreds of flight hours in representative missions and climatic conditions over an eight-month period, the Army was well positioned to judge credibility of the production proposals. Chapter 9 summarizes the results of that judgment process.

Chapter 9

FINAL SELECTION AND PRODUCTION

The last major effort to win the second and most critical award of the UTTAS program got underway in February 1976 when the Army sent letters of instruction to Boeing Vertol and Sikorsky outlining the scope of their proposals for the UTTAS production program. These proposals together with the results of the prototype fly-off evaluation would provide the basis for the Army's final selection. The stakes could not have been higher as the winner would become the sole source supplier for all production UTTAS helicopters for the Army. Also at stake was the opportunity to produce derivative models of this new utility helicopter for other missions and for other operators. The long-term destiny of both companies would clearly be determined by the Army's final selection.

Throughout the UTTAS program, the Army's stated production requirements, referred to as the basis of issue, specified a total of 1107 aircraft. That number was intended to fill the Army's operational units plus provide for maintenance float and for attrition. Although that quantity was extremely significant to the bidders, no one could have forecast the ultimate size of the market for what became the Black Hawk helicopter and for its many derivative models. Nor could anyone have imagined how far beyond the late 1980s, when production of the 1107 was initially scheduled to end, would production continue without interruption. Thirty years later, a definitive market assessment for Black Hawk helicopters still cannot be made as production of new advanced models continues.

The Army set the submittal date of May 1976 for the Sikorsky and Boeing Vertol production proposals. Best and final offers were due in November 1976, and the production contract was scheduled to be awarded in December 1976. Proposal preparation and contract negotiations with both companies took place while the prototypes were still undergoing Army flight testing. That overlap resulted in many proposal revisions and design improvements to address key findings coming out of the Army's fly-off evaluation. Correction of these findings continued to be the essence of Sikorsky's win strategy as was correction of the problems uncovered during the flight development phase.

The award date of December 1976 had been in Army planning for the prior five years, and that date was holding up well. It was holding up despite the turbulent development phase just concluding that witnessed crashes of both the YUH-60A and YUH-61A prototype aircraft as well as incorporation of major configuration changes. Negotiations with both companies began on time four months ahead of the award date. The production contract was planned to include the first year of low-rate initial production along with fixed-price options for the next three years. That total of the first four production years was for 353 helicopters.

The Black Hawk qualification program, started during the design/development phase, was to be completed during what the Army called the maturity phase. Completion of the qualification work concurrent with low rate production would only be performed by the company selected for production. Also to be awarded to the selected company was the final portion of the production engineering and planning (PEP) phase whose purpose was to construct production tooling and to prepare the documents needed for hardware procurement and production.

Contract negotiations with the Army's Source Selection and Evaluation Board (SSEB) began in August 1976 and continued through November. The Army's major evaluation areas were technical, operational suitability, cost, logistics support, and management. Cost was to have a 50% weighing factor in the Army's decision. However, negotiations over technical issues were the most intensive of all and likely may have had a greater impact on the aircraft finally selected than envisioned. Discussions regarding aircraft weight, performance, and guarantees were especially intense. Data from Army performance measurements and R&M data collection were still trickling in as Army testing was in its final stages. These data had to be analyzed, interpreted, sometimes disputed, corrected, and finally agreed upon as contract negotiations were underway. But the contentious issues all were resolved one by one, some to Army benefit and some to Sikorsky.

The emergence of aircraft performance guarantees and reliability assurance warrantees for the production aircraft were unexpected and not enthusiastically embraced. It was the Army's plan that the winner would earn or lose fee depending on how certain performance and R&M attributes were achieved for all 353 units of the initial low rate production. There were penalties and rewards set for each attribute.

The Army's intent was to make sure that critical flight performance and reliability values would continue to be achieved during at least the early stages of UTTAS production. Both clauses proved to be difficult to negotiate. The subject of performance guarantees was of the greatest concern because of measurement uncertainties. The variability of flight instruments, ambient weather conditions, and other factors could produce inaccurate results. The type of statistical method for interpreting performance data caused concerns as well. In the end, fee adjustments were agreed upon for aircraft empty weight and for the two key performance parameters of hover ceiling and cruise speed at the hot and high conditions. Incentives were established for fee if the aircraft performed better than the specified values while penalties would be levied if they did not.

The weight and performance guarantees turned out to have a profound effect on how the Sikorsky UTTAS detail design was modified as it transitioned from prototype to production configuration. The early focus on weight saving without question helped make a better aircraft for the reasons described in this chapter. It also earned the company additional fee as did the reliability and maintainability warrantee clauses.

WEIGHTS AND PERFORMANCE

Within the technical area, aircraft weight and flight performance were the most contentious issues that dominated meetings with the SSEB. Accurate prediction of the production aircraft's weight was important because the Army's most critical performance parameters of vertical rate of climb and mission cruise speed were dependent on mission gross weight. Complicating matters was the fact that Sikorsky's proposed production design was not an exact duplicate of the prototypes weighed and tested by the Army. Many minor design improvements were planned for the production configuration reflecting changes requested by the Army during its eight months of testing. In addition, there were design changes proposed by Sikorsky to reduce aircraft weight and manufacturing cost as well as to improve flight performance.

The net result of these changes was that the weight of the proposed production UTTAS was several hundred pounds lighter than the prototype. Each pound of this weight difference had to be agreed to by the Army team before negotiations on flight performance could be concluded. Agreement was reached after two months of discussions on the weight empty and primary mission gross weight of the Sikorsky production design, which ended up 300 lb lighter than the prototype weight. Tabulated in Table 3 is the downward progression from the actual prototype weights to the weights committed to in Sikorsky's contract specification and agreed to by the Army as achievable values.

Table 3   Weight evolution

	Empty weight, lb	Gross weight, lb
YUH-60A actual wt.	11,182	16,750
May 14, 1976 Proposal	10,955	16,500
Sept 9 Proposal update	10,918	16,460
Sept 27 Addendum	10,866	16,420
Oct 20 Addendum	10,892	16,450
Oct 25 Final contract spec.	**10,900**	**16,450**

As the weight issues were being resolved, performance negotiations focused on the Army's methods and instrumentation used to acquire data as well as on the computer programs used to calculate performance. Power loss measurements for engine inlets, gearboxes, and accessories became heated negotiation issues together with drag corrections for design changes. The most significant performance issue was prediction of aircraft vertical-rate-of-climb capability at the specified ambient altitude and temperature conditions of 4000 ft and 95°F. Data were compared and critiqued from tethered and free-hover test flights as well as actual vertical-climb testing by both the Army and Sikorsky. The amount of power correction for the type of screws used to attach the rotor-blade tip caps was the subject of intensive discussion and represents the level of detail that was needed to reach agreement on critical performance capabilities. Power corrections for blade surface quality, instrumentation wires and gauges, nose instrumentation boom, and tip Mach number were all issues that needed to be resolved. Eventually agreement was reached on the vertical-rate-of-climb derivatives to be used to account for changes in weight and in power.

The Army's performance requirement to hover with one-engine-inoperative (OEI) at a 5-ft wheel height with full fuel but without payload also became a textbook discussion issue. For this issue the Army held the winning hand. The author discussed that requirement in Chapter 3 and pointed out that Sikorsky's 1972 proposed UTTAS prototype could not meet the 5-ft OEI height requirement unless fuel was consumed or offloaded to lighten the aircraft. However Sikorsky estimated that a 2-ft wheel height could be achieved with a full fuel load. That was Sikorsky's position with which the Army agreed at the time. However this issue was still simmering in the minds of Army aerodynamicists. During the production proposal negotiation in 1976, four years later, the Army made it clear that not only could Sikorsky not meet the 5-ft requirement, but it could not achieve the 2-ft capability promised in its proposal.

The Army's aerodynamics expert from its flight-test facility at Edwards Air Force Base presented a comprehensive analysis of thrust augmentation in ground effect based on a half-dozen different methods used by industry and by the Army. His conclusion was that the weight of the Sikorsky design was too heavy at 13,780 lb (gross weight of 16,420 minus 2640 representing the 11-man squad) to achieve a 2-ft hover. To meet the 2-ft value, the Sikorsky design would have had to be about 500 lb lighter. This weight reduction was not felt by company engineers to be achievable by lightening the structure.

The solution to this problem argued by the company was to assume that a quarter of the 2000-lb full fuel load was burned off or offloaded when the takeoff with a single engine was to be attempted. Although technically correct, that solution clearly violated the Army's conditions for its demanding OEI performance requirement. At that point the leader of the Army's SSEB technical team, Bob Wolfe, observed that "*Sikorsky was beating the wrong dead horse.*" That observation ended the discussion, and the Army advised that it would record it as a deviation for the company but it would accept the fuel burn-off rationale.

Two important changes to Sikorsky's production design came out of the performance negotiations. The first was a 4-in. increase in main-rotor diameter to increase lift capability. That was achieved by making the blade-swept tip caps each 2 in. longer. That was an easy improvement to make and its benefits were measured by the Army at its AEFA facility at Edwards Air Force Base while proposal negotiations were going on.

The second and perhaps the most important design improvement was a slight change in the reduction ratio of the main gearbox for the production aircraft. That came about when the Army's technical team leader pointed out that Sikorsky was not taking full advantage of the T700-GE-700 engine provided by the Army. He indicated that nearly 50 more horsepower was available at the high-altitude and temperature conditions if the engines were operated at a slightly higher rotational speed. When the UTTAS gearbox was designed, the company's propulsion engineers had not noticed that opportunity in the engine performance data. It was very easy to take advantage of that improvement by slightly changing the main gearbox reduction ratio at no weight or cost penalties. That change by itself was worth nearly 300 lb of gross weight capability that produced substantial performance benefits to all follow-on H-60 models.

SSAC VISIT

During contract negotiations, the Army's Source Selection Advisory Council (SSAC) visited both companies to assess readiness for production. The council visited Sikorsky on 29 September, 1976, Figs. 160 and 161, to look over the company's production facilities and judge its production planning. The council also reviewed Sikorsky production experience as well as its management structure and specific assembly line plans to build the aircraft. Its assessment would then be presented to the Source Selection Authority who was the Secretary of the Army.

Along with becoming acquainted with features and performance of the UH-60A proposed by Sikorsky, the SSAC needed to verify the company's production facilities and its capacity to produce up to 168 UTTAS aircraft per year. It had been many years since the company enjoyed that level of production for a single model. At the time of this visit, Sikorsky Aircraft was operating at 22% capacity, and its total employment was down to below 6000 people. Factory space and facilities were employed to build spare parts and limited helicopter production for the Navy. The main final assembly line was empty as seen in Fig. 162.

Fig. 160   U.S. Army SSAC visitors welcomed from left to right by Robert F. Daniel, Sikorsky vice president; Harry J. Gray, UAC chief executive officer; Robert Stewart, UAC vice president; Gerald J. Tobias, Sikorsky president; and Robert J. Torok, Sikorsky senior vice president. (©Igor I. Sikorsky Historical Archives, Inc.)

Figure 163 shows the SSAC viewing a detail factory model of planned UTTAS production that included all the fit-out stations in the final assembly line.

FINAL SELECTION AND CONTRACT AWARD

At the conclusion of negotiations, the Army invited both contractors to sign the production contracts in advance of announcing the winner. Figure 164

Fig. 161   Harry Gray pointing out UTTAS features to Major General Willard Latham. (©Igor I. Sikorsky Historical Archives, Inc.)

Fig. 162 Empty final assembly line at Sikorsky's main facility viewed by the Source Selection Advisory Council three months before UTTAS production award. (©Igor I. Sikorsky Historical Archives, Inc.)

pictures Sikorsky's president signing the contract that represented the last company step of a 52-month effort to win one of the most important contracts in its history.

On Thursday, 23 December 1976, Maurice Schnieder called Tobias to congratulate the company on being selected as the final winner. He called immediately after he added his signature to the draft Sikorsky contract making it official.

Fig. 163 Eugene Buckley briefing the SSAC on the UTTAS final assembly stations planned to produce the required production rate. (©Igor I. Sikorsky Historical Archives, Inc.)

Fig. 164   Sikorsky production contract signing ceremony with the principals, Maurice D. Schnieder, Army contracting officer seated on the left, and Gerry J. Tobias, Sikorsky president signing for the company. Standing is the author center and Charles P. Martin to the right, Sikorsky UTTAS contract manager. (©Igor I. Sikorsky Historical Archives, Inc.)

At the same time that the company was called, the Assistant Secretary of the Army (R&D), Edward A. Miller held a press conference at the Pentagon to announce the UTTAS production decision. He described the basic production contract awarded to Sikorsky as a one-year fixed-price incentive contract for $83.4 million to deliver 15 aircraft. In addition, fixed-price options were included for three years of production totaling 353 aircraft with 56 in the second year, 129 in the third year, and 168 in the fourth year [25]. Secretary Miller also indicated that the contract included performance incentives on weight empty, hover ceiling, and cruise speed of the helicopter. In addition to the production contract, Sikorsky was also awarded a producibility engineering phase and maturity phase contracts to prepare for production and to complete the UTTAS qualification started earlier during the basic engineering development phase.

In response to reporters' questions about why Sikorsky was selected over Boeing Vertol, Secretary Miller responded as follows:

> Sikorsky offers lower risk and greater maturity in terms of the helicopters that were tested. They offered lower risk in the technical area as a whole, lower risk in operational suitability, lower risk in the maturity phase costs and lower risk in production costs. The source selection board found that the Sikorsky helicopter was clearly ready for production and the other was not [26].

On 7 January 1977 the Army briefed Sikorsky at AVSCOM in St. Louis on the UTTAS Source Selection and Evaluation Board's results. This was without doubt the most enjoyable and least stressful visit to AVSCOM in nearly five years. The SSEB described how data from testing conducted by Sikorsky was integrated with Army data acquired during performance testing at AEFA, from development testing at TECOM and from operational testing at OTEA. All of those data were used to evaluate and adjust the production proposal through the negotiation process. The SSEB presented its assessment of the Sikorsky proposal as follows: 1) meets essentially all requirements and is suitable for all intended missions; 2) significantly fewer changes for production configuration; 3) excellent reliability and crashworthiness; 4) meets air transportability preparation times but exceeds some man-hour requirements; 5) lower risk maturity program with at least $10M lower cost; 6) slightly higher investment cost; 7) lowest O&S and life-cycle cost, but differences within estimate accuracy; and 8) slightly exceeds DTC objective ($660,000 vs $600,000).

The selection rationale presented by Secretary Miller and the SSAC confirmed that Sikorsky's key strategies to win were correct and well executed. The company's full-scale flight testing of all advanced technologies clearly helped reduce risk. The Sikorsky and UTC corporate directive to create a design responsive to all Army requirements helped ensure a best-value configuration. Finally, the company's decision to incorporate all major design changes in the prototypes before they were delivered to the Army set the stage for the Army's confidence that transition to production would be at low risk.

The good news of December 23 was shared with all Sikorsky employees and with the local community in many personal and public ways. One was to spotlight the winning aircraft on the company front lawn alongside the Merritt Parkway in Stratford, Connecticut, for all travelers to see. Figure 165 shows

Fig. 165   One of the three Sikorsky YUH-60A prototypes on display on the evening of production selection. The UTTAS would soon after be renamed the UH-60A Black Hawk. (©Igor I. Sikorsky Historical Archives, Inc.)

the scene that made that holiday season a special and memorable event for thousands of people.

INITIAL PRODUCTION PERIOD

When the UTTAS program transitioned from a prototype to a production program, several key management changes were made. At Sikorsky, Eugene Buckley was appointed vice president of the UTTAS program prior to the aircraft being renamed Black Hawk by the Army. He was appointed Sikorsky executive vice president in 1985 and then company president.

Eugene Buckley

Ken Rosen who had been part of the UTTAS design team since the prototype UTTAS award in 1972 was appointed to lead the engineering team during the transition to a stable production configuration. Reporting to Rosen were Robert Tynan, who supervised design activities; Jim Faulk, who managed system attributes; and William Groth, who supervised all test activities.

Following the production selection, Col. Richard D. Kenyon was assigned to manage the Army UTTAS Project Office. Its technical team continued to be directed by Chuck Musgrave who had led that team since the prototype program was launched in 1972. The Army's Flight Standards organization continued to be led by Charlie Crawford with responsibilities for all qualification and airworthiness activities.

At the General Electric Company, Bill Crawford continued to manage the T700 engine team as it made the transition from a development program to the status of a world-class engine in its power category.

Along with the production award on 23 December, 1976, Sikorsky Aircraft was also awarded contracts for the second producibility engineering phase (PEP) and for the maturity phase. Both phases had been planned for award to the one contractor selected for production. The purpose of the PEP contract was to modify the YUH-60A prototype design where necessary to make it more suitable to volume production. In addition this phase included design and construction of low-rate initial production tooling and preparation of work instructions for all manufacturing operations.

The Army had set four primary objectives for the maturity phase, the most significant of which was completion of the UH-60A qualification program that had begun during the earlier basic engineering and development (BED) phase. Certain test activities not associated with flight safety had been deferred to the maturity phase. Those test activities covered the range of component-, subsystem-, and system-level testing. A second Army objective was to verify through instrumented flight testing that the required aircraft performance and flying qualities would be achieved. The Army's third maturity-phase objective was to verify that the aircraft would be capable of operation in hostile weather environments including desert, arctic, and tropic climates. The final objective involved the development and qualification of the mission flexibility kits that were planned for installation on the production aircraft.

Qualification testing during the maturity phase, when added to testing conducted earlier during the BED phase, earned UTTAS the distinction of being the most tested helicopter ever to enter Army service. By the time that the maturity phase ended in 1979, total YUH-60A flight time grew to 2437 hours. Operation of the ground-test vehicle totaled 2044 hours during the course of the transmission and propulsion system qualification. Laboratory testing of aircraft rotor, transmission, and flight controls included nearly 300 fatigue test specimens.

System-level testing conducted during the maturity phase resulted in significant design improvements to the basic YUH-60A configuration. These changes were beyond those incorporated during the BED phase and described in Chapter 7. Improvements were made to correct deficiencies found both during the Army's GCT flight evaluations and during final qualification testing. Many design improvements were also made to reduce aircraft weight in order to create a cushion to absorb the inevitable weight increases that historically accompany the early phases of a new program.

VIBRATION REDUCTION CONTINUES

The intense efforts to reduce aircraft vibrations during the BED phase described in Chapter 7 did not end upon award of the production contract. Refinements to the vibration control package continued into the maturity phase. They were aimed at improving performance of the bifilar main-rotor absorber and at correcting newly uncovered stabilator response to main-rotor 4P excitation as well as reducing overall vibration levels.

One of the vibration-related changes made early during the BED phase was to increase the output of the main-rotor bifilar absorber to try to reduce rotor-induced vibrations. That change involved lengthening the arms of the bifilar and increasing the weight of each pendulum to 35 lb. That increased weight helped offset the bifilar's tendency to detune itself when operating at high pendular amplitudes up to 18 deg. Later, during maturity-phase testing, an improved design that reshaped the bushings about which the pendulums moved from a circular to a cycloidal shape evolved. This new shape significantly improved the bifilar's performance during large-motion amplitudes to the extent that its weights were able to be reduced from 35 to 25 lb each. This overall weight saving of 40 lb was used to partially offset the weight of a spring-mass absorber that was installed in the fuselage nose to further reduce cockpit vibrations.

As the vibration levels continued to be reduced during the maturity phase, 4P excitation at the tail of the aircraft became a problem. The excitation was accompanied by high local stresses in the stabilator attachment fittings and support structure. As it turned out, the stabilator's natural frequency just happened to be close to main rotor 4P, reminiscent of the proximity of the transmission roll and pitch modes to 4P found during the BED phase.

While experiments to detune the stabilator using tip-mounted weights were underway, an unexpected but fortunate event took place. During one of many flight tests involving no change to the baseline design and for no apparent reason, significant reductions in both stabilator vibrations and stresses were measured. In following Igor Sikorsky's classic advice to respect the facts when theory and facts disagree, Ken Rosen's team, and in particular John Marshall, dug into the stabilator installation on that particular aircraft to find the reason for the marked reduction in response.

What was found was that the stabilator attachment bolts had become loosened, suggesting that the stabilator had detuned itself. Under Marshall's direction, a prototype elastic isolator integral with the attachment fittings was quickly fatigue tested and cleared for installation on the aircraft. With the isolators installed, the stabilator's natural frequency was reduced to near 3P, providing significant reductions in both vibration and stresses. This fix was quickly made part of the production configuration.

The final change to the vibration reduction package to emerge from the maturity phase was the addition of spring-mass absorbers in each of the landing-gear stub wings. This was done to keep roll vibration levels within specification on a consistent basis. With that addition, the vibration control suite was complete and was installed in the first production UH-60A. This suite remained essentially unchanged for a quarter-century. The next major change to vibration management took place in 2001 when the UH-60M began its development. As described in Chapter 10, the M model was equipped with Sikorsky's newly developed active vibration control system that improved vibration at a reduced weight penalty.

STABILITY AUGMENTATION SYSTEM EVOLUTION

Among the innovations incorporated in Sikorsky's UTTAS proposal in 1972 was a new concept for an aircraft stability augmentation system (SAS) based on fluidics technology. This innovation, pioneered by the Honeywell Company, provided rate stabilization without any moving parts and without dependence on electrical power. The fluidic gyro sensed the rotational movement of an oil flow through an orifice that, because of the Coanda effect, produced a pressure difference. The pressure difference was then fed to control servos to null out the unwanted aircraft rate change.

This fluidic SAS was flight tested by Sikorsky on a CH-54 Flying Crane helicopter with excellent results prior to submitting the UTTAS proposal in 1972. This new concept was well received by the Army because of its simplicity and promised reliability. The fluidic SAS was incorporated in the YUH-60A prototypes and remained the baseline stability augmentation system up through the maturity phase. During that phase of the UTTAS program, limitations of both the fluidic approach and of a simple SAS system began to surface. Chief among these was the adverse effect of oil viscosity changes with ambient temperature and the corresponding SAS gain changes. The government-directed changeover from SAE 5606 fluid to SAE 83286 fluid worsened the adverse viscosity effect. This fluid change was made to provide superior fire protection to all military aircraft. A concerted effort to maintain relatively constant fluid temperature through the fluidic system by use of thermal barriers helped, but they were not sufficient. Installation of flow-compensation devices to offset temperature induced viscosity changes was also insufficient.

As this effort to overcome the viscosity problem was underway, there was a growing feeling that the fluidic approach precluded taking advantage of many functions that were achievable with electronic stability augmentation systems. Functions such as attitude hold were desired by Army pilots and needed electronic-based systems for incorporation.

Because of the desire to expand SAS functions coupled with the limitations of the fluidic system, the decision was made during the maturity phase to convert to an all-electronic system. The initial change was to a separate analog system, designed by Bendix, together with a digital system designed by Hamilton Standard. Each system had approximately 5% control authority. Many important new functions were added to the Black Hawk flight-control and vehicle-management systems as a result of this change. Later during the production program, a change was made to an all-digital system typical of current aircraft.

READY FOR PRODUCTION

The intense effort to reduce component weights during the PEP phase produced extraordinary results that benefited the Black Hawk program for years to come. The production contract awarded in December 1976 specified an empty weight of 10,900 lb for the UH-60A model. However the actual empty weight of the first production UH-60A delivered in 1978 was 10,387 lb. That weight included all of the design improvements to the vibration reduction suite as well as the improvements to the stability augmentation system described earlier. It also included all design changes found to be needed as the qualification program progressed to completion. The production program therefore started with a qualified aircraft that was 513 lb below specification weight. As a result, aircraft performance was excellent, especially vertical climb rate. At the critical 4000-ft, 95-deg ambient condition, vertical rate of climb exceeded specification by a factor of two, increasing from 480 to over 1000 ft/min.

Because of this substantial weight margin, the UH-60A was able to accommodate many additions to equipment as well as provisions for new systems and design improvements during the course of delivering 1000 UH-60A models. The impact of these additions on system weight is described in Chapter 10, and that impact provided the impetus for the Army to develop the UH-60L model.

The low-rate initial production deliveries took place essentially on contract schedule. As planned, the Army exercised options for the second- and third-year production quantities. Sikorsky and Army personnel celebrating signing of the second-year option for 56 Black Hawk helicopters on 17 October 1977 are shown in Fig. 166.

Each successive year required a ramp up in annual deliveries reaching a planned peak of approximately 177 units during which years an average of 15 UH-60As were delivered each month. In retrospect, it seems hard to believe that the Army's initial estimate of 1107 Black Hawks had planned to be completely delivered over an eight-year period. When the production award was made in 1976, the end of the Army's Black Hawk production program was expected to occur in 1986. For many reasons, not the least of which was the Black Hawk's

Fig. 166   Standing L to R: Robert J. Torok, senior vice president, Government Programs; Eugene Buckley, vice president, Black Hawk Program; Gerald J. Tobias, president, Sikorsky; Charles P. Martin, manager, Contract Administration; Col. Richard Kenyon, Black Hawk program manager; Marquis Hilbert, Sikorsky rep. St. Louis; Donald E. Sorel, Sikorsky rep., St. Louis; Philip Locke, vice president, Contracts and Counsel. Seated is Melvin Storch, U.S. Army contacting officer. (©Igor I. Sikorsky Historical Archives, Inc.)

versatility and performance, production continued long beyond initial planning and in configurations not conceived of during the earlier periods.

FULL PRODUCTION AND MULTIYEAR PROCUREMENT

At the end of the first three years of low-rate initial production, the Army chose to award contracts to Sikorsky covering several years of production rather than the typical single year contracting practice. It did so because of the greater leverage on cost that multiyear procurement promised. Both prime and subcontractors would come to the negotiating table with pencils sharpened by the promise of stable and predictable long-term production bolstered by a more aggressive long term capital investment plan. Multiyear contracts for Black Hawk were so successful that six such contracts were awarded to Sikorsky covering more than 25 consecutive years of uninterrupted production and more are planned.

Figure 167 is a happy group of Sikorsky representatives who were present at the signing of the first multiyear contract for UH-60A Black Hawks.

Fig. 167   Present at the first multiyear contract signing were as follows. First row: William Minter, vice president, Black Hawk; Gregory Coca, Finance; James E. Campion, manager, New Product Pricing; Donald Sorel, St. Louis representative. Second row: Charles P. Martin, manager, Contract Administration; Mark Hilbert, Sikorsky St. Louis representative; Allan K. Poole, vice president, Government Logistic Support; Daniel Zsebik, Sikorsky St. Louis representative; and Philip Locke, vice president, Contracts and Council. (©Igor I. Sikorsky Historical Archives, Inc.)

At that time neither they nor the Army had any idea of how many times this event would be repeated.

The first multiyear contract was awarded in 1981, and since then every Black Hawk production award by the U.S. government has covered more than a single year. They began as three-year production periods and increased to five-year periods. These contracts also began to include U.S. Navy Seahawk and foreign military sales as well. All multiyear contracts for the Black Hawk and its derivative aircraft awarded to date are listed next:

1) Multiyear 1 was awarded in December 1981 for 294 UH-60A aircraft for $950 million. It covered aircraft deliveries from FY 1980 through FY 1983.

2) Multiyear 2 was awarded in October 1984 for 234 UH-60A and 54 EH-60A aircraft for $832 million. It covered aircraft deliveries from FY 1984 through FY 1987.

3) Multiyear 3 was awarded in January 1988 for 252 UH-60A aircraft, but during this period, production was changed over to the uprated UH-60L model. This award was for $983.2 million, which happened to be the largest single contract ever awarded to Sikorsky. Deliveries were scheduled from FY 1988 through FY 1991.

4) Multiyear 4 was awarded in April 1992, and it was the first to cover a five-year production period. It was for 300 UH-60L aircraft with an option for an additional 180 aircraft. Contract value was $1.54 billion, which now became Sikorsky's single largest contract. Deliveries were from FY 1992 through FY 1997.

5) Multiyear 5 was awarded in July 1997, again for a five-year period. Initially this contract covered 108 UH-60Ls for the Army and eight for the Air Force, and its value was $745 million. The government's plan was to complete production of the UH-60L and turn the production line over to MH-60S for the U.S. Navy halfway through this five-year contract. However the Army decided to continue producing the UH-60L model, so that both Army and Navy aircraft were produced. Eventually, 252 Black Hawks and derivative Hawk models, including the UH-60M MEDIVAC helicopter and 85 foreign military sales (FMS) were delivered under this contract whose total value reached approximately $2.3 billion.

6) Multiyear 6 was awarded in September 2002. This five-year contract was for 80 Army UH-60L and 82 Navy MH-60S aircraft as well as additional UH-60M MEDIVAC in addition to more FMS aircraft. Contract value was $1.5 billion and included low-rate initial production of the new UH-60M model for the Army.

7) Multiyear 7 is scheduled to be awarded in mid-2007. It will be a five-year joint service contract to include the UH-60M and HH-60M models for the Army plus the MH-60S and MH-60R models for the Navy. This contract is expected to cover 531 aircraft with a potential for 800 aircraft

to be delivered. This will also be the first multiyear contract to include spare parts. Should all contract options be exercised, the value of this contract will approach $12 billion.

The duration and expansion of multiyear procurements summarized above demonstrate two important factors. First they confirm the customers' confidence that the prime and subcontractor base can be counted on to produce aircraft at the expected quality and schedule requirements. Second, they demonstrate conviction that manufacturing as well as overhead costs can be reduced at a steeper rate than would be expected for single-year contracts.

Steeper-than-normal cost reduction should be expected as a result of the longer-term planning horizon that multiyear procurement provides. The assurance of continued production beyond a single year can accelerate cost reduction by providing a greater incentive to invest in more efficient capital equipment, to improve manufacturing methods and training, and to implement design changes to improve producibility. The net result can be achievement of steeper learning curves as well as purchased material costs than would be achieved with single-year contracts.

Long-term contracting at fixed prices provides a powerful incentive for the contractors to reduce cost because the cost savings from accelerated learning curves fall to the bottom line as profits increased. But on the next contract, cost negotiations start where the last contract cost performance ended, so that the customer shares in the benefits of a steeper learning curve when it is achieved. Multiyear contracts for Black Hawks created a win-win situation for all parties. They likely also helped foreign governments decide in favor of buying Black Hawks and Seahawks if they were leaning toward those models.

Chapter 10

BLACK HAWK LINEAGE

The Black Hawk production award in 1976 has turned out to be the most important contract ever won by Sikorsky. It created the foundation of the company's production base that has grown to be larger and has endured longer than initially thought possible. It opened new U.S. military as well as international markets for derivatives of this new utility helicopter. By winning this program, the company was able to offer a high-technology utility transport, qualified by the U.S. Army, to a worldwide market. As a result of the Army's stringent requirements, met with a good aircraft design, the UH-60A proved to be extraordinarily adaptable to a broad range of military missions. Its performance and strength margins, along with a cabin configuration of usable proportions, have made it an especially versatile helicopter. Moreover, its reliability and survivability features were unmatched by any other utility helicopter in the world.

Those operational benefits, superior in comparison to alternative helicopters then available, were the main reasons that Black Hawk derivatives have been widely accepted in markets open to competition. In addition, the U.S. government's long-term commitment to the Black Hawk and Seahawk programs has been an important consideration for international customers. Their confidence in the government's sustained support and product improvement helped the Hawk models to become the utility helicopters of choice.

Production of Black Hawk and Seahawk models with their many derivatives brought about a dramatic improvement in Sikorsky's business base. Figure 168 shows the long decline of production from the late 1950s to the time when the company won the UTTAS production competition in 1976. The reasons for that decline were outlined in Chapter 3. Since that award, production has been dominated by H-60 models, which have helped restore factory output to near historic quantities. Because the empty weight of these models is approximately twice the average weight of the earlier S-55 and S-58 high-volume models, total Sikorsky output has actually exceeded earlier production when measured in pounds of helicopters delivered rather than in number delivered. Total sales have also exceeded historic values measured in constant year dollars.

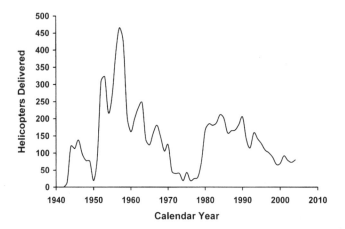

Fig. 168 Annual deliveries of all Sikorsky helicopter models are shown starting with the R-4 in 1943. The first production UH-60A Black Hawk was delivered in 1978 and started the rapid upswing in deliveries. From 1984 a gradual decline began as U.S. military inventories of H-60 models were filled. From 2000 an upward trend resumed as newer H-60 models were introduced coupled with increasing sales of Sikorsky's S-92 and S-76 models.

This chapter describes key derivative versions of the Black Hawk helicopter in chronological order of their development to meet the operational needs of all branches of the U.S. military. Many of these derivatives were later selected by over 25 international customers with modifications to suit their unique mission requirements. International sales of the various S-70 models have either been direct purchases from Sikorsky or purchases through the U.S. government as foreign military sales (FMS). Chapter 11 describes how international customers have configured their Black Hawk and Seahawk models and the missions that they perform.

The mission equipment, weapons systems, communications/navigation systems, avionics systems, and special features of the derivatives described in this chapter are snapshots of configurations existing at a point in time. Upgrades and enhancements are continuously being made as technology offers improved features and as missions require new capabilities.

Every new Black Hawk derivative model that is designed, qualified, and put in production has had the potential of spawning its own family lineage. Some derivatives have in turn produced newer U.S. military variants, and some have spawned new international models. Each new derivative adds distinct features, equipment, and capabilities that set the stage for more advanced models. In reviewing the Black Hawk lineage described in this chapter, three derivatives in particular stand out as having had the greatest impact in expanding the marketplace. They are the SH-60B, the UH-60L and the UH-60M models.

The SH-60B Seahawk created a significant increase in potential markets for the new H-60 utility helicopter. The Seahawk was especially important because it opened the door to ship-based operations for which compactness, automatic rotor-blade folding, and many marinized features are critical. In addition, the Navy's Seahawk development included more powerful engines as well as a 20% uprated transmission system together with strengthened flight controls. All of these enhancements then became basic building blocks for a new improved U.S. Army Black Hawk model designated as the UH-60L.

The UH-60L version entered production after approximately 1000 UH-60As were delivered. The L model more than recovered performance lost by the A model due to its unusual weight growth discussed in this chapter. The UH-60L demonstrated outstanding flight performance as a result of its basic Seahawk propulsion system that far surpassed A model capabilities. With this uprated performance, the UH-60L was able to create a new Black Hawk lineage for the U.S. Army and for international operators.

The third Black Hawk derivative that likely will have a major impact on the utility market is the UH-60M model. The M model is the latest derivative to be developed as of this writing and might become one of the most important. This derivative is the first to incorporate new aerodynamic and electronic technologies. The M rotor system is the first of the Black Hawk/Seahawk line to take advantage of major advancements in rotor-blade aerodynamic and structural materials technologies that were not available when the Black Hawk was first designed. It also incorporates major advancements in vibration control technologies developed by Sikorsky for its S-92 commercial program. In addition, its integrated cockpit and avionic systems could be crucial to success in battlefields of the future. The UH-60M's performance margins together with planned enhancements including a fly-by-wire flight control system set the stage for its own family of derivative models.

U.S. NAVY SH-60B SEAHAWK

The Seahawk was the first Black Hawk derivative, and its configuration required significant modification to the UH-60A. Unique Seahawk features and equipment, designed to provide shipboard compatibility, opened up worldwide market opportunities for ship-based operation. Those capabilities in turn led to several major derivatives of the SH-60B for both the U.S. and for international naval forces. The result was that the Seahawk helicopter spawned its own family of derivative models. More than 600 naval hawks are in service worldwide, of which the U.S. Navy flies over 350 units. Sikorsky's designation for the basic naval Hawk line is the S-70B.

As the UTTAS prototype was being developed during the 1970s, the U.S. Navy began planning for a new-generation helicopter system to succeed the

Kaman SH-2 Seasprite helicopter. Requirements of this new system were tailored around the basic Army UTTAS specification in order to reduce costs by capitalizing on the Army's investment and plan for long term production. The Navy's planning recognized that changes to the basic Black Hawk helicopter would be required to operate in its maritime environment and to carry the unique electronic airborne sensors and weapons needed for antisubmarine warfare (ASW) and antisurface ship targeting (ASST) missions. Out of that planning emerged a series of naval Hawks specially configured to protect carrier task forces and to perform rescue, re-supply of ships, and other naval missions.

Soon after winning the UTTAS production contract in 1976, Sikorsky began to focus on creating a new ASW/ASST helicopter for the U.S. Navy based on its UTTAS design. It was assumed that Boeing Vertol would also respond to the Navy's requirement with a marinized version of its YUH-61A UTTAS prototype. There was some concern within Sikorsky that the Department of Defense might be reluctant to rely on the same company to develop and produce new utility helicopters for both the Army and Navy. It was also known that despite the loss of the UTTAS production award, Boeing Vertol was continuing to refine its YUH-61A. That effort was understood to focus on vibration reduction through a unique transmission-to-airframe isolation system. Progress was rumored to have been made without raising the main rotor as Sikorsky had done in evolving its Black Hawk configuration two years earlier.

Frederick Silverio

At Sikorsky, the task of designing what was to become the SH-60B was assigned to Fred Silverio, who was a young engineer with ASW avionics integration experience associated with the Kaman LAMPS Mark 1 helicopter. His design team responded to the Navy's request for proposal with the same management guidance that helped lead to the Sikorsky UTTAS win, which was to be completely responsive to all Navy RFP requirements. In addition the team's goal was to achieve 60% commonality with the Army UTTAS helicopter.

Along with the Sikorsky and Boeing Vertol proposed offerings, both derived from their UTTAS prototypes, the Navy examined versions of existing models from Bell, Kaman, Westland in the United Kingdom, and MBB in Germany. However, they were too small, being in the 12,000 lb weight category, to perform the required missions.

Proposals were submitted in April 1977, and following a lengthy evaluation period, the Navy made its selection in early 1978. Sikorsky's Seahawk design was selected because it offered significantly lower life-cycle cost as a result of parts commonality with UTTAS and because it was most responsive to the Navy's requirements.

The Navy authorized full-scale development of the Seahawk in February 1978. Sikorsky's YSH-60B Seahawk prototype first flew in December 1979, 22 months after contract award. The first production SH-60B flew in February 1983 and entered service in 1984.

The SH-60B, Fig. 169, was developed to perform the Navy's ASW and ASST missions while secondary missions included search and rescue and logistical support. In its basic role of ASW, the Seahawk was intended to be the platform for the Navy's Light Airborne Multi-Purpose System referred to as LAMPS Mark III.

This system consists of acoustic sensors for detecting submarines, as well as radar for detecting ships. It includes equipment for data processing and secure data relay back to the fleet and carries acoustic homing torpedoes for destroying submarines. Its purpose is to search and clear the outer zone area to a distance of approximately 30 n miles from an aircraft carrier battle group. The radome installed beneath the cockpit contains search radar that gives the battle group commander an extended picture of the surface threat situation. It also provides a standoff targeting capability for the battle group's surface-to-surface missiles.

The Seahawk was designed to operate from new classes of Navy ships, the FFG-7 Oliver Hazard Perry class guided missile frigates, the DD-963 Spruance class destroyers, the DDG-993 Kidd class guided missile destroyer, and the CG-47 Ticonderoga class guided missile cruiser. Many of Seahawk's configuration features were designed to achieve compatibility with these new

Fig. 169   U.S. Navy SH-60B Seahawk equipped for outer zone protection of a carrier task force was the first of a long lineage of naval hawks. The sonobouy launcher with 25 tubes can be seen above the torpedo support wing, and the large search radar dome is visible below the cockpit. (©Igor I. Sikorsky Historical Archives, Inc.)

ships. Shipboard hangar dimensional limits of height, width and length ultimately defined Seahawk's overall folded configuration similar to how the Army's air transport requirements affected the UTTAS design. However, hangar height did not require a low rotor position like that needed for the Black Hawk helicopter when ferried by cargo transport aircraft.

The Navy implemented a new and unusual approach to manage Seahawk's weapons systems integration during the design and production phases. The Navy became the overall prime contractor over both Sikorsky Aircraft, who was the air vehicle contractor, and over IBM, who was selected to integrate the ship and aircraft electronics systems. Both companies reported to the Navy. An interface control document (ICD) proved to be the most important document of the Seahawk program. That document specified installation, performance, weight, and maintainability requirements and controlled the integration of the airborne electronics system, referred to as the "mission equipment package." During the production program, Sikorsky flew relatively bare Seahawk aircraft to IBM's facility in Owego, New York, where the mission equipment package was installed and tested. Completed SH-60Bs were then delivered to the Navy from the IBM facility that later became Lockheed Martin Systems Integration – Owego.

The most significant areas of design change needed to create a Seahawk were in airframe, rotor, propulsion, and weapon systems. Figures 170 and 171 show the key UH-60A airframe features that were changed to create the SH-60B. The tail landing gear was relocated 13 ft forward to minimize footprint for the small shipboard landing areas. In addition, the tail gear was

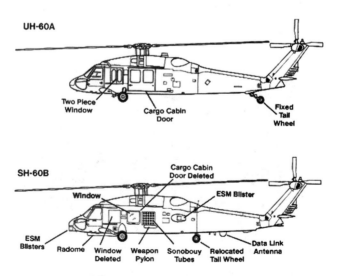

Fig. 170 Design modifications shown were needed to facilitate flight operations from small ships and to accommodate special ASW and ASST sensors and weapons.

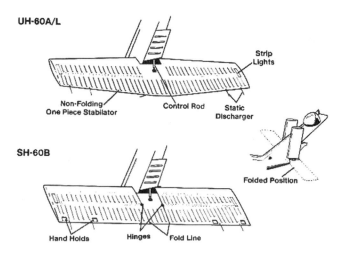

Fig. 171 This figure shows the areas of stabilator design change for the Seahawk. All sensors, actuators, electronics, and stabilator control laws from the UH-60A were retained.

changed to a dual-wheel arrangement in order to meet the ships' deck plate and support panel structural criteria. But landing loads also had to be limited by providing an unusually long oleo stroke, which in turn required a special cylinder coating to minimize friction. As noted in Chapter 5, the UH-60A landing gear was designed for a 38-ft/s vertical impact to meet crashworthiness requirements. That high energy level was achieved by use of dual energy-absorbing oleos. But for Seahawk, the requirement was 17-ft/s crash capability, and as a result only a single oleo was needed, significantly reducing weight.

The Black Hawk fuselage was also modified to permit use of larger crashworthy fuel cells and installation of the sonobouy launcher equipment along with sensor operator crew stations and equipment. Two weapons pylons were added for carrying external stores such as torpedoes, depth charges, and air-to-surface missiles. The sonobouy launcher was first intended to be the Navy system in use on fixed-wing aircraft such as the S-2 and P-3 series. Sonobouys are expendable acoustic sensors launched into the water to detect and localize submarines. That Navy launcher, although a safe and reliable cartridge actuated device, was too heavy for the Seahawk. Each explosive cartridge weighed 3 lb, and 25 were required to launch the 25 sonobouys. Because of this weight penalty, Sikorsky designers pursued a pneumatic approach to fire the sonobouys out of their tubes. This pneumatic concept was successfully developed, and it was the first such unit to enter the fleet. It saved 92 lb over a conventional explosive approach.

The decision to fold the main rotor blades using a powered automatic system, as opposed to manual blade folding, was made when the Navy conducted shipboard trials with a YUH-60A prototype. What was found was that personnel working at the rotor head to prepare for manual blade folding would be subjected to a high risk of falling because of very high ship rocking motion. The spring rate of the landing gear coupled with ship motions during sea state 2 to 3 conditions created a hazardous situation for maintenance personnel working up at the rotor head. So the decision was made to develop a fully automatic system similar to other ship-based helicopters. But for the Seahawk a novel power system was used.

Figure 172 shows the magnitude of deck rolling motions that can be experienced during and after shipboard landings with the SH-60B.

Prior Sikorsky ship-based helicopters have all used hydraulic actuators to fold the rotor blades; however, for the Seahawk an innovative approach using

Fig. 172   The need to avoid crewmen working up at the rotor head is apparent in a) the photo showing a crewman preparing to attach a cable to the Seahawk's RAST system for winch down to the deck and b) the photo showing the deck securing process prior to blade folding. (©Igor I. Sikorsky Historical Archives, Inc.)

an all-electric system was designed. This turned out to be a very successful "first," which produced significant weight saving. Reducing weight at the rotor is an important objective for helicopters having the ability to make emergency landings on the water. That is because the higher the topside weight, the lower will be the critical turnover angle during emergency flotation in high-sea states in the event that the helicopter is forced to land on the water and deploy its flotation bags.

The Navy initiated a program to increase the power of the UH-60A's T700-GE-700 engines and to incorporate features to improve engine durability in the harsh marine environment. That program produced the T700-GE-401 engine whose power was 1690 hp up from the 1543 hp used in the UH-60A Black Hawk. But engine growth continued, and starting in mid-1988 Seahawks were powered by the T700-GE-401C rated at 1890 hp.

To cope with this increased power, the Seahawk transmission system was concurrently uprated from the UH-60A's main gearbox rating of 2828 hp to a rating of 3400 hp. This was done by selectively increasing gear face widths, strengthening shafting, and enlarging gearbox housings in selected areas. The successful upgrading of the engine, transmission system, and flight control system components led the Army to incorporate many Seahawk features in its UH-60L version discussed later in this chapter. These upgraded components became the standard for many follow-on Black Hawk and Seahawk derivatives.

U.S. ARMY EH-60B SOTAS

The Army developed two unique derivatives of the UH-60A for special electronic missions during the early 1980s. The first was the YEH-60B configured to carry the Army's Stand Off Target Acquisition System (SOTAS) featuring a large rotating radar antenna designed to detect moving targets on the battlefield. Figure 173 shows the antenna pod retracted up against the fuselage underside. The UH-60A main landing gear was lengthened to provide sufficient ground clearance for the antenna pod, but the gear oleo struts are retracted when the antenna is deployed.

Figure 174 shows the radar antenna deployed and in the rotating mode. Only one YEH-60B was built, and it never was put in production, but instead the Army transferred its support to the proven JSTARS program.

U.S. ARMY EH-60A/C QUICK FIX

The Army's second electronic derivative, the EH-60A/C Quick Fix, was put in production and placed in service with armored cavalry regiments. The purpose of this derivative is to carry the Army's Quick Fix IIB system to intercept, monitor, locate, and jam enemy radio transmissions. It does

Fig. 173   U.S. Army YEH-60B SOTAS with long radar antenna stowed beneath cabin. The lengthened main landing gear provides ground clearance for the antenna pod. (©Igor I. Sikorsky Historical Archives, Inc.)

this by the four dipole antennas mounted on the tailcone and the retractable whip antenna, providing the jamming function, mounted below the airframe shown in Fig. 175. First flight of this derivative was made in September 1981 when it entered a full qualification program for production release. Production ended seven years later in September 1988 after 66 were produced.

Fig. 174   The YEH-60B SOTAS with antenna extended and rotating. The main landing-gear oleos are retracted to provide clearance for the rotating antenna. (©Igor I. Sikorsky Historical Archives, Inc.)

Fig. 175 EH-60A Quick Fix in flight with its whip antenna deployed. (©Igor I. Sikorsky Historical Archives, Inc.)

U.S. NAVY SH-60F CV HELO

Two years after the SH-60B Seahawk entered service, the U.S. Navy started development of the SH-60F model to provide close-in ASW protection of aircraft carrier groups to replace its aging Sikorsky SH-3H Sea King helicopters. The key feature of the F model was the installation of a dipping sonar system to detect submarines that might be close to the carrier task force where waterborne noise is high and where sonobouys would be less effective.

First flight took place in March 1987, and first fleet deployment began in 1991 aboard the USS NIMITZ. Production deliveries continued until December 1994 at which time a total of 76 were produced.

The basic airframe, propulsion, and rotor systems of the SH-60B were retained, but major changes were made to the mission sensor equipment and weapons package. Because the SH-60F was to operate from carrier decks, it did not need the recovery assist secure and traversing (RAST) system needed by Seahawks to land on small vessels in high sea states. In addition, the magnetic anomaly detection (MAD) equipment and search radar were removed and replaced by an AQS-13F active dipping sonar, seen deployed in Fig. 176. In addition to dipping sonar, the SH-60F can deploy active or passive sonobouys if required. A manually loaded gravity launcher holding six sonobouys replaced the pneumatic sonobouy system, developed for the SH-60B described earlier. A new tactical data and communication system, auxiliary fuel system, and an additional weapons pylon were also installed.

Some years after the SH-60B and SH-60F models entered service, the Navy elected to consolidate their predominantly antisubmarine missions into a single naval Hawk designated as the MH-60R. This Seahawk variant, launched in 1999, performs all undersea warfare and antisurface ship warfare missions. The Navy's plans call for conversion of all B and F models to the MH-60R design.

Fig. 176   Unique wave pattern beneath the SH-60F is caused by rotor downwash as the helicopter lowers its sonar transducer into the water. (©Igor I. Sikorsky Historical Archives, Inc.)

U.S. NAVY HH-60H RESCUE HAWK

The Navy began development of a special version of the SH-60F Seahawk in 1986 whose primary mission was to provide combat strike rescue and special warfare support in all weather and in combat conditions. The HH-60H, seen in Fig. 177, is equipped with an infrared jamming system, chaff/flare dispensers, radar warning receivers, and with the engine infrared suppression system similar to the Black Hawk helicopter. Defensive weapons include provisions for the 7.62-mm M60D machine gun and 7.62 GAU-17 Gatling guns. First flight was made in August 1988, and it entered service in March 1989. Approximately 45 HH-60Hs have been deployed since then. As part of the Navy's consolidation plan already mentioned, the HH-60H is being replaced by the MH-60S which entered service in 2002.

U.S. COAST GUARD HH-60J JAYHAWK

In 1986 the U.S. Coast Guard started development of a new medium-range rescue helicopter based on the Navy's HH-60H airframe. Its mission was to fly out 300 miles, conduct search operations for one and a half hours, rescue as many as six people, and return to base. To do this in adverse weather conditions,

Fig. 177   U.S. Navy HH-60H configured for special warfare operations was derived from the SH-60F ASW version. (©Igor I. Sikorsky Historical Archives, Inc.)

the HH-60J Jayhawk is equipped with search/weather radar giving its cockpit nose area a very distinctive appearance. It also can carry a forward-looking infrared (FLIR) turret mounted below and aft of its radome seen in Fig. 178.

Jayhawks can carry two 120-gallon fuel tanks on their port-side stores rack plus a similar tank on the starboard rack. Rescue operations over water are performed with a 600 lb capacity hoist mounted on the starboard side above

Fig. 178   HH-60J Jayhawk search and rescue helicopter alongside a full-scale model of the VS-300 flown by Igor Sikorsky in 1939. His vision of rescuing people in distress by the helicopter has been achieved to an unbelievable extent by the 40 years of helicopter technology advancements since his first flight as well as by dedicated and well-trained pilots and crewmen. (©Igor I. Sikorsky Historical Archives, Inc.)

the sliding door and in view of the pilot. In addition to search and rescue, Jayhawks are used for law enforcement missions including drug interdiction and environmental surveillance and protection. The Coast Guard has received approximately 35 Jayhawks during the period from 1990 to 1993, which are deployed at air stations across the country.

Of the many helicopter rescue missions performed by the Coast Guard, few took more courage or taxed the Jayhawk more than one performed on 17 December, 2000. On that date, the 600-ft cruise vessel SeaBreeze was 225 n miles east of Virginia when its engine room began to flood during gale force winds. The ship with a crew of 34 and no passengers was sinking, listing and rolling helplessly in 35-ft waves and 60-kn gusts. In response to a distress call, the Coast Guard dispatched two HH-60Js 30 min apart and a C-130 Hercules. The first Jayhawk on scene, SN 6031, realized that there was not enough time to make 34 separate hoists before the ship's crew would be under water. So it lowered a rescue swimmer and basket to the ship's afterdeck and hauled up two crewmen at a time taking just two minutes per haul. This was repeated during severe wind gusts with wave peaks that splashed over the Jayhawk's cockpit. Finally the cabin was packed with survivors, and remaining fuel was becoming critical. The flight crew was barely able to slide the cabin door closed. An accurate count could not be made until after landing when the rescuees spilled out of the cabin and could be counted.

Aircraft 6031 had pulled up 26 of the stricken ship's crew, which set a single-aircraft record for the Coast Guard HH-60J. The second Jayhawk on scene, SN 6001, rescued the remaining eight crewmen under the same weather conditions. The SeaBreeze sank shortly after the aircraft departed.

The heroism and proficiency of the Coast Guard personnel were honored in many ways. One was by the American Helicopter Society when it in 2001 presented the pilots with its Frederick L. Feinberg Award that is given to the helicopter pilot(s) who accomplished the most outstanding achievement during the prior year.

Sikorsky Aircraft helped honor the crews with its Winged-S Rescue Award. That award, symbolized by a gold winged-S lapel pin with "RESCUE" written within the company logo, is a badge of honor among pilots and aircrews around the world. It is awarded to aviators who take part in the saving of human life with a Sikorsky helicopter. Handing out this award was a tradition started by Igor Sikorsky in the 1950s, and bestowing that award continued to be his most enjoyable and fulfilling honor.

U.S. MARINE CORPS VH-60N

Excellent survivability and performance made the UH-60A a natural candidate for the executive transport mission. Design of the VH-60N pictured in Figure 179, was started in 1986 using the best features of the SH-60B/F

Fig. 179   VH-60N fleet, derived from the Army's Black Hawk, is operated by the Executive Flight Detachment of Marine Helicopter Squadron One (HMX-1) based at Quantico, Virginia. (©Igor I. Sikorsky Historical Archives, Inc.)

and the UH-60A configurations. Many of the proven UH-60A ballistic and crashworthiness features were retained including the hover infra-red suppression system. In addition, special design features were incorporated to provide additional hardening against potential electromagnetic pulse threats. Because of the need to quickly position executive transport helicopters where needed, all of the UH-60A air transportability features were kept to facilitate rapid deployment.

The VH-60N entered service in 1988, and nine were delivered. It uses the Seahawk's uprated engines, transmission system, and flight controls and is internally configured with an executive style interior including extensive soundproofing. Many upgrades to avionics systems were installed including secure worldwide communication capability, which is controlled by a radio operator located in the forward portion of the cabin.

U.S. AIR FORCE MH-60G/HH-60G PAVE HAWK

Development of the USAF MH-60G for its Special Operations Command began in 1986 as a modified version of the UH-60A tailored for special missions. Those missions included long-range infiltration and resupply and recovery of special operations forces as well as recovery of downed pilots. Special equipment was installed to permit operation in night and in virtually all weather conditions. Figure 180 shows the MH-60G's unique features for long-range rescue operations. Later in the program, the uprated UH-60L became the baseline airframe for Pave Hawks, and the specialized HH-60G version was created. It was assigned the primary mission of search and rescue backed up by the MH-60G, which retains its primary mission of inserting and

Fig. 180   MH-60G equipped with in-flight refueling boom along with optional internal fuel tanks, FLIR system, weather radar, and rescue hoist with a 200-ft cable capable of lifting 600 lb. (©Igor I. Sikorsky Historical Archives, Inc.)

recovering special operation personnel. Both Pave Hawks can be outfitted with two 7.62-mm miniguns in the gunners' window or two 0.50-caliber machine guns in the cabin door for suppressive fire. Approximately 100 Pave Hawks have been delivered, most of which are HH-60Gs.

U.S. ARMY MH-60K BLACK HAWK

The Army MH-60K is similar in many respects to the Air Force MH-60G model and was configured to perform similar missions for the Army Special Operations Command. Early versions of the MH-60K were UH-60As modified to carry an infrared sensor, night-vision equipment, infrared jammer, and special navigation/communication equipment. These early versions were identified as the MH-60A, of which approximately 30 were made. Development of its replacement, the MH-60K, began in 1987, and the first prototype flew in August 1990 beginning a two-year flight development program during which the IBM Federal Systems Division and Sikorsky Aircraft were both contractors to the Army.

Its special features for long-range operation include enlarged internal fuel cells (360 gallons), aerial refueling probe, and ability to carry the external

Fig. 181   U.S. Army Special Forces MH-60K equipped with in-flight refueling probe and 250-gallon external fuel tanks for long-range covert operations. (©Igor I. Sikorsky Historical Archives, Inc.)

tank system (ETS) from the fuselage mounting provisions for the Army's external stores support system (ESSS). The MH-60K also is equipped with terrain-avoidance radar and mounted below its radome is a FLIR turret that can be seen in Fig. 181. Defensive equipment in addition to suppressive-fire guns includes a missile warning receiver, a chaff/flare dispenser, and a radar warning system.

U.S. ARMY UH-60L BLACK HAWK

The UH-60L, initiated in 1987, was the first major upgrading of the basic Black Hawk helicopter since the UH-60A model was first delivered in 1978. This upgrade, primarily in installed power, was needed to restore performance lost by the A model due to many weight increases during its 11-year production run of nearly 1000 units. During that period, the Black Hawk configuration went through a maturing phase reflecting combat service experience and the rigors of high flight time.

The Army's operational experience indicated the need for features and equipment that were not envisioned when the program began. In addition, service experience showed that reliability and durability of certain aircraft components needed to be improved. As equipment and features were added, and certain components strengthened, their associated weight increases began to extract a toll on aircraft flight performance. It became clear that an upgrade to the UH-60A's propulsion system was needed to regain performance. That realization led to development of the UH-60L model. The Black Hawk production line changed from the A to the L model in 1989, which marked the beginning of a production run of UH-60Ls that is expected to approach 20 years.

The main building blocks selected to create the L model were the uprated engines, improved durability main gearbox, and strengthened flight controls developed earlier for the Navy SH-60B Seahawk program. The uprated Seahawk engines, identified as the T700-GE-701C for the Army, had an intermediate rated power of 1857 SHP compared to 1622 SHP for the T700-GE-700 engines that they replaced. The Navy's improved durability gearbox was rated at 3400 hp compared to 2828 hp for the A model gearbox. With this substantial power increase, the UH-60L not only recovered performance lost by a decade of weight increases, but it provided performance margins that extended mission capabilities much above the A model. For example, external load capacity increased from 8000 to 9000 lb permitting the L model to transport the Army's weaponized M1036 High Mobility Multipurpose Wheeled Vehicle (HMMWV) including the AVENGER HMMWV shown in Fig. 182.

The Black Hawk weight history from contract award in 1976 to the end of UH-60A production is a story of trading weight and performance margins for improved mission capability and product reliability. During its 11-year production period, the A model's empty weight increased nearly 1 lb for every

Fig. 182   UH-60L carrying the M1036 High Mobility Multipurpose Wheeled Vehicle (HMMWV) weighing 8750 lb. (©Igor I. Sikorsky Historical Archives, Inc.)

aircraft delivered on essentially a linear basis. Each pound that was added reduced performance, particularly vertical climb capability. Yet even at the end of its production, the A model still performed reasonably well but not to the Army's material need minimum requirements.

The UH-60A was able to accept weight growth for 11 years because of a very successful weight reduction program put in place when the first production contract was signed. That weight reduction program achieved a 513-lb underweight status for the first production Black Hawk helicopter delivered. The effect of this appreciable weight "kitty," almost 5% of empty weight, acted like a vacuum that needed to be filled. And filled it was with such enthusiasm that an inertial overshoot of an additional 353 lb was incrementally added. The first UH-60A delivered weighed 10,387 lb against a specification weight of 10,900 lb. With an empty weight 513 lb below spec, mission gross weight was correspondingly below its specification value of 16,540 lb. This resulted in vertical climb increasing from the contract value of 480 fpm to over 1000 fpm and cruise speed increasing from 147 kn to over 150 kn.

However as weight was added incrementally as illustrated in Fig. 183, performance finally fell below the Army's material need minimum requirement of 450 fpm vertical climb and 145 kn cruise speed. The last UH-60A delivered weighed 11,253 lb against a specification weight that had increased over the years to 11,284 lb, reflecting the sum total of all engineering change proposals and specification change notices issued since production started in 1976.

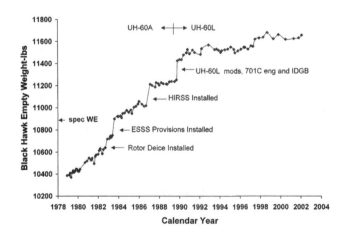

Fig. 183 Added equipment and structural improvements increased UH-60A empty weight nearly 1 lb for every unit produced. The highlighted equipment are a) full provisions for main- and tail-rotor deice capability, b) full structural and electrical provisions to install the external stores support system, and c) the new hover infrared suppression system. Also noted are the T700-GE-701C engines and the improved durability gearbox that were part of the modifications to the A, which created the L model.

Achievement of the UH-60A's initial underweight status and the extent to which it benefited the program is an instructive lessons-learned experience. It was especially important to start the new UH-60A production program with substantial underweight and overperformance margins in order to help keep the program viable. The early creation of positive margins for empty weight, performance, and reliability was a result of guarantees and warranties written into the production contract. As mentioned in Chapter 9, financial incentives and penalties provided strong incentives. Probably these incentives were stronger than would be expected from simply the application of good program management practices. In any case the results helped the Black Hawk helicopter mature into a more mission-capable aircraft.

Sikorsky designers aggressively pushed for weight reduction in every part of the design starting during the production contract negotiation process. The same was true in performance and reliability with the result that additional fee was earned during the low-rate initial production (LRIP) period. However, the added fee was not as important as keeping the program sold in the Army and in the Congress. There is no doubt that the positive weight margin helped keep the program healthy. If Sikorsky had delivered the first UH-60A at its contract value of empty weight instead of 513 lb underweight, it would have found itself not meeting material need performance minimums early in the program as features were added and as weight began to increase. Had the critical vertical-climb performance fallen much below MN minimums, there likely would have been suggestions of a program stretch-out or even cancellation. But the substantial weight margin provided time to mature the A model and to find the best way to re-establish positive performance margins. That was achieved with a new baseline model that was to become the UH-60L. The extent to which the first L model recovered critical performance is tabulated in Table 4.

Figure 183 plots the empty weight trend of the A model through its production life and of the L model during the first 12 years of its production. Highlighted are the most significant configuration changes that increased weight during the UH-60A production period.

Table 4   UH-60L Performance gains

	Last production UH-60A 1989	First production UH-60L 1989
Empty weight	11,253 lb	11,426 lb
Mission gross Wt.	16,803 lb	16,976 lb
Speed 4000 ft-95°F	139 kn	152 kn
VROC 4000 ft-95°F	390 fpm	1550 fpm

The data points in Fig. 183 include UH-60L models manufactured from 1989 through 2001 shown on the right half of the data plot. The slope of the L weight growth is seen to be less than half that of the A model, indicating that the UH-60L configuration has been much more stable than that of the UH-60A. That favorable trend would suggest a longer production life of the L before its replacement is needed.

As can be inferred from Fig. 183, there was no shortage of ideas to improve the Black Hawk, and its early underweight status provided the motivation to make the aircraft more versatile and more durable. Early operational experience showed that several aircraft subsystems had to be modified to achieve acceptable reliability. The two most important were the stabilator automatic control system and the main-rotor spindle assembly. Reliability of the stabilator control system was an early problem involving inadvertent shutdown of the automatic incidence-setting feature. Reversion to manual operation required pilots to use the panel-mounted slew switch to adjust stabilator incidence during flight, which was a safety concern. A comprehensive improvement package was installed to significantly enhance reliability of the stabilator amplifiers, sensors, and other components. In addition, manual slew switches were added to the cyclic control sticks so that pilots could rapidly control stabilator incidence without taking their hands off the flight controls in the event of a system failure.

Structural redundancy added to the main-rotor titanium spindles was another design improvement having a significant weight impact. The spindles provide the load path for blade centrifugal force to the elastomeric bearings. Fatigue strength of the spindles was found to be affected by production manufacturing anomalies associated with machining of the inboard threads that could cause uneven load distribution within the threads. In addition to tightening up the thread manufacturing and inspection processes to eliminate such anomalies, internal tie-rods were added to provide fail-safe load paths to alleviate safety concerns.

Many other improvements were made to the airframe and other systems to correct failure modes revealed during early service experience. They all contributed to a pronounced trend of increasing weight compounded by additions in mission equipment and in provisions for new equipment.

During the early years of production, provisions were added to the airframe to allow future installation of new special equipment being developed for the UH-60A. In some cases the equipment itself was installed as the aircraft were being built. Among the most important survivability features added was the hover infrared suppressor system (HIRSS) to reduce engine exhaust IR signature in all flight regimes down to hover flight. The initial suppressor system was designed to provide effective signature reduction only at cruise speeds above 80 kn by using ram air to mix with and cool the exhaust plume. However the Army tightened its requirement when new technology permitted achievement of required signature levels down to zero flight speed by using air entrainment and mixing features integral with the engine installation. With this major improvement, the highly desirable HIRSS became part of the aircraft configuration. Also becoming part of the production configuration was the rotor deicing system. All of the equipment to de-ice the main-and tail-rotor blades was installed as an integral part of the aircraft rather than as an optional kit as initially planned. Permanent installation of the de-icing package permitted Black Hawk helicopters to be deployed anywhere in the world and to fly safely during moderate icing conditions.

Additional features added during the early UH-60A production period included cable cutters above the cockpit and on the landing-gear drag beams for protection against wire strike. Also added were provisions for a rescue hoist, a flight data recorder, installation of M134 miniguns in place of M60 machine guns, and various other features.

An important new equipment package installed early was the external stores support system (ESSS) making it possible for Black Hawk to carry external fuel tanks, shown in Fig. 184, or a variety of weapon systems. Although the ESSS, constructed of graphite-epoxy-composite materials, was produced and delivered as a kit, the structural and electric provisions for later installation were incorporated in every UH-60 model. These provisions were installed on the production line while earlier built aircraft had the ESSS provisions installed in the field.

Fig. 184   Operational versatility of the external stores support system, shown carrying four external fuel tanks, encouraged the Army to incorporate the structural attachment points in all production Black Hawk helicopters so that every aircraft built would be able to accommodate the ESSS either to extend operational range or to carry weapons or both. (©Igor I. Sikorsky Historical Archives, Inc.)

The external stores support system was designed to carry approximately 5000 lb per side. It was qualified to carry two 450-gallon tanks on the inboard pylons and two 230-gallon tanks on the outboard pylons. With this fuel load added to the internal tanks, the UH-60 models can fly over 1100 n miles.

The load-carrying capacity of the ESSS quickly led to the development and qualification of a variety of weapon systems that could be carried externally. The first weapons system to be demonstrated and qualified for the Black Hawk was the Hellfire missile. Sikorsky and the Tactical Systems Division of Rockwell International performed the ground and flight testing at Redstone Arsenal required for the Army to qualify the Hellfire installation shown in Fig. 185. Other weapons that can be carried on the ESSS include Stinger, Maverick, and Sidewinder missiles as well as twin-pod 2.75-in. unguided rockets on each of the four stations.

UH-60 models have been qualified to carry cabin-mounted weapons as well as ESSS-mounted systems. Guns capable of being installed in Black Hawk cabin windows include the standard M-60D 7.62-mm machine gun, the GAU-19 0.50 cal 3-barrel Gatling gun with up to a 2000-round-per-minute

Fig. 185   Sixteen Hellfire anti-armor missiles can be carried with four on each of the ESSS pylon mounts as shown above, with an additional reload of 16 Hellfire missiles carried in the cabin. The lower picture shows the variety of weapons that can be carried on the ESSS pylon mounts. (©Igor I. Sikorsky Historical Archives, Inc.)

firing rate. Other weapons include the GAU-2B 7.62 minigun and the M-230 30-mm chain gun can be carried on the ESSS as well.

U.S. ARMY UH-60Q DUSTOFF

Second to the troop assault mission, aeromedical evacuation from the combat zone was the Black Hawk helicopter's most important mission. During early UH-60A production, MEDIVAC capability was achieved by converting troop assault UH-60As to MEDIVAC helicopters by the Army. These early conversions had neither the medical facilities nor equipment needed to provide the fullest medical care possible, nor were the early A models outfitted with stores support system to carry range extension fuel tanks. Because of these limited capabilities, specifications were established for a dedicated MEDIVAC derivative taking advantage of the added performance capabilities of the newly created L model. This new UH-60Q DUSTOFF (dedicated unhesitating service to our fighting forces) was created and placed in service in 1993.

The UH-60Q was configured and equipped with high-technology medical equipment including an oxygen generation system, an intravenous (IV) solutions warming and cooling unit, cardiac monitoring system, a powered litter lift system, and outlets for 28-V dc as well as 110/220-V ac electrical power and night-vision compatible lighting. Six litter stations for acute care patients and seating for several ambulatory patients are available. This Black Hawk variant, Fig. 186, is equipped with cockpit-mounted FLIR, weather radar, satellite communications, and global positioning system.

Fig. 186   UH-60Q DUSTOFF showing the FLIR and radar sensors mounted on cockpit structure as well as the ESSS carrying two 230-gallon fuel tanks from the outer two stores attachment fittings. (©Igor I. Sikorsky Historical Archives, Inc.)

The UH-60Q's medical systems, range extension fuel system, and all-weather capability enable it to perform battlefield evacuation, combat search and rescue, forward surgical team transport, as well as performing disaster and humanitarian relief missions.

S-70A FIREHAWK

One of the more specialized derivatives of the Black Hawk is the firefighting version pictured in Fig. 187 releasing a load of water from its 1000-gallon tank over a brush fire. This helicopter is one of three S-70A FIREHAWKS operated by the Los Angeles County Fire Department (LACFD). The FIREHAWK is a unique combination of an airborne fire truck and a medivac aircraft that is created by installing two kits to a UH-60L helicopter. These kits convert it to both a firefighter and a medical evacuation helicopter complete with rescue hoist and state-of-the-art medical equipment to diagnose and treat injured rescuees.

The use of helicopters to fight fires in areas inaccessible by conventional land-based equipment has been well refined and is employed worldwide. Special water containers such as Bambi Buckets, suspended from a helicopter, as well as special water tanks attached to the helicopter, have been developed that allow precision water and fire-retardant drop where needed. High-capacity water pumps to quickly refill these containers while hovering over

Fig. 187   S-70A FIREHAWK, made from a newly built U.S. Army Black Hawk, is one of two purchased in 2001 by the Los Angeles County Fire Department for both firefighting and emergency medical evacuation. In 2005, a third FIREHAWK was purchased by the LACFD. (©Igor I. Sikorsky Historical Archives Inc.)

ponds, swimming pools, or almost any body of water permit rapid flights to and from the fire zone.

This capability to conduct drop and refill cycles in minutes is what makes helicopters especially well suited to fighting fire in remote areas. The Los Angeles County covers 4000 square miles populated by over 10 million people. Its extensive mountainous rugged terrain makes firefighting by conventional equipment nearly impossible. Similar geography in other western states has helped encourage shared solutions that focused on using fixed-wing aircraft and helicopters as the airborne "fire trucks." The Oregon National Guard was the first military organization worldwide to convert UH-60L aircraft to FIREHAWKS for firefighting missions. Fifty kits to convert UH-60L helicopters to firefighting machines were built with funds allocated by the U.S. Congress. Likewise, the Los Angeles County Fire Department was the first municipal organization to put S-70A FIREHAWKS in routine service and to employ a trained and dedicated staff for their operation.

The idea of using the Black Hawk as a firefighting helicopter was advanced soon after Sikorsky developed the ESSS for the U.S. Army. The ESSS permits nearly 1500 gallons of fuel to be carried in external tanks for long-range missions. A design engineer at Sikorsky, Denton Delong, first proposed what seemed like a far-out idea during the early 1990s. He reasoned that the Black Hawk's significant useful load, speed, and altitude performance together with high structural margins were exactly the right attributes needed by a firefighting helicopter. Moreover, the ESSS structure had more than adequate strength to carry water-filled external tanks.

Armed with back-of-the-envelope sketches and calculations, Delong visited the LACFD to get their thoughts about a possible Black Hawk firefighter. The LACFD firefighters were very enthused about this aircraft's performance, but Delong's idea of using four water tanks suspended from the wing-like external structure drew a negative reaction. They much preferred using a single large tank attached to the bottom of the fuselage to facilitate rapid refilling as well as to make it easier to inject fire retarding chemicals into the water tank. Precise control of water release would also be facilitated through a single tank. The LACFD encouraged development of the one tank idea and recommended the Aero Union Corporation in Chico, California, as a possible source because of their extensive experience with firefighting helicopters.

Aero Union and Sikorsky created the configuration depicted in Fig. 188 that first flew in 1999. With the help from the LACFD pilot and maintenance staff, the team was able to overcome unexpected technical problems by the end of a three-month test-and-fix development period.

The 1000-gallon tank, made of aluminum, is attached to the Black Hawk cabin tub section at its four corners. The attachment fittings together with local frame reinforcements are installed as part of a structural kit. Opening

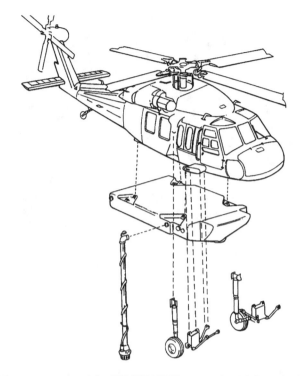

Fig. 188 Main components of the FIREHAWK conversion kit include the rectangular 1000-gallon water tank with an integral 30-gallon tank for chemical fire retardants, a 10-ft snorkel with a pump at the bottom, 20-in. extenders for the main landing gear, and cockpit switches for the crew to control water release rates and to initiate water refill.

and closing of the tank doors by a hydraulic motor can be controlled by the pilots for releasing the water at a wide range of drop rates. Switches on the helicopter's cyclic stick control the snorkel up and down movement, tank door opening, and emergency water dump. The pilot can select any of four coverage levels in either the full-, half-, or quarter-drop modes. Water is dropped in what is called a constant-flow delivery process wherein the doors open and close against head pressure in the tank to control the quantity of combined water and fire retardant that is released. The coverage level is selected by the crew depending on the type of fire, flame height, weather, and flight routes in and out of the fire zone.

The water tank is refilled in less than 60 s through the snorkel tube while hovering over any accessible body of water as pictured in Fig. 189. A thumb switch on the helicopter's collective pitch stick actuates the snorkel water pump.

During early flight testing, the operational procedure was to let the snorkel hang free while flying to and from the fire zone. However, the dynamics of

Fig. 189   High-capacity electric pump is at the bottom of the snorkel tube about to enter the water. This jet pump, using three-phase 120-V ac power, is capable of a 1000-gpm. flow rate, and it can draw from water as little as 8 in. deep. It is a "trash"-type pump designed to handle whatever sand, gravel, or debris that it might ingest as a result of its high pumping capacity. (Aero Union photo)

the snorkel/pump combination in conjunction with the helicopter's main-rotor downwash rotation produced pendulum and rotational oscillations that limited flight speed to less than 60 kn. During one early flight, the snorkel swung back far enough to hit the underside of the airframe. Even without the oscillation problem, the aerodynamic drag of the snorkel reduced the aircraft's performance.

After experimenting with several modifications, the solution finally adopted was to get the snorkel out of the airstream by retracting it immediately after refilling the tank. The 6-in.-diam snorkel is made from soft nylon that flattens as it is rolled up by a motor-driven retraction drum. The electric wires that power the pump wind up with the snorkel tube. This solution eliminated the special flight speed restriction, but a snorkel twisting problem still remained. When it is being lowered by the drum, the snorkel tends to twist counter-clockwise as driven by the rotation of the rotor slipstream. Excessive twist can restrict water flow up to the tank, but this is avoided by actuating the pump switch intermittently as it is lowered into the water. When the crew chief sees the snorkel begin to develop a twist, he advises the pilot to hit the pump switch a few times, which quickly straightens the now pressurized snorkel tube.

Sufficient space under the Black Hawk cabin to mount the water tank was achieved by adding extenders to the normal UH-60L main landing gear, which is used as is. The extenders add another 20 in. to the UH-60L fuselage-to-ground clearance, which is sufficient to accommodate the 30-in.

high tank. This provides approximately a 6-in. ground clearance below the tank and permits the landing-gear oleo cylinders to absorb crash energy if needed. In the firefighting mode, aircraft gross weight is limited to 22,000 lb on the ground but can increase to 23,500 lb when filling the water tank from hovering flight. The water is regarded as an external load that can be jettisoned if required, similar to a typical helicopter sling load.

The LACFD conducted a three-month evaluation of the first prototype FIREHAWK helicopter in 1999 with the help of Sikorsky test pilot Chip Washington and under the leadership of Lee Benson, then LACFD senior pilot. Aero Union provided the tank, snorkel, and controls while the Air Methods Corporation of Englewood, Colorado, provided the custom-designed medical interior package. The Breeze-Eastern Company of Union, New Jersey, provided the exterior rescue hoist, and Sikorsky supplied the landing-gear extenders. The Air Methods EMS interior included a life-support system with built-in suction, oxygen, and vital parameter monitoring. In addition to the medical equipment, 10 passenger seats were installed along with a para-medic seat. All are fully crashworthy as in military Black Hawks.

During the LACFD evaluation, the demonstration and training FIREHAWK was placed in the real-life situation pictured in Fig. 190.

Following this evaluation, the LACFD ordered two S-70A FIREHAWKS including training, initial spare parts, and the full medical and firefighting packages, which were delivered in 2001. Total cost was approximately $25 million. What these specialized helicopters provide the LACFD is an

Fig. 190 S-70A FIREHAWK extinguishing a brush fire in a remote area. This demonstrator aircraft was an Oregon National Guard UH-60L before being repainted. It is back with the Guard in Army green and still a firefighter. (Photo by Richard Rogers)

all-purpose fire and rescue capability with the size and performance to carry 10 to 12 firefighters at 150 kn and to be able to refill 1000 gallons in less than a minute. Equally important is that the same helicopter can perform life-saving rescue and medical evacuation missions with state-of-the-art equipment. Demand for these services led the LACFD to purchase a third FIREHAWK in 2005.

One such mission involved a commuter van with 10 NASA employees that plummeted 200 ft over the side of a mountain. Witnesses summoned help, and LACFD aircraft N160 was the first helicopter on scene. Of the 10 victims, one was able to get out without help, and three perished; one was hoisted out by an LACFD Bell 412. Five victims were hoisted out by the FIREHAWK, which stayed on station and continued the extrication of three additional litter patients, one of whom is pictured in Fig. 191 about to be brought into the cabin. It was also able to lower the Jaws of Life to ground personnel to extricate passengers trapped in the van. All living victims were brought out within 90 min.

The Oregon National Guard put its UH-60L FIREHAWK to use soon after receiving it back from the LACFD demonstrations. On 9 August, 2001, it was called to assist the Portland Fire Bureau fight an urban wildfire [27]. The wildfire threatened 100 homes and the University of Portland. Every fire-fighter, 167 in total, responded as did all available equipment. That included one FIREHAWK, Fig. 192, and one UH-60L carrying a 750-gallon Bambi

Fig. 191   This S-70A FIREHAWK is the same firefighting aircraft pictured in Fig. 187, now rescuing victims of a van that crashed down a mountain gorge. Firefighter, paramedic, and helicopter crew chief Mike Dubron is pictured lifting a litter basket with the rescue hoist mounted over the cabin door. (LACFD photo)

Fig. 192   Portland, Oregon, 2001 wildfire was the first operational use of the FIREHAWK in that state, and it too confirmed the effectiveness of that special Black Hawk configuration. (Wide World photo)

Bucket. Drawing water from the Willamette River, together they dropped nearly 20,000 gallons of water saving lives and property.

U.S. NAVY MH-60S KNIGHTHAWK

During the 1990s, the Navy evolved a helicopter master plan calling for consolidation of its requirements into two basic helicopter configurations that would enhance mission capabilities and reduce procurement, training, and support costs. Its plan called for phasing out seven existing different airframes by acquiring two new Sikorsky models: the MH-60S and the MH-60R. Both models are multimission helicopters planned to perform all antisubmarine warfare, antisurface ship warfare, medivac, logistics, and search and rescue missions for the Navy. They share the same propulsion and dynamics systems as well as newly developed cockpit display systems.

The MH-60S is a combination of the best features of the Black Hawk helicopter and Seahawk configurations to create a multimission Navy helicopter capable of a wide variety of missions formerly performed by a wide variety of helicopters. Its missions include vertical replenishment of ships, vertical onboard delivery, carrier search and rescue, as well as remote site logistics missions. Missions will likely be expanded to include organic airborne mine countermeasure, armed helicopter operations, combat search and rescue, and special warfare support.

The MH-60S was the first Navy derivative that departed from the Seahawk configuration and instead used the Army UH-60L airframe complete with its aft-mounted tail landing-gear assembly. This selection provides the MH-60S with a more spacious cabin, dual large sliding doors, 9000-lb capacity cargo hook, plus full provisions for the Black Hawk external stores support system. Retained from Seahawk are the automatic folding main rotor, T700-GE-401C engines and drive system, folding tail, and flight control system.

The MH-60S made its first flight in January 2000, and it was accepted for fleet service in 2002. Total procurement of 237 is planned, which will gradually replace the Navy's fleet of four different helicopter models. Figure 193 shows its close resemblance to the basic Army UH-60A/L configuration.

U.S. NAVY MH-60R STRIKEHAWK

After initiating the MH-60S just described, the Navy began development of the MH-60R as the second of its two models intended to consolidate essentially all of its missions into two basic configurations of the earlier SH-60

Fig. 193   U.S. Navy MH-60S designed to consolidate missions performed by an aging fleet of H-46, H-1, H-3, and HH-60H helicopters. This derivative uses the Black Hawk fuselage with its larger cabin, external cargo hook, and aft-positioned tail landing gear. (©Igor I. Sikorsky Historical Archives, Inc.)

series. The MH-60R is derived from and resembles the basic Seahawk, and it consolidates the missions performed by the SH-60B and SH-60F Seahawks.

The first prototype MH-60R flew in July 2001, having been built at Sikorsky by remanufacturing an SH-60B to the new standard. Initial planning called for building the new R model by remanufacturing either SH-60Bs or SH-60Fs, which is the origin of the R designation. The plan envisions remanufacturing all or some B and F Seahawks to the R configuration plus building brand new MH-60Rs to satisfy a total requirement of approximately 250 aircraft. Fleet introduction is planned for mid-decade.

The MH-60R, seen in Fig. 194 artist rendition, will operate from the Navy's frigates, destroyers, cruisers, and aircraft carriers. Its purpose is to perform all undersea warfare (USW) and antisurface warfare (ASuW) missions conducted by the SH-60B and SH-60F Seahawk versions. The MH-60R carries new mission improvement equipment including sonar, radar, electronic support, and integrated self-defense equipment. Deliveries of the MH-60R began in August 2005.

The MH-60R's major upgrades to flight and mission avionics and to offensive and defensive weapons and countermeasures are identified in Fig. 195.

U.S. ARMY UH-60M BLACK HAWK

In March of 2001, the U.S. Defense Acquisition Board approved the Army's plan to upgrade the Black Hawk configuration to a level significantly above the capabilities of the UH-60L developed 12 years earlier. The Army's

Fig. 194 U.S. Navy MH-60R designed to consolidate missions performed by the SH-60B and SH-60F models. The latter two models are being remanufactured to create the MH-60R in addition to newly manufactured R models. (©Igor I. Sikorsky Historical Archives, Inc.)

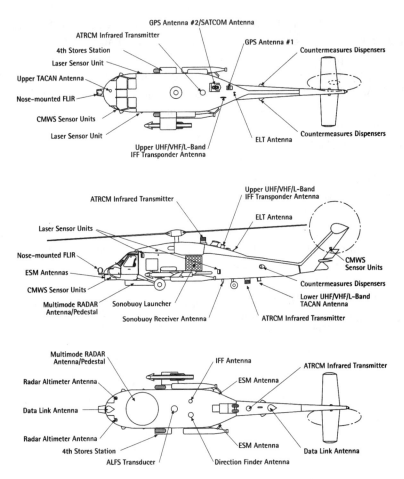

Fig. 195 Among the most discernable features of the MH-60R are the nose-mounted FLIR sensor, multimode radar below the cockpit, sonobouy launcher as well as dipping sonar, and a missile-carrying station in addition to the torpedo-carrying station.

planned upgrades included improved flight performance, full compatibility with the emerging digital battlefield, enhancement of survivability, as well as other improvements to increase Black Hawk operational effectiveness while reducing operation and support costs. Shortly after its plan was approved, the Army awarded Sikorsky a $200M contract to develop and evaluate a new Black Hawk model identified as the UH-60M that could be produced both as a new helicopter as well as by remanufacturing older models. This M model first flew in 2003, Fig. 196, and began to be produced in mid-decade with first delivery achieved on 31 July, 2006.

The UH-60M is one of the most significant UH-60 versions because of the extent to which it incorporated new technologies developed since the program

Fig. 196   First flight of the UH-60M took place on 17 September 2003 at Sikorsky's West Palm Beach test facility. The aircraft shown is the first prototype, identified as M1 that was rebuilt from an early UH-60A. It was later joined in the flight development program by M2, a rebuilt UH-60L, and by M3 a new build UH-60M. (©Igor I. Sikorsky Historical Archives, Inc.)

began in the early 1970s. In particular, advancements in rotor system aerodynamic and materials technologies, vibration control technology, cockpit display, and information integration and propulsion technologies became available for infusion into the UH-60 design. Use of these proven advancements was intended to ensure that Black Hawk helicopters will meet the requirements of the changing battlefield for the next quarter-century.

One of the factors behind the need for a new troop assault Black Hawk model was the increasing cost of operation resulting from the aging of the UH-60A and L models as they approach their design service lives, hastened by the increased operational tempo during the conflicts in the Middle East. Another major driver was the need to restore performance that was lost because of weight growth. This factor of weight growth is similar to the main reason that the UH-60L was developed to replace the UH-60A model. However, the cause of this weight growth is very different. The weight issue for the L came about not because of growth in empty weight, as was the case for the A model, but because of growth in useful load needed to be carried during the primary troop assault mission. That growth was caused by an increase in the number and in the unit weights of the crew and troops as equipped for the air and land warrior roles and capabilities.

PERFORMANCE GROWTH TO MEET NEW ARMY REQUIREMENTS

Two operational changes that required this increase in useful load occurred during the 1990s. The first was recognition that an additional crew member was needed to serve as a dedicated second gunner during operations in the battlefield. This fourth crew member would be able to provide suppressive ground fire in the zone not covered by a single gunner who has visibility only to one side.

The second change was that the weights of both the crew and the 11-man squad had to be increased to reflect the equipment escalations of the new air and land warrior concepts. Unit weight of the future land warrior has increased to 290 from the 240-lb value allocated for each soldier when the Black Hawk helicopter was initially designed in 1972. This increase accounts for body armor and improvements in communications, enhanced vision capability, GPS positioning, and other new features of the soldier's equipment package. In addition, the upward trend of body weight over time had to be considered.

All together, the weight of the added gunner plus the heavier unit weights of crew and troops added approximately 900 lb to the lift requirement for an 11-man squad regardless of which UH-60 model carries this newly defined squad and crew. With that increase in useful load added to the improvements made to cockpit displays and integration, flight control systems, survivability equipment, airframe strengthening and other needed changes, the challenge for the design of the M model was not only to restore flight performance but to provide margin for growth.

That performance challenge was met by use of new-technology main rotor blades that produce a 4% higher efficiency as well as greater speed and maneuver capability plus installation of T700-GE-701D engines that produce 4% more power as well as improved durability. Together, the new rotor blades and the new engines increased lift by approximately 1000 lb to more than compensate for weight growth. The improvements in useful load and changes in weight empty and gross weight for each of the three Army troop assault versions are compared in Table 5.

Cruise speed and climb performance are compared in Table 6 with speed based on 100% maximum continuous power and vertical climb based on 95%

Table 5   Escalation in mission weights

Weight	UH-60A	UH-60L	UH-60M
Useful load, lbs	5,710	5,924	6,882
Empty weight, lbs	11,284	11,782	12,500
Mission weight, lbs	16,994	17,706	19,382
Max gross weight, lbs	20,250	22,000	22,000

Table 6 Performance improvements

Performance	UH-60A	UH-60L	UH-60M
Cruise speed at GW of 16,800	140 kn	155 kn	153 kn
Vertical Rate of Climb at GW of 16,800 lb	377 ft/min	1315 ft/min	1646 ft/min
Vertical Rate of Climb at GW of 18,000 lb	0 ft/min	592 ft/min	994 ft/min

intermediate rated power in accordance with Army performance ground rules. Ambient conditions are 4000 ft altitude and 95° F. The slight drop in cruise speed of the M compared to the L is caused by acknowledgment of the drag of added antennae and external systems present on the L but not factored into flight manual performance at the time.

The UH-60M design takes advantage of several features developed for Sikorsky's S-92 helicopter. This new medium-transport model, Fig. 197, was developed during the 1990s as a private venture by Sikorsky together with a team of major aerospace companies from Japan, China, Brazil, Taiwan, and Spain. Its configuration was optimized for the commercial-transport market with a 19-passenger cabin as well as for the military medium-transport market. It is aimed at those missions requiring significantly larger cabin volume and useful loads than can be provided by Black Hawk models. Special features were designed into the S-92 helicopter to meet the most current requirements of the FAA and its foreign counterparts and also to achieve

Fig. 197 S-92 was first flown in December 1998. Its cabin is configured to accommodate 19 passengers in a civil version and 22 or more troops in a military configuration. It can be equipped with a rear ramp to permit rapid loading of troops and vehicles. (©Igor I. Sikorsky Historical Archives, Inc.)

military standards of survivability and multimission capability and battlefield operability.

The S-92 incorporates many of the UH-60 design innovations, but its technology base clearly represents a new helicopter generation. This is particularly true in rotor-blade and rotor-head design as well as in vibration control methodology and in cockpit displays and integration. The structural design of its elastomeric rotor head with emphasis on fail-safe design features helped earn the S-92 the Collier trophy in 2002 for the safest helicopter ever developed. Its high-performance main rotor blade formed the basis of the UH-60M after that new blade was test flown on a UH-60L to confirm performance expectations and dynamic compatibility with the UH-60 airframe and drive system.

The infusion of technology developed by Sikorsky for its S-92 commercial program into the UH-60M military program is a departure from normal practice. The norm has been to apply qualified military-developed technology to commercial programs. However the S-92, benefiting from technologies developed for earlier UH-60 models, now reciprocates by providing technology advancements to extend military UH-60 performance and to improve vibration control.

INCREASED PERFORMANCE ROTOR

The original UH-60A design, as described in Chapter 4, was able to achieve a record high rotor aerodynamic efficiency that resulted in excellent aircraft vertical as well as cruise performance. It achieved that efficiency by using cambered airfoil shapes, high nonlinear blade twist plus an unusual swept-tip design that improved performance in both hover and high-speed flight modes. During the 1990s, Sikorsky demonstrated further advances in rotor efficiency through refinement of all of these critical blade parameters, particularly airfoil shape and blade-tip geometry.

The company also made the transition from an all-titanium blade spar to an all-composite spar to reduce manufacturing cost while retaining the torsional stiffness, fatigue strength, and survivability characteristics of the Black Hawk's original titanium blade spar. This new blade technology was selected for the Sikorsky S-92 utility transport. Figure 198 compares the key features of this new blade with the original main rotor blades for the UH-60A/L models.

ADVANCED VIBRATION CONTROL SYSTEM

The S-92 also pioneered a major improvement in aircraft vibration control engineering through the application of active self-adaptive technology to achieve lower vibration levels. With this technology, acceptable vibration levels can be achieved with far less of a weight penalty than earlier Black Hawk derivatives were forced to carry. This new system utilizes an active

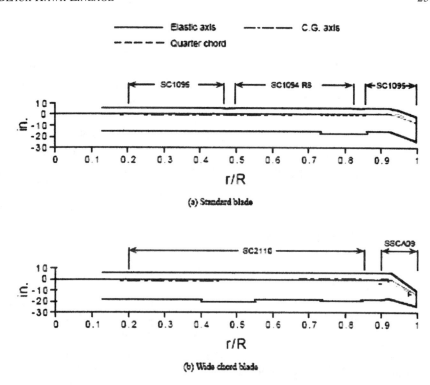

Fig. 198   Chord of the composite blade for the M model is 1.75 in. (16%) wider than the A and L blades, increasing cruise speed and maneuverability as well. Its new airfoil contour and blade-tip airfoil and dihedral shape further improve hover and vertical-climb performance.

vibration control system (AVCS) to reduce 4/rev vibration throughout the airframe. The AVCS eliminates the need for the passive spring-mass units carried in all prior Black Hawk models, thereby significantly reducing weight. The AVCS further maintains consistent vibration performance when rotor speed deviates from its nominal 100% value and avoids the loss of effectiveness characteristic of passive absorbers when operating at off-design frequencies.

The AVCS achieves lower vibration at lower weight because it is a distributed system able to attenuate vibration in selected zones within the airframe. Force generators of the AVCS can be located wherever necessary throughout the fuselage to generate forces to cancel out local vibrations. The heart of the system is a closed-loop algorithm that calculates the force generator commands required to minimize vibrations as measured by accelerometers located throughout the cockpit and cabin. A feedback control algorithm processes a tachometer signal, providing frequency and phase information, and also processes accelerometer signals that feed back local vibration conditions.

The AVCS computer calculates the required force generator commands and sends them digitally to an electronic unit. This unit then converts the digital signals to analog signals, which then are sent to electric motors within the force generators. These motors drive counter-rotating eccentric masses to generate forces of appropriate magnitude and frequency to cancel fuselage vibrations.

In the UH-60M, a force generator capable of producing 1000 lb is located in the forward cabin overhead, replacing a heavy spring-mass absorber. In addition, generators able to produce 450 lb are located one in the left landing-gear stub wing and one in the cockpit nose. Figures 199–201 show where the major AVCS components are located in the M model.

The relative sizes of the electronic units and force generators used in both the S-92 and the UH-60M are shown in Fig. 202.

DIGITAL AVIONICS AND INTEGRATED DISPLAYS

All key aspects of the UH-60M cockpit have been brought up to latest military aviation standards with regards to display technology, digital avionics, digital flight control components, and modular open architecture systems. This major upgrade offers the capability to achieve standardization of equipment and training across Black Hawk derivative models as well as with other Army helicopters. Its new cockpit incorporates dual digital data busses and advances in digital avionics architecture together with a much improved flight control system. Four-color multifunction displays (MFDs) are used in the

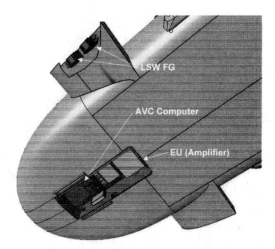

Fig. 199 AVCS computer and electronic unit are located below the cockpit floor between the longitudinal skid beams, and one force generator is mounted in the landing-gear stub wing. (©Sikorsky Aircraft Corporation)

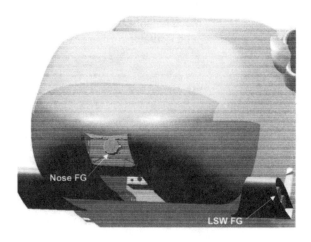

Fig. 200   Additional small force generator is installed forward in the cockpit support structure between the two longitudinal skid beams. (©Sikorsky Aircraft Corporation)

new cockpit designed to increase pilot situational awareness and interoperability with joint forces on and in the battlefield area. Among the main objectives of this cockpit upgrade was to significantly improve the UH-60M's ability to communicate and operate on what is referred to as the 21st-century digital battlefield. Digitized features and equipment ensure more precise long-range navigation, command and control interoperability, and are

Fig. 201   Main UH-60M force generator is located in the cabin overhead replacing the original 4P spring-mass absorber. (©Sikorsky Aircraft Corporation)

**Moog Amplifier
and Actuator**

**Hamilton
Sundstrand Computer**

Fig. 202   The UH-60M force generators are pictured on either side of the amplifier with the computer shown in the foreground. (©Sikorsky Aircraft Corporation)

compatible with future air traffic management requirements. The new cockpit incorporates an improved message and data-transfer capability as well as dual embedded global positioning and inertial navigation systems.

Significant improvements in pilot workload and operational capability were achieved by major upgrade of the aircraft's flight control system. Dual digital computer flight control computers were installed, along with a fully coupled flight director system, providing stability augmentation, trim, and flight-path stabilization functions. A major benefit of the new control system and the integrated displays is the ability to conduct combat operations during degraded visual conditions with more precision and safety.

Figure 203 shows the redesigned and smaller instrument panel containing the four MFDs, all of which are 6×8 in. active matrix liquid crystal displays. The traditional communication and navigation avionics installed in earlier UH-60A/L models including many flight instruments have been replaced by the MFDs. They provide primary flight, navigation, and tactical information, and they are fully integrated with a digital moving map displaying real-time aircraft position and terrain information, a Stormscope for detecting lightning activity, and a radar warning system.

The enhanced downward visibility through the chin windows, made possible by the shortened panel, is noted by comparing Figures 203 and 204.

HIGH LIFE STRUCTURE

Early in the UH-60M design process, it was found that a new cabin and transition section primary structure made largely of high-speed machined frames and longitudinal beams would be less expensive than continuing to

Fig. 203 Four displays as well as a shortened instrument panel that provides greater visibility of terrain and ground personnel. Two control display units (CDUs) are installed in the center console. A FLIR can be installed to permit safer operations during decreased visibility and night conditions. (©Sikorsky Aircraft Corporation)

produce the original design that was almost all built-up riveted structure. The cost reduction from this machined structure approach helped offset the increased cost of the new integrated cockpit. This new cabin/transition section will be used as well for all Black Hawks remanufactured to the

Fig. 204 Cockpit arrangement and displays shown are typical of earlier UH-60 A and L versions that were based on conventional analog instruments as well as nonintegrated avionic units. (©Sikorsky Aircraft Corporation)

M standard to in effect "zero time" that part of airframe structure subject to damaging vibratory loading as well as to provide added strength margins for the heavier troop assault mission.

In addition to new airframe structure, the UH-60M will also be equipped with new crashworthy crew and troop seats containing adjustable energy absorption features. These features provide protection for a wider weight range to accommodate both male and female occupants. Provisions for air bags in the cockpit, deployed during rapid deceleration, are included.

Gradual phase-in of the UH-60M began in 2006 as UH-60L production started to taper off. In addition to new production build, consideration is being given to rebuilding older UH-60A and L models to the UH-60M configuration to provide all of the operational cost and performance benefits of this new model plus significant service life extension of a large fleet of old, high-time Black Hawk helicopters.

Figure 205 recaps the major configuration features of the UH-60M incorporated in the first M delivered in July 2006. The planned product improvement program that adds fly-by-wire, composite primary structure and many other features will help production of this model reach a planned quantity of 1200 units.

BEYOND THE UH-60M BLACK HAWK

The U.S. Army has significantly refined the effectiveness of air mobility using helicopters ever since their earliest use in the 1950 decade. During the Korean conflict, experimentation with helicopters in the battlefield proved the value of their unique flight capabilities. During the Vietnam conflict a decade later, helicopter air mobility became the primary role of the venerable

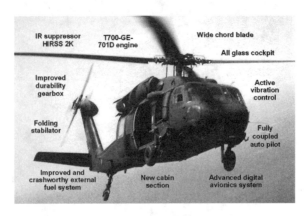

Fig. 205   Features noted extend performance margins, improve reliability and occupant comfort, and significantly enhance compatibility with the digital battlefield. (©Sikorsky Aircraft Corporation)

Bell UH-1 Huey. Starting in the 1980s, the effectiveness of the airmobile doctrine was demonstrated by Black Hawk helicopters in every battlefield conflict since it first saw combat in Grenada in 1983. That experience was followed by Panama in 1989, Somalia in 1993, Afghanistan in 2001, and Iraq in 2003.

In spite of the progress made to date, significant improvements in flight safety, battlefield interoperability, payload, speed and range, and operation in all-weather and limited visibility operations are still needed. Technology coupled with design ingenuity and imaginative tactics are still the engines that drive operational capability and effectiveness.

Successive versions of the UH-60 have provided significant operational improvements and will continue to do so as new design innovations and proven technology advancements are integrated into the Black Hawk helicopter and into its mission systems. Perhaps freed from the physical constrains of air transport in obsolescent transport aircraft, future Black Hawk derivatives can be envisioned to have more spacious cabins to accommodate more equipment and more troops. Future Black Hawk versions will have significantly more performance capability especially in mission range as more efficient rotor systems and more powerful engines are developed. Future Black Hawks will be more survivable as proven concepts are incorporated to reduce radar, infrared, and acoustic signatures as well as new weapon countermeasures to defeat RPV threats. Future Black Hawk models will exhibit far greater operational safety by virtue of fly-by-wire control systems coupled to ground proximity and obstruction detection sensors using the right control laws to prohibit accidents.

The Black Hawk configuration that will replace the UH-60M can begin to be envisioned now, and the right technology is under development to turn that vision into reality.

Chapter 11

INTERNATIONAL HAWK FAMILY

The world market for new-generation utility helicopters began to expand during the 1980 decade for the same reasons that spurred the U.S. Army to develop the Black Hawk. Operators of earlier generation helicopters also sought major improvements in flight performance, survivability, reliability, and operational cost. It had been nearly a quarter century since the last all-new utility helicopter was designed and it was time for a change. Faced with the obsolescence of earlier models and the need for improvements, it was no surprise that the Black Hawk and its variants found ready markets in many countries.

The U.S. Army set high standards for the Black Hawk design requirements when it launched this program in 1972. Many helicopter experts felt that the specification was much too demanding and that some attributes were mutually exclusive. What was agreed upon was that only a new and innovative helicopter using new rotorcraft technologies would have a chance of meeting those requirements. When the Black Hawk completed its growing pains in 1978 in what the Army aptly called the maturity phase, this new utility helicopter demonstrated achievement of all critical attributes. The international helicopter community became aware of the UH-60A as it began operational service with its very enthusiastic acceptance by the U.S. Army.

When the Black Hawk and Seahawk models achieved full rate production early in the 1980s, they clearly stood out as the new-generation utility helicopters that many countries of the world were waiting for. Both models were found to be quite adaptable to a wide range of land-based and ship-based missions. Many foreign military organizations began to look at the Black Hawk, and later the Seahawk, as the aircraft of choice for modernizing their helicopter fleets. Those evaluations led to foreign variants of both models with new features and new equipment added to meet specialized operational needs. It further led to coproduction and licensed production agreements with those countries that operated large aircraft fleets.

Along with the demonstrated and publicized capabilities of these new models, the commitment of the U.S. military to the Black Hawk and Seahawk programs was an important consideration for potential foreign customers. They appreciated the fact that the Hawk series would be produced, operated, supported, and improved by the largest helicopter operator in the world. That realization significantly increased their confidence in acquiring these new-generation helicopters. In addition, the U.S. government encouraged foreign procurement either through the foreign military sales (FMS) process or by direct purchase from Sikorsky Aircraft.

The countries presently operating the largest fleets of the Hawk series are Japan, Australia, South Korea, Turkey, and Colombia. The first three have produced these models in country under license to meet the needs of their defense forces. In total, 24 countries have selected Black Hawk and Seahawk variants to date and more are expected. This chapter provides a brief country-by-country description of the Hawk models summarized in Table 7 and their primary missions.

What is apparent in reviewing the operational experience of each country is the broad commitment to use helicopters for humanitarian missions especially by those countries with large fleets. Most countries operating Hawk variants have equipped their aircraft to perform long-range search and rescue as well as general humanitarian missions. This chapter describes such missions that have saved lives and helped thousands of people in distress. Several such missions have saved people in record numbers, and many have been performed in the most adverse weather conditions imaginable. They continue to show what trained and dedicated flight crews can accomplish with highly capable helicopters.

As they have for 60 years, helicopters around the world have led the way in easing human suffering in the aftermath of both natural and manmade disasters. These remarkable machines are indeed living up to the helicopter's highest calling as envisioned by Igor I. Sikorsky from the beginning of his pioneering helicopter achievements.

Table 7   International Hawks: models and missions

Country	Government service	Base model	Delivered units	Missions
Argentina	Presidential Air Group	Black Hawk	1	VIP transport
Australia	Royal Australian Navy	Seahawk	16	Antisubmarine
	Royal Australian Army	Black Hawk	39	Antisurface ship
				Search and rescue
				Utility transport
Austria	Austrian Air Force	Black Hawk	9	Search and rescue
				Utility transport
Bahrain	Bahraini Air Force	Black Hawk	2	VIP transport
			9 planned	Utility transport

(*Continued*)

Table 7 International Hawks: models and missions (*Continued*)

Country	Government service	Base model	Delivered units	Missions
Brazil	Brazilian Army	Black Hawk	10	Search and rescue
	Brazilian Navy	Seahawk	6 planned	Surveillance
				Antisubmarine
				Coastal surveillance
Brunei	Royal Brunei Air Force	Black Hawk	10	VIP transport
				Search and rescue
				Firefighting
Chile	Chilean Air Force	Black Hawk	1	Search and rescue
				Utility transport
Colombia	Colombian National Police	Black Hawk	6	Counternarcotics
	Colombian Air Force	Black Hawk	4	Search and rescue
	Colombian Army	Black Hawk	60 (100 planned)	Counterinsurgency
				Medical evacuation
				Armed attack
Egypt	Egyptian Air Force	Black Hawk	8	Utility transport
				VIP transport
Greece	Hellenic Navy	Seahawk	11	Antisubmarine
				Antisurface ship
				Search and rescue
Israel	Israeli Air Force	Black Hawk	49	Utility transport
				Medical evacuation
				Armed attack
Japan	Japanese Maritime Defense Force	Seahawk	101	Antisubmarine
	Japanese Air Self Defense Force	Black Hawk	35	Antisurface ship
	Japanese Ground Self Defense Force	Black Hawk	70 planned	Search and rescue
				Utility transport
Jordan	Jordanian Royal Squadron	Black Hawk	13	Utility transport
				VIP transport
Malaysia	Royal Malaysia Air Force	Black Hawk	2	VIP transport
Mexico	Mexican Air Force	Black Hawk	6	VIP transport
				Special forces
				Disaster relief
Morocco	Royal Moroccan Police Air Squadron	Black Hawk	2	VIP transport
People's Rep. of China	People's Liberation Army Air Force	Black Hawk	24	Utility transport
Philippines	Philippine Air Force	Black Hawk	2	VIP transport

(*Continued*)

Table 7   International Hawks: models and missions (*Continued*)

Country	Government service	Base model	Delivered units	Missions
Republic of China-Taiwan	Republic of China Air Force	Black Hawk	21	Search and rescue
	Republic of China Air Navy	Seahawk	21	VIP transport Antisubmarine Antisurface ship
Republic of Korea	Republic of Korea Army	Black hawk	130	Utility transport
	Republic of Korea Air Force	Black Hawk	10 planned	Medical evacuation
	Republic of Korea Navy	Black Hawk	10	VIP transport Search and rescue Special operations
Saudi Arabia	Royal Saudi Land Forces and Royal Saudi Air Force	Black Hawk	21	Utility transport Medical evacuation VIP transport
Spain	Spanish Navy	Seahawk	12	Antisubmarine Antisurface ship
Thailand	Royal Thai Army	Black Hawk	7	Utility transport
	Royal Thai Navy	Seahawk	6	Antisubmarine Search and rescue
		Seahawk	6 planned	Maritime defense Disaster relief
Turkey	Turkish Jandarma	Black Hawk	6	Border control
	Turkish National Police	Black Hawk	6	Urban area control
	Turkish Land Forces	Black Hawk	95	Utility transport
	Turkish Navy	Seahawk	8 (24 planned)	Search and rescue Antisubmarine Antisurface ship

AUSTRALIAN HAWKS

Models and missions in Australia

Service	Base model	Aircraft delivered	Missions
Royal Australian Navy	SH-60B Seahawk (S-70B-2)	16	Antisubmarine Antisurface ship Search and rescue
Royal Australian Army	UH-60L Black Hawk (S-70A-9)	39	Utility transport

Fig. 206   The Royal Australian Mk 50 Sea King was designed by Sikorsky in the 1950s as the first turbine-engine-powered AWS helicopter as well as the first amphibious helicopter. It was overtaken by new rotorcraft technology and a desire by all navies to have a multipurpose antisubmarine and antisurface ship helicopter that would be smaller and yet more capable than the venerable Sea King. (Australia Museum of Flight photo)

ROYAL AUSTRALIAN NAVY SEAHAWKS

In 1984, the Australian Department of Defense began to evaluate new antisubmarine warfare helicopters to replace its fleet of prior generation machines. That aging fleet, operated by the Royal Australian Navy (RAN), consisted mainly of Sikorsky Sea King helicopters, Fig. 206, manufactured under license by Westland in the United Kingdom. Similar Sea Kings have been in service with most countries that were engaged in airborne submarine detection and warfare operations.

The Australian Department of Defense held a competition among international helicopter manufacturers to select a replacement for the Sea King. The new helicopter was referred to as a role-adaptable multipurpose weapon system with autonomous operating capability. The RAN's requirements were partially shaped by the capabilities demonstrated by the new U.S. Navy's SH-60B Seahawk that had just entered service.

The competitive evaluation conducted by the Australian Department of Defense included both European and American designed helicopters. It concluded with the selection of the basic U.S. Navy Seahawk. In that same year, Japan and Spain also selected the Seahawk to replace their Sea Kings for antisubmarine, antisurface ship, and search and rescue missions. The obsolescent Sea Kings were gradually relegated to a utility transport role.

In September 1985, Sikorsky was contracted to deliver the initial eight multimission S-70B-2 Seahawks. All eight aircraft were completely assembled by Sikorsky and delivered from its Florida completion center. However

Fig. 207   Royal Australian Navy S-70B-2 externally resembles the U.S. Navy Seahawk including its search antenna radome mounted beneath the cockpit. The weapon pylons on either side of the fuselage can carry Penguin and Sea Skua anti-surface ship missiles as well as torpedoes. (Royal Australian Navy photo)

follow-on RAN Seahawks were shipped by Sikorsky in major sections for assembly and delivery in country by Aerospace Technologies Australia (ASTA) at Avalon in Victoria. The RAN Seahawks had substantially different avionic systems than the U.S. Navy Seahawk. These systems included the MEL Super Searcher radar, new acoustic processors, and strap-down inertial heading and position reference systems.

A total of 16 S-70B-2 Seahawks similar to pictured in Fig. 207 were placed in service and operate from Adelaide and Anzac Class frigates. For submarine detection, the S-70B-2 is equipped with radar, acoustic processors, and magnetic anomaly detector, and it can use a wide range of expendable sonobouys deployable from the aircraft. Once detected and classified as an enemy submarine, the S-70B-2 can launch an attack with Mk46 lightweight torpedoes. The avionics system is built around a dual MIL-STD1553B data bus controlled by two computers. In the aircraft's role of antisurface ship warfare, its radar system is capable of automatically tracking as many as 32 surface contacts. The radar can detect targets at ranges far beyond the coverage provided by surface ships in a task force. All critical information is processed onboard the Seahawk and transmitted in high-speed bursts by a secure data link to the RAN frigates. The S-70B can launch Penguin or Sea Skua missiles against surface ship targets.

With these capabilities, the helicopter becomes an extension of the ship's sensor and weapons systems, thereby greatly extending the ocean area in which enemy submarines and surface ships can be detected and attacked.

The aircraft's navigation suite, which integrates data from its global positioning system, Doppler radar, and air-data computers, produces constantly updated position information allowing for accurate targeting for a ship's Harpoon missiles. Later upgrades included installation of integrated protection systems with electronic support measures, forward looking infrared sensor, and a missile countermeasures dispensing system. Night-vision goggles are being provided to all Navy Seahawk aircrews as well as external lighting installed on the fleet of 16 Seahawk helicopters. This addition enhances safety and improves operational effectiveness during search and rescue missions as well as other operations conducted under limited visibility conditions.

With its electronic equipment and built-in rescue hoist, the RAN Seahawks have been well suited to perform search and rescue missions to which they responded on many occasions. One in particular needed two flights to complete the rescue when the crew of a RAN Seahawk rescued 19 passengers from a sinking ferry in the Solomon Islands archipelago in the South Pacific [28].

The guided missile frigate HMAS Melbourne launched an S-70B-2 Seahawk on 16 August 1999 upon receiving an urgent request for assistance. After a 40-min search, the aircrew caught sight of a distress signal from survivors clinging to a 20-person life raft and small aluminum vessel. An initial group of 12 survivors including four young children were winched aboard the aircraft and flown to nearby Malaita Island. The Seahawk crew then returned to the scene, hoisting another seven people aboard and guiding a local vessel to the remaining 33 survivors who were still awaiting rescue. Those ferry passengers had been in the water for six to eight hours, but tragedy was avoided when the Seahawk directed the rescue vessel to the scene just as darkness was falling. This Seahawk was from the Nowra-based 816 Squadron.

ROYAL AUSTRALIAN AIR FORCE BLACK HAWKS

Two years after the RAN selected the Seahawk for its maritime missions, the Royal Australian Air Force (RAAF) selected the Black Hawk to perform its utility transport missions. An initial order for 14 S-70A-9 aircraft for the RAAF, placed in 1986, was followed in January 1987 by an order for an additional 25 units. Aircraft kits and equipment were shipped by Sikorsky to Hawker de Havilland's Bankstown facility in Australia for final assembly and delivery to the RAAF.

The RAAF Black Hawk helicopters contained many features to increase commonality with the RAN Seahawks as well as to improve mission flexibility. Key configuration changes from the U.S. Army baseline UH-60L, which already included the strengthened Seahawk flight controls, further added a rescue hoist, rotor brake, folding stabilator, and special communication and navigation equipment. The Sikorsky ESSS was also part of the RAAF configuration as well as an external rescue hoist. During 1989, all of the

Fig. 208   Black Hawk joined the Australian Defense Force with the Seahawk shortly after its first flight in September 1987. The S-70A-9 variants are basically UH-60Ls with the engine's hover infrared suppression system (HIRRS), cable cutters, the Seahawk automatic flight control system and folding stabilator, an external rescue hoist, and Australian-specified avionics. (RAAF photo)

S-70A-9 units were transferred from the RAAF to the Royal Australian Army. Figure 208 pictures one of the Royal Australian Army's Black Hawks flying alongside a RAN Seahawk.

The Australian Defense Force (ADF) dedicated much of its Black Hawk fleet to the largest emergency relief effort ever conducted by Australia when it came to the aid of Papua New Guinea [29]. The drought that enveloped that country during the later months of 1997 was described as a once-in-a-century disaster. Black Hawks from the 5th Aviation Regiment were critical contributors to the drought relief operations that began late that year and extended into 1998. Carrying food, medicine, and cargo, the Black Hawks delivered urgently needed supplies to drought-stricken areas in the country's remote highlands.

Each Black Hawk, crammed with up to two tons of rice, flour, and cooking oil, flew to remote locations accessible only by helicopter. Estimates were that the ADF distributed more than 1.5 million pounds of aid throughout five provinces during what was called the largest emergency relief effort in Australia's history. Local relief organizations estimated that as many as 660,000 people faced danger of starvation from the drought, which devastated food crops, particularly in the highland areas of the country. One hundred thousand of these were considered to be in a critical, life-threatening situation. Figure 209 shows one of the aircraft delivering lifesaving food and medical supplies.

Soon after the drought relief operations in Papua New Guinea, the ADF contributed to a major humanitarian mission in the highlands of Indonesia. This mission, named Operation Ausindo Jaya, was a three-month effort to bring food, medicine, and other essentials to over 90,000 people in a drought-ravaged area of Irian Jaya in western New Guinea [30].

Fig. 209 Australian Black Hawk brings life-saving relief supplies to Papua New Guinea during a prolonged severe drought. (Australian Defense Forces photo)

The backbone of the relief effort was three RAA Black Hawks from the 5th Aviation Regiment together with one Caribou transport aircraft from the RAAF No. 35 Squadron. Both units were based in Townsville, and just earlier both had received national acclaim for their six-month involvement in the drought relief operations in Papua New Guinea. The ADF pilot found that unpredictable weather conditions in the highlands of Indonesia made flying extremely hazardous especially with a nearly nonexistent air traffic control system. The Australian Army and Air Force pilots, who were veterans of the drought relief efforts in Papua New Guinea, considered the higher-altitude Indonesian relief work to be considerably more hazardous. In spite of the hazards, they made hundreds of accident-free flights over the three-month period bringing in more than 450 tons of food and cargo to the beleaguered residents. Figure 210 shows the typical terrain and weather.

Fig. 210 Bales of rice delivered to the remote mountain village of Langda with clouds obscuring most of the sky and the ceiling down to 200 ft. The ADF pilots described return flights as "flying through pea soup, the weather was atrocious and there was no visibility." (Australian Defense Force photos)

The Australian Defense Force did more than delivering food and supplies. They wanted to leave behind a lasting benefit to the people beyond the immediate gift of life. Health teams were deployed with the food-carrying helicopters to conduct clinics and develop malaria eradication programs. Australian Air Force engineers looked for airstrip sites to make some of the more remote villages accessible to larger fixed-wing aircraft. These and other initiatives helped provide the people with a greater quality of life and gave them hope for a better future.

AUSTRIAN BLACK HAWKS

Models and missions in Austria

Service	Base model	Aircraft delivered	Missions
Air Force	UH-60L Black Hawk (S-70A-42)	9	Search and rescue Utility transport Int. Peacekeeping

The Austrian Federal Ministry of Defense selected the Black Hawk after a competitive evaluation. Its decision was a landmark event because it occurred in a geographical region that typically favors European manufacturers. That selection was the first instance in the Black Hawk's 25-year production history to that time that it was selected by a European country over a helicopter manufactured in Europe.

Historically, the central region of Europe had been especially difficult to penetrate by a U.S. manufacturer because that is home to several well-established helicopter companies. They are Aerospatiale in France, MBB in Germany, Augusta in Italy, and Westland in the United Kingdom. In spite of a natural domestic bias, Austria chose the U.S. Army's UH-60L on the basis of performance, particularly at high altitude, which was demonstrated to be superior to alternative helicopters.

Prior to making its selection, the Austrian Ministry of Defense was able to observe the Black Hawk in rescue operations when the U.S. Army provided assistance in that country. Ten UH-60L Black Hawks based in Germany came to the aid of Austrian people during the Tyrolean valley avalanche crisis in the winter of 1998–99 [31]. Carrying up to 25 survivors at a time, the UH-60Ls operated in swirls of snow from blocked-off sections of the Austrian autobahn. Food and medical supplies were loaded for return flights. Operating continuously during daylight hours and flying at high altitudes, the Black Hawks evacuated thousands of stranded skiers, residents and tourists. They proved to be especially well suited to high-altitude personnel evacuations, cargo supply, and medical evacuation missions.

Fig. 211 Austrian S-70A-42 is equipped with weather radar, a Rockwell Collins glass cockpit, rescue hoist, skis, armored pilot seats, crash-resistant cabin seats, hover infrared suppression system, rotor de-icing system, and the external stores support system. (©Igor I. Sikorsky Historical Archives, Inc.)

That catastrophe spurred Austria into buying new, larger, and more capable transport helicopters. It conducted a competitive evaluation that included a Eurocopter Cougar and the Sikorsky UH-60L. The UH-60L was officially announced the winner in October 2000. The evaluators concluded that the Black Hawk better met the technical as well as the military requirements. Its critical advantages were said to be its greater flexibility allowing adaptation to different missions. In addition, the wide range of weapon options qualified on the UH-60L by the U.S. Army were felt to be important considerations. Its well-documented survivability, including safety in the event of crash landings, was highly rated.

In addition to performing military and civilian transport missions within Austria, the Black Hawks were planned to be deployed in international peacekeeping and peace support operations. Nine Black Hawks were purchased by the Austrian Federal Ministry of Defense directly from Sikorsky Aircraft and were designated as S-70A-42 models. They are configured as pictured in Fig. 211.

BAHRAIN BLACK HAWKS

Models and missions in Bahrain

Service	Base model	Aircraft delivered	Missions
Bahrain Royal Flight	UH-60A/L Black Hawks	2	VIP transport
Royal Bahraini Air Force	UH-60M Black Hawks	9 planned	Air mobility

Fig. 212   Bahrain Black Hawk is a VIP version of the UH-60L with four executive-style swivel seats and four fixed seats along the rear cabin bulkhead. (©Sikorsky Aircraft photo)

The Bahrain Defense Forces purchased the first of two Black Hawks in 1990 through the foreign military sales program soon after Sikorsky changed its production line from the UH-60A to the L model.

The Bahrain aircraft, Fig. 212, was fitted with an executive-style, eight-passenger interior for use as a transport for the Crown Prince of Bahrain, Shaikh Salman bin Harmad Al-Khalifa. The Crown Prince was an accomplished Black Hawk pilot who was taught to fly this aircraft by Sikorsky pilot John Dixson. The Crown Prince became King Hamid I of Bahrain in 2002.

Fig. 213   This weaponized WS-70 was assembled by Westland under license from Sikorsky and first flew in April 1987. It was demonstrated by Westland in Kuwait, Bahrain, Abu Dhabi, Dubai, Aman, and Quatar. (Westland photo)

In 1994 the Bahrain Defense Forces purchased a second Black Hawk that was added to its executive transport fleet. This second aircraft was a previously owned UH-60A offered for sale on the open market. It had been originally purchased by Westland Helicopters as a kit from Sikorsky in conjunction with a license for production and sale of Black Hawks in market areas traditionally served by Westland. This kit was fully assembled by Westland at Yeovil in the United Kingdom. Westland used it as a demonstrator and equipped it with the armament installation seen in Fig. 213. It was flown at the 1987 Paris Air Show and during both the 1988 and the 1990 Farnborough Air Shows.

Without sufficient orders to justify creation of a Black Hawk assembly line, Westland sold the WS-70 demonstrator to Bahrain without the weapons but with the external stores support station pictured in Fig. 213.

The government of Bahrain converted this UH-60A into a VIP aircraft with basically the same eight-passenger interior of its newer UH-60L and painted it to match. The Crown Prince frequently used this earlier Black Hawk for hunting expeditions in the islands of Bahrain during which 230-gallon fuel tanks were installed on the stores support system to ensure sufficient flight range and endurance.

In 2006, Bahrain requested the purchase of nine UH-60M Black Hawks. These new versions of the Black Hawk are superceding the UH-60L model in production. They are planned to increase Bahrain's air mobility and to implement the country's helicopter modernization program.

BRAZILIAN BLACK HAWKS

Models and missions in Brazil

Service	Base model	Aircraft delivered	Missions
Army	UH-60L Black Hawk (S-70A-36)	10	Utility transport Search and rescue
Navy	SH-60 Seahawk	Planned to replace SH-3 Sea Kings	Antisubmarine Coastal surveillance

A dramatic demonstration of the Black Hawk's lift capability that helped sell the Brazilian Army on the UH-60L was performed in country in 1992. Sikorsky flew a borrowed U.S. Army UH-60L to the military base in Manaus, Brazil, which is just below the equator at the confluence of the Amazon and Rio Negro Rivers. One particular demonstration flight was performed in response to Brazil's question concerning the number of troops that the Black Hawk could carry in typical conditions of the Amazon area.

This particular UH-60L was equipped with the external stores station but carried no external fuel tanks. The internal fuel tanks, at the time of the troop-carrying demonstration, were partially full. After removing all cabin seats, Sikorsky pilot John Dixson and program representative Don Berger urged the Brazilians to fill the cabin with troops as best they could. And fill they did. When every square inch of cabin floor was occupied and the doors were barely able to be closed, there were 53 Brazilian troops aboard plus the cockpit flight crew. The troops were not armed and carried no equipment, and so their total weight was not critical. Because the Black Hawk was not yet at its weight limit, John Dixson moved the demonstration one notch up by carrying a jeep as a slung load from the cargo hook in addition to the 53 troops crammed in the cabin. Flying copilot was Major Pavanello of the Brazilian Army who later became squadron commander.

This flight, consisting of a normal vertical takeoff and fly-around at altitude, was the high point of the demonstration that impressed the Brazilian Army as well as the Sikorsky employees on site. It still can stand as a record for the number of adult people carried in a UH-60 model. It exceeded the 43 fully armed troops carried earlier by a Black Hawk in 1988. That was also a demonstration flight but under combat conditions in Diyarbakir, Turkey. In that flight for the Turkish Jandarma, Sikorsky's Gary Kohler and Andy Evans were pilot and copilot.

In August 1997 Brazil began modernizing its helicopter fleet by purchasing four UH-60L models. These aircraft were needed to help Brazil perform a peacekeeping operation along the disputed border between Ecuador and Peru. That region is located in the Condor Mountains of southeast Ecuador. This operation, named the Military Observer Mission Ecuador and Peru (MOMEP) program, was created in 1995. Before its turnover to the Brazilian Army, the peacekeeping duty was led by a U.S. government task force. This program was created by the United States, Brazil, Argentina, and Chile because of the threat to regional stability posed by a century-old border dispute that intensified with a brokered treaty in 1942.

With Black Hawks now in its inventory, the Brazilian Army took the lead in MOMEP operations. Under the direction of program manager Don Douglas, Sikorsky provided training and a five-year total maintenance program including an in-country team to perform all support activities [32]. It created a fully equipped maintenance and hangar facility in a remote jungle area of Patuca, Ecuador, partly visible in Fig. 214. Brazil's Black Hawks were outfitted to perform aerial surveillance, resupply, and search and rescue missions. They also provided safe transport for multinational observer teams to and from camps located 30 km from Patuca. The border area had been heavily mined making transport by helicopter the only safe means to move MOMEP personnel and equipment.

While performing their peacekeeping missions, one of the Black Hawks was redirected to undertake a rescue mission involving Ecuadorian civilians

Fig. 214   Black Hawks assigned to the MOMEP peacekeeping operations in the demilitarized zone between Ecuador and Peru. (PFC K.K. Rockett photo)

[33]. A truck carrying seven people plunged into a river gorge when a bridge collapsed. Alerted by local authorities, a Brazilian Army crew finally located the truck. All seven victims were hoisted into the Black Hawk and flown to a hospital in Macas, Ecuador, for treatment, and they all survived. The flight crew members who performed the rescue are pictured in Fig. 215.

The MOMEP peacekeeping program worked well in preventing conflict between thousands of troops mobilized on both sides of the border. The program provided time for a comprehensive peace treaty to be developed and signed between Peru and Ecuador in October 1998. The treaty led to a formal demarcation of border regions in May 1999. In June 1999 the MOMEP was formally closed at a ceremony in Ecuador with the declaration that this successful multinational effort set the stage for a lasting peace [34]. At that point the four Black Hawks were transferred to the Brazilian Army airbase in Manaus.

Fig. 215   Standing with their Black Hawk are from left to right: Sgt. Waack; Cpl. J. Antonio; Maj. Luciano Pinto, pilot; Capt. Marcio Melo, copilot; Sgt. Mendes; and Sgt. Paulo Roberto. Together they rescued seven Ecuadorian civilians from a river gorge. (Brazilian Army photo)

Fig. 216   Brazilian Army Black Hawks are configured similar to the U.S. Army UH-60L baseline aircraft. Each S-70A-36 carries a global positioning system, long-distance high-frequency radio, an internal rescue hoist, and weather radar. (©Igor I. Sikorsky Historical Archives, Inc.)

In 2005, the Government of Brazil purchased six UH-60L models through the foreign military sale program. They planned to be equipped with T-700-GE-701C engines, 7.62-mm M134 miniguns, search and rescue equipment, litters, and hoists. All six aircraft similar to the S-70A-36 pictured in Fig. 216 are scheduled to be delivered by 2007.

The government of Brazil is planning to increase its inventory of Black Hawks by four in the near term. It plans to introduce Seahawks into its naval forces by 2010 to replace 12 of the older generation SH-3 Sea King helicopters for antisubmarine warfare, coastal surveillance, and other missions.

BRUNEI BLACK HAWKS

In 1986 the Brunei Ministry of Defense purchased two S-70A-14 Black Hawks, one dedicated to support travel requirements of the Sultan of Brunei

Models and missions in Brunei

Service	Base model	Aircraft delivered	Missions
His Majesty the Sultan's Flight (HMSF)	UH-60A Black Hawk (S-70A-14)	2	VIP transport
Royal Brunei Air Force (RBAF)	UH-60L Black Hawk (S-70A-29) (S-70A-33)	8	VIP transport Search and rescue Firefighting

Fig. 217 Royal Brunei Air Force Black Hawks are equipped with the external stores support system to carry auxiliary fuel tanks for long-range missions. They also are fitted with forward-looking infrared and radar mounted in the cockpit nose. (©Igor I. Sikorsky Historical Archives, Inc.)

and his Royal Family while the other was outfitted for search and rescue missions flown by the Brunei Air Wing. During 1994 and 1998, eight more Black Hawks, basic UH-60L models, were added to the Brunei inventory. Some were equipped to perform long-range search and rescue missions in the configuration pictured in Fig. 217, and some were configured as VIP aircraft to replace and augment the earlier A model.

In addition to search and rescue missions, the RBAF Black Hawks have been pressed into firefighting service with the installation of external water containers. Using the Bambi Bucket system designed for fast water fill by helicopter from any body of water, the Royal Brunei Air Force has demonstrated an impressive capability to control wild fires.

In 1998, four RBAF Black Hawks flew 594 sorties and dropped more than 392,000 gallons of water in the 38-day firefighting mission that saved 14,000 acres of forest and residential land [35]. These were S-70A-33 Black Hawk helicopters, carrying water-filled Bambi Buckets similar to the Oregon National Guard UH-60L seen in Fig. 218 fighting a wildfire in Portland, Oregon.

The helicopters dedicated to transporting the Brunei royal family are operated by His Majesty the Sultan's Flight (HMSF) that was formed in 1980 when the Sultan took delivery of his first Sikorsky S-76A VVIP aircraft. In 1984 that S-76A was replaced by a Mark II version, which in turn was replaced by an S-76A+ with Arriel engines. Later, in 1991, it was replaced by an S-76B with the more powerful Pratt and Whitney PT6 engines for better hot-day performance.

Fig. 218 Bambi Bucket suspended from this Black Hawk is similar to those used by the RBAF and holds 660 gallons of water. It can be quickly refilled from local bodies of water using an electric-driven pump built into the lower portion of the bucket. (Oregon National Guard photo)

Four of the newer Black Hawks purchased in 1995 were UH-60L models identified by Sikorsky as S-70A-29 models, one of which is pictured Fig. 219 in its distinctive blue and silver colors.

The Black Hawk's sliding cabin doors were replaced by hinged doors, Fig. 220, to provide more options for interior arrangement of seats, side consoles, and other amenities.

Figures 221 and 222 show the seat and interior decor selected for the Sultan and Royal Family.

Fig. 219 Newer VIP Black Hawk UH-60L models, operated by service, are equipped with range extension fuel tanks and nose-mounted radar and forward-looking infrared sensor. (©Sikorsky Aircraft Corporation)

Fig. 220 Left-side hinged door provides access to the executive-style eight-passenger interior. Two swivel seats are on either side of the isle, and four seats are back against the rear cabin bulkhead. (©Sikorsky Aircraft Corporation.)

Fig. 221 Interior colors and sweeping curved patterns match those of the aircraft exterior. The last of the aft row of four seats is visible behind this swivel seat. (©Sikorsky Aircraft Corporation)

Fig. 222   One of the consoles with its controls for the overhead lighting and cabin climate is seen along the side wall behind the door opening. (©Sikorsky Aircraft Corporation)

CHILEAN BLACK HAWKS

Models and missions in Chile

Service	Base model	Aircraft delivered	Missions
Chilean Air Force	UH-60L Black Hawk (S-70A-39)	1	Search and rescue

The Chilean Air Force accepted one UH-60L in July 1998, Fig. 223, equipped with external fuel tanks for extended range rescue missions. Those fuel tanks would prove their value for the Chilean Air Force's record flight to the South Pole.

The UH-60L was acquired to start a major aircraft upgrade program for the Chilean Air Force. Chile plans to replace its UH-1 Huey fleet with more capable helicopters for a variety of transport and rescue missions.

Training for rescue missions was conducted with U.S. National Guard together with Air Force Medical Centers. In November 2000 a mass casualty evacuation was simulated in Santiago, Chile. Figure 224 shows pararescuemen from the California Air National Guard carrying "victims" from a crash to a

Fig. 223   Chilean Air Force Black Hawk configuration is similar to that of the U.S. Army UH-60L and is equipped with external fuel tanks for long-range search and rescue missions. (©Igor I. Sikorsky Historical Archives, Inc.)

medical facility in the Atacama Desert, north of Santiago. The mass casualty evacuation exercise was part of a medical and pretrauma hospital response training exchange between the Chilean Air Force, California Air National Guard, and the Wilford Hall Medical Center of Lackland Air Force Base, Texas.

One of the most difficult missions performed by the Chilean Air Force was a flight to the South Pole along the route indicated in Fig. 225.

In January 1999, the Chilean Black Hawk, commanded by General Fernando Rojas Vender chief of the Chilean Air Force, landed at Amundsen-Scott Air Base at the South Pole.

Fig. 224   Simulated mass evacuation performed in the Atacama Desert by Chilean Air Force and California Air National Guard personnel. (U.S. Air National Guard photo)

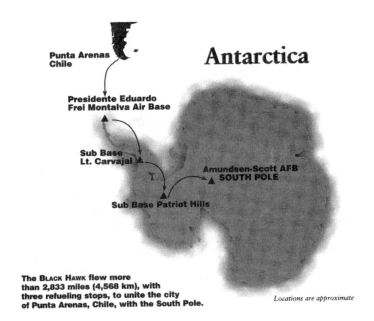

The BLACK HAWK flew more than 2,833 miles (4,568 km), with three refueling stops, to unite the city of Punta Arenas, Chile, with the South Pole.

Locations are approximate

Fig. 225   Route from southernmost Chile to the Amundsen-Scott base at the South Pole covered over 2800 miles with three refueling stops. The round trip took a month hampered by weather conditions.

Flying more than 2833 miles (4568 km) from Punta Arenas, his flight marked the first time a helicopter united another continent with Antarctica and the South Pole [36].

The Black Hawk was outfitted with the four 230-gallon tank configuration of the external stores support system along with the standard winterization kit, skis, and electric pumps for the external tanks. Although the extra two tanks were not felt to have been absolutely necessary from a time and distance standpoint, they provided operational flexibility to compensate for headwinds. They also provided more options when it came to refueling from some of the forward bases that had very limited fuel supplies. Much of the flying was at gross weights of 23,000 lb after refueling and often with the rotor deicing system in operation.

Along the way, three stops were made to refuel at makeshift bases on the Antarctica Peninsula. The Black Hawk made its first refueling stop at Presidente Eduardo Frei Montalva, a distance of 768 miles from Punta Arenas covered in 4.4 h. But five days were spent there waiting for improved weather.

A second stop was made at Sub Base Lt. Carvajal, 481 miles closer to the pole. Much of the refueling was from drums visible in Fig. 226. At Carvajal, bad weather caused another five-day delay. The last refuel stop was at Patriot

Fig. 226 One of the refueling stops where 55-gallon drums and few creature comforts constituted the fuel depot. The Chilean Air Force pilots who took turns flying during the trip over the Antarctic were Hugo Rodriguez and Claudio Avendano. (©Igor I. Sikorsky Historical Archives, Inc.)

Hills Station, which was 912 miles and 6.2 flying hours from the prior stop at Carvajal. Finally after flying an additional 672 miles, the helicopter landed at the South Pole.

Four hours later, after visiting with the people manning the Amundsen-Scott Air Base, the Black Hawk took off for the long trip back to Chile. Its round-trip flight covered nearly 6000 miles during a month of flying in difficult weather conditions. It marked the first time that a helicopter successfully reached the South Pole from Chile. Upon returning to his air base, General Rojas identified the hero of this mission as the Black Hawk from their Aviation Group 9, which had only recently been acquired by the Chilean Air Force.

This flight provided invaluable experience to the Chilean Air Force for conducting long-range rescue missions under Antarctic weather conditions. Lessons were learned with radio communication and navigation by the global positioning system in the South Pole region. Critical information was learned about operation, checkout, and maintenance of aircraft systems whose operation becomes essential for flight in Antarctic. Essential systems included the rotor deicing and the aircraft's anti-icing systems as well as the external fuel tank pumping systems. The pilots reported that the absence of contrast between clouds and snow-covered mountains created a pronounced flight hazard because every base visited was next to mountains. Several fixed-wing aircraft had in the past flown into mountains believing them to be cloud formations. The similarity in color and texture makes it difficult to tell the difference, and this awareness of lack of contrast should help helicopter rescue crews perform their missions more safely.

COLOMBIAN BLACK HAWKS

Models and missions in Columbia

Service	Base model	Aircraft delivered	Missions
National Police	UH-60A/L (S-70A-41)	6	Counter narcotics
Air Force	UH-60L	4	Search and rescue
Army	UH-60L Black Hawk	60 (100 planned)	Counterinsurgency Medivac Armed attack

Utility and armed versions of the Black Hawk have become major factors in Colombia's war on drug trafficking and in counterinsurgency operations. Colombia, in 1987, was the first South American country to integrate the UH-60 into its armed forces as well as the first to develop and place in service an integrated armed Black Hawk pictured in Fig. 227. Approximately 70 Black Hawks have been delivered to Colombia, and more are planned. These aircraft are a combination of the U.S. Army's UH-60A and UH-60L models. Some of the UH-60L aircraft have been converted to attack helicopters, named "Arpia," which carry impressive armaments and sensors for all-weather and night operations.

In their counternarcotics role, the Black Hawks can reach the altitudes necessary to eradicate the coca and poppy fields in the Andes Mountains, where it is grown and processed. Aid packages from the United States have provided training for special army battalions to help destroy drug plantations and laboratories in guerrilla-controlled areas of southern Colombia.

Fig. 227   Colombian Black Hawks can be equipped with rescue equipment, weapons, and special avionics and sensors as needed for their missions. The aircraft pictured is carrying pylon-mounted weapons and has a nose-mounted radar for navigation and an infrared sensor package for night vision. (©Igor I. Sikorsky Historical Archives, Inc.)

Excellent performance at high altitudes and temperatures has encouraged operators to use Black Hawks for rescue missions that might not have been attempted with prior-generation helicopters. Such a rescue performed by the Colombian Air Force in February 2002 reflects the combination of crew skill and aircraft performance that made the difference between a miracle and a tragedy on a harsh mountainside [37].

After two weeks of surviving temperatures ranging from 0 to 5°C at an altitude of 12,000 ft, a stranded rescue team of six Ecuadorians searching for a crashed Ecuadorian aircraft were themselves fighting for their lives. The unforgiving weather and thick cloud cover would neither allow them to leave nor allow them to be rescued from the icy grip of nature. They managed to survive on rainwater and whatever vegetation that could be found. A rescue effort by well-trained Colombian crewmen and skilled pilots made a successful rescue on the 14th day of searching for the Ecuadorian team in frigid winds and dense cloud cover.

For the two UH-60A Black Hawks, serial numbers 4101 and 4106, manned by 10 members of the Colombian Air Force that made up the extended rescue effort, day 14 of the rescue mission would turn uncertainty into nothing short of a miracle. After 38 rescue sorties flown day and night using night-vision goggles anguish turned to joy as one of the Black Hawks, number 4101, balanced between gusts of wind and aircraft power limits, managed at last to hoist the gaunt survivors into the aircraft's cabin. As the clouds closed in once again, the aircraft departed in very limited visibility amid the hugs and screams of joy exchanged between the rescuers and the rescued. All six Ecuadorian soldiers, safely aboard the Black Hawk, miraculously survived.

That heroic rescue was recognized in a special presentation of the Sikorsky Winged-S Rescue Award on 12 July 2002 in Rio Negro, Colombia, to the crew of 10 airmen, Fig. 228.

Recognizing the need for increased helicopter fire power to combat insurgency forces, the Colombian Air Force began to experiment with weapon systems on the UH-60L. Early versions that first flew in August 1995 were called Arpia I. With the help of the Elbit Company and Sikorsky Aircraft, the Air Force developed improved configurations referred to as the UH-60L Arpia II followed by the Arpia III, which was able to carry more ammunition and advanced sensors.

Counterinsurgency operations using the UH-60L Arpia I were first performed in November 1995. The fire power delivered by this new weapon system proved to be a decisive factor prompting the Colombian Air Force to convert more of their UH-60 inventory to that configuration. It further led to continued development and improvement of their armed Arpia I leading to the Arpia III model pictured in Fig. 229. The Arpia III incorporates helmet-mounted sights and displays for both flight crew members along with a nose-mounted infrared sensor and navigation radar. With these sensors and with cockpit displays compatible with night-vision goggles, the Arpia III can engage targets at night and under obscured visibility conditions.

Fig. 228   Colombian Air Force crews receive the Sikorsky Winged-S award for their rescue of six stranded Ecuadorians, themselves searching for a crashed aircraft. (©Igor I. Sikorsky Historical Archives, Inc.)

The normal Arpia III weapons load is four 12.7-mm machine guns, two 7.62 machine guns, and two launchers each capable of firing 19 2.75-in. rockets. Figures 230 and 231 show the weapons installed on the UH-60L external stores support station. The name "Arpia" refers to an eagle native to Colombia that lives on the mountain peaks. It is regarded as a fierce, ferocious, and skilled predator that has aptly become the symbol of the Colombian armed Black Hawk fleet.

The UH-60L Arpia III weapons load takes full advantage of the Black Hawk's maximum takeoff gross weight and its operational ceiling of over 19,000 ft. It has proven to be a very formidable and feared helicopter in Colombia's counterinsurgency warfare.

Fig. 229   External stores support system designed to carry fuel tanks is more than capable of carrying a variety of weapons including the rocket launchers and heavy 0.50-caliber machine guns shown in this picture of a UH-60L Arpia III. (Colombian Air Force photo)

Fig. 230   Two three-barrel GAU-19 12.7-mm (0.50 cal) machine guns are suspended from the inboard stations, and two more are mounted in the cabin doorway, which provides a wide field of fire. Ammunition for the pylon-mounted guns is fed by flexible chutes from a container in the cabin holding 1500 rounds for each gun. (Colombian Air Force photo)

Fig. 231   Two M-60 7.62-mm machine guns are mounted in the cabin windows, one on either side of the cabin. One LAU-19 rocket launcher carrying 19 2.75-in.-diam rockets is mounted on each of the outboard stations. The muzzle of the General Electric 12.7-mm machine is seen on the inboard weapon station. (Colombian Air Force photo)

EGYPTIAN BLACK HAWKS

Models and missions in Egypt

Service	Base model	Aircraft delivered	Missions
Egyptian Air Force Transport Brigade	UH-60L (S-70A-21)	8	VIP transport

Fig. 232   Black Hawks purchased were UH-60L models equipped with communication and navigation systems as specified by the Egyptian Air Force. The two steps mounted on both sides of the cabin indicate that the aircraft are dedicated to transporting government executive personnel. All Egyptian Black Hawks have VIP-type finished interiors with seating for eight people. (©Igor I. Sikorsky Historical Archives, Inc.)

In 1996, the government of Egypt selected the U.S. Army UH-60L for utility and executive transport missions. Its initial purchase through the foreign military sales program was for two Blacks Hawks. They were designated by Sikorsky as S-70A-21 models, pictured in Fig. 232, and delivered in 1990.

The government of Egypt ordered an additional two Black Hawks in 1996 which were delivered in 1997. Two more Black Hawks were ordered and delivered in June 2000 followed by another two aircraft in 2003 bringing Egypt's inventory to eight Black Hawks. All appear to be dedicated to executive transport and are attached to the Egyptian Air Force Transport Brigade.

GREEK SEAHAWKS

The Hellenic Navy began an extensive modernization program during the 1990s to meet the demands of national security and Greece's NATO

Models and missions in Greece

Service	Base model	Aircraft delivered	Missions
Hellenic Navy	SH-60B/F Seahawk (S-70B-6)	11	Antisubmarine Antisurface ship Search and rescue

responsibilities. A major part of that program involved replacing an aging fleet of destroyer and frigate ships along with upgrading the navy's antisubmarine warfare (ASW) capability.

The ship replacement program included four Meko-200H class frigates; the first of which was delivered from Germany in 1993. These frigates would be the platform from which dedicated new-generation ASW helicopters would operate. To that point in time, the Hellenic Navy operated AB 212 ASW helicopters, which were of original Bell Helicopter design but modified and equipped for ASW missions by Agusta in Italy.

Following a competitive evaluation in 1991, the Hellenic Navy selected a hybrid of the U.S. Navy's SH-60B and F Seahawk models to perform both the antisubmarine warfare and antisurface unit warfare (ASuW) missions. Designated as the S-70B-6 and named the "Aegean Hawk," this aircraft was to operate from the Hellenic Navy's new frigates.

An initial order for five Aegean Hawks was placed with Sikorsky in August 1992 with an option for an additional three that was converted to a firm order. Five S-70B-6 aircraft similar to that shown in Fig. 233 were delivered in 1995. They were followed by one in 1997 and two in 1998. The avionic systems for these eight Aegean Hawks included dipping sonar (AN/AQS-18V-3) for submarine detection, search radar (AN/APS-143V-3) for surface ship detection, and electronic support measures (AN/ALR-6GV-2) for detecting hostile missiles. Omitted were the magnetic anomaly system and 25-tube sonobouy launching system carried by the U.S. Navy SH-60B Seahawk for submarine detection in the outer zone of an aircraft carrier task force. Weapons carried by the Aegean Hawks include Penguin antiship missiles and torpedoes.

During mid-2000, an additional three Aegean Hawks were ordered with significant improvements to both cockpit displays as well as defensive and offensive capabilities. The new aircraft increased the Hellenic Navy's inventory to 11 aircraft but of two different configurations that spurred modification of the first eight S-70B-6 models. In addition to a four-cathode-ray tube glass cockpit with a Collins FMS-800 flight management system, the Aegean Hawks incorporated an AAS-44 FLIR system with laser designator and the capability to launch Hellfire missiles. They were further upgraded to include an ALE-47 countermeasure dispensing system, improved electronic support measures and an improved navigation system with embedded global positioning and integrated inertial navigation systems.

The Aegean Hawks are well-equipped to perform humanitarian as well as military missions. They support civilian search and rescue operations including rescuing passengers and crews from ships in distress as well as air transport of patients from remote islands to mainland medical facilities. Maritime rescue operations have become almost routine peacetime missions for both Black Hawk and Seahawk variants of most of the countries that operate them.

Fig. 233   External configuration of the Aegean Hawk, seen approaching for landing aboard a Greek frigate, is typical of ASW and ASuW Seahawks with cockpit-mounted search radar and a dipping sonar system. Missiles and torpedoes are carried on the stores pylons on either side of the fuselage. (Hellenic Navy photos)

The largest peacetime search and rescue operation in the history of the Greek military organization was conducted in January 2002 by the Hellenic Navy. Its Aegean Hawks played a vital role in setting a record for the number of people saved from a disabled Turkish vessel [38].

Using their rescue hoists, two Aegean Hawks lifted more than 20 migrants from the deck of a Turkish ship as it pitched and rolled in a turbulent Mediterranean Sea 30 miles southeast of Crete. Deteriorating weather conditions led Greek authorities to order the evacuation of the ship's most vulnerable passengers. Rescue helicopters airlifted 43 persons in all.

The ship Aydin Kaptan, bound from Turkey to Italy, was carrying 246 people, when it sent out a distress signal late on New Years Day after experiencing

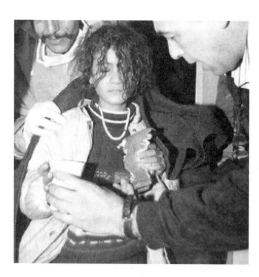

Fig. 234 Among the 43 people rescued by the Hellenic Aegean Hawk were children hoisted up into the helicopter from the ship in distress, the Aydin Kaptan, and flown to local hospitals. (©Igor I. Sikorsky Historical Archives, Inc.)

engine failure. It also began taking on water. Helicopters were dispatched to the ship in order to begin transferring women, children, and injured persons. The evacuees were lifted from the ship by rescue hoist during heavy sea states and extremely poor weather conditions. One seriously injured woman had to be lifted into the helicopter by a Stokes Litter. The young girl pictured in Fig. 234 was airlifted by helicopter to shore still clutching her doll.

After completing their rescue hoist evacuations, the Seahawks were put to work ferrying fuel to the ship, so that it could attempt to make port under its own power. The ship began making its way to Crete with more than 200 exhausted migrants after crew members of a British navy survey vessel boarded the ship to make temporary repair to its hull and to its engine. The Aydin Kaptan eventually arrived in port at the end of a towline, marking the successful completion of a record-setting rescue operation.

ISRAELI BLACK HAWKS

Models and missions in Israel

Service	Base model	Aircraft delivered	Missions
Air Force	UH-60A	10	Utility transport
	UH-60L	15	Medivac
	(S-70A-50)	24	Armed attack
	UH-60L		
	(S-70A-55)		

The Israeli Air Force (IAF) began considering the Black Hawk soon after it entered service with the U.S. Army. In 1983 a single U.S. Army UH-60A visited Israel and was evaluated by IAF pilots. They recommended it as a replacement for the Bell 212, but lack of funding postponed Black Hawk procurement for more than a decade.

The IAF received its first Black Hawks in August 1994, when 10 U.S. Army UH-60As were given to Israel after the Gulf War. The helicopters were shipped to Israel in August 1994 onboard two USAF C-5 Galaxies. The 10 aircraft, manufactured between 1977 and 1979, had logged some 2000 flight hours before arriving in Israel. They were consequently overhauled and equipped to perform IAF missions. The UH-60A models, nicknamed "Yanshuf," meaning Owl, entered service with the 124th "Rolling Sword" Squadron, operating alongside the squadron's Bell 212 utility helicopters.

Changes to the overhauled UH-60As included a new communication system, a moving map display, and a self-protection electronic suite. The 10 Black Hawks soon entered operational service as both assault and evacuation helicopters. They saw their first combat use in April 1996 in southern Lebanon.

In 1997 Israel ordered 15 newly built 15 S-70A-50 Black Hawks under a foreign military sale agreement between the U.S. Army and the IAF. The S-70A-50 pictured in Fig. 235 is similar in configuration to the UH-60L but modified to include Israeli communication and ECM systems and an HH-60G rescue hoist. The first helicopter was formally accepted by the IAF at

Fig. 235   Later Israeli Black Hawks are variants of the U.S. Army UH-60L but outfitted with defensive weapons and communication/navigation systems compatible with IAF operations. (©Igor I. Sikorsky Historical Archives, Inc.)

Sikorsky's Connecticut facility in March 1998, and the first five new aircraft arrived in Israel that May. With deliveries complete by early July, the new helicopters immediately became operational with Israeli systems. They were renamed Yanshuf-2, and they allowed the Rolling Sword Squadron to become an all-Black Hawk operator passing down its Bell 212 helicopters to other squadrons.

In 1999 the IAF began a major improvement program of its new UH-60Ls, equipping the 15 aircraft with in-flight refueling probes and shoulder-mounted fuel tanks that allow easy access to the cabin and the use of cabin-mounted machine guns. The first upgraded Yanshuf-2 prototype flew in early 2000. Tests on the new aircraft were carried out by the IAF flight-test center and included the first in-flight refueling demonstration in March 2000. The following May, a number of Israeli Black Hawks were deployed to Turkey using their new in-flight refueling capabilities.

In March 2000, three Israeli Black Hawks were assigned to transport Pope John Paul II during his visit to Israel. One aircraft carried the Pope, another his medical team, and a third remained on standby. One aircraft was adapted to the role by removing several troop seats, adding cushioning to others and laying wall-to-wall carpeting inside the helicopter's cabin. The Pope was flown during his stay in Israel by the commanding officer of the 124th Squadron.

In 2001 the IAF ordered an additional 24 Black Hawks, identified as S-70A-55, under an FMS agreement with the U.S. Army. These new UH-60L based aircraft were equipped with T700-GE-701C engines, rescue hoist provisions, and the rotor brake system. Fifty new Israeli-designed systems were incorporated in production. When the new Black Hawks began to arrive in 2002, the IAF opened a second all-Black Hawk squadron. The new aircraft and squadron became operational as the aircraft arrived in country. Total Black Hawk inventory of the IAF was 49 aircraft when this order was completed.

JAPANESE HAWKS

Models and missions in Japan

Service	Base model	Aircraft delivered	Missions
JMSDF	SH-60J Seahawk	101	Antisubmarine Antisurface ship
JASDF	UH-60J Black Hawk (S-70A-12)	35	Search and rescue
JGSDF	UH-60J	70 planned	Utility transport

JMSDF SEAHAWK

The primary task of the Japanese Maritime Self-Defense Forces (JMSDF) is to maintain control of the nation's sea lanes and territorial waters. Essential missions of JMSDF helicopter fleet include antisubmarine and antiship warfare as well as mine clearing.

The JMSDF began to conduct ASW helicopter operations in 1958 with Sikorsky SH-3 Sea King helicopters pictured in Fig. 236. The Sea King model was the naval version of Sikorsky's amphibious S-61 helicopter that was developed for the U.S. Navy during the late 1950s specifically for ASW missions. It was later used extensively by other maritime countries as well as by the U.S. Air Force as a cargo transport, by the U.S. Marine Corps as an executive transport, and by commercial operators as well.

After acquiring operational experience with Sea Kings produced by Sikorsky, the JMSDF elected to build additional Sea King helicopters in Japan. Sikorsky then licensed Mitsubishi Heavy Industries (MHI) to produce Sea Kings to meet the operational needs of the JMSDF. Between 1964 and 1987, MHI produced over 150 Sea Kings that were identified as HSS-2A/B models.

When the U.S. Navy developed the SH-60B Seahawk and made it operational in 1983, the JMSDF and other countries saw it as the natural successor to their fleets of aging Sea King helicopters. The Seahawk embodied the latest rotorcraft technologies, as well as the latest sensors and weapons systems to counter both hostile surface ships and submarines. The ship-based Seahawks provided the capability to detect and combat both threats and are equipped to process acoustic and radar data for transmittal by secure links back to the fleet.

Fig. 236   JMSDF HSS-2B helicopters built by Mitsubishi Heavy Industries under license from Sikorsky. Used for antisubmarine warfare and patrol/surveillance missions. (JMSDF photo)

In 1983, the JMSDF selected the SH-60B Seahawk as the basic airframe with which to modernize and upgrade its ASW and ASuW capabilities. Japan was the first international country that selected the Seahawk later followed by five other countries. The initial order from the JMSDF was for two prototype XSH-60J Seahawks to be built by Sikorsky and equipped with a mix of Japanese-and American-built electronic systems. Its first flight, shown in Fig. 237, at Sikorsky's flight-test facility was followed by extensive development and demonstration flying in Japan.

The avionics suite of the SH-60J includes dipping sonar and search radar systems as well as magnetic anomaly detection capability to help detect submarines. Some of the Japanese-built cockpit systems include displays, datalink, flight managements systems, and ring laser gyro attitude and heading reference systems.

Like the Seahawk, the SH-60J is capable of operating from the helicopter platforms of Japanese frigates and destroyer ships. Over 100 SH-60J models have been placed in service of the JMSDF, and all but the two prototypes were built by MHI in Japan from kits supplied by Sikorsky. The first flight of the production SH-60J took place in May 1991.

In August 2001, Mitsubishi began flight testing an upgraded version identified as the SH-60K with an enlarged cabin to hold a new avionic installation with enhanced capabilities. Its cabin was lengthened by 13 in. just behind the cockpit and raised in height. This expansion was intended to accommodate a substantially revised avionics system, including a datalink.

Other new features include integrated flat panel cockpit displays, missile warning and defensive systems, and antiship missiles along with more

Fig. 237   First flight of the XSH-60J took place in August 1987. Tailored to meet the mission needs of the Japanese Maritime Self Defense Force, it was the first international variant of the U.S. Navy SH-60B Seahawk to be produced. (JMSDF photo)

powerful engines. The first flight of the SH-60K was reported to have been made by MHI in September 2001 with development testing in process.

JASDF BLACK HAWKS

The Japanese Air Self-Defense Force JASDF, like the JMSDF, examined the U.S. Army Black Hawk model as a way to modernize its fleet of earlier-generation utility transport and search and rescue helicopters. In 1988 the JASDF selected the basic U.S. Army UH-60L to replace its aging Sikorsky S-62 model and the Kawasaki-Vertol KV-107 Sea Knights for search and rescue missions.

Like the SH-60J, the Japanese UH-60J was to be produced by Mitsubishi under license from Sikorsky. Its special configuration features, noted in Fig. 238, include Japanese electronic systems as well as external fuel tanks on upswept ESSS mounts, external rescue winch, Japanese-built radar, a FLIR turret in the nose, and bubble side windows for observers. Its General Electric T701 engines for the JASDF and marinized 401C engines for the JMSDF are also built under license in Japan by Ishikawajima-Harima.

Approximately 35 UH-60J helicopters are in service with the JASDF.

JGSDF BLACK HAWKS

The largest of the three services of the Japanese Self Defense Force, the Japanese Ground Self-Defense Force (JGSDF), began to modernize its large

Fig. 238 Underside of the air defense UH-60J models are painted in high-visibility yellow and white to help its recognition by rescuees. The sensor and search radar dome are clearly visible in the cockpit nose. (JASDF photo)

fleet of utility helicopters. The JGSDF operates a wide variety of helicopters from small observation to large transport to armed support helicopters. The Kowasaki-Vertol KV-107 served as the medium transport helicopter for 36 years when in 1995 the JGSDF initiated a program for its replacement.

In that year, the JGSDF ordered a utility variant of the UH-60J from Mitsubishi, designated the UH-60JA. It featured a UH-60J airframe but incorporated improved avionics, including forward-looking infrared sensor, color weather radar, GPS navigation receiver, and a cockpit compatible with night-vision goggles. The first model was delivered in 1997 for flight evaluation followed by production models of the configuration pictured in Fig. 239. The JGSDF plans to acquire a total of 70 UH-60JA Black Hawks to operate alongside the UH-1J as its standard utility helicopter.

Fig. 239 Black Hawk used by the Japanese Ground Self Defense Force is a U.S. Army UH-60L model modified and built by Mitsubishi Heavy Industries. The UH-60JA includes external fuel tanks, nose-mounted FLIR sensor, weather radar, and cabin-mounted large caliber weapon seen in the lower picture. The external stores support structure is upswept in order to provide easier troop and crew access to the cabin. (JGSDF photos)

JORDANIAN BLACK HAWKS

Models and missions in Jordan

Service	Base model	Aircraft delivered	Missions
Royal Jordanian Air Force	UH-60A Black Hawk (S-70A-11) UH-60L	3 10	VIP transport Utility transport

The government of Jordan operates a growing fleet of Black Hawk helicopters used for a variety of missions. These missions, flown by the Jordanian Air Force, include executive and utility transportation, emergency medical service, search and rescue, armed helicopter support, and special operations. Fig. 240 shows one of the executive transport versions in a desert camouflage paint pattern.

Jordan acquired its first three UH-60A model Black Hawks as a direct purchase from Sikorsky in 1986 configured for VIP executive transport missions.

Jordan's fourth VIP Black Hawk, a UH-60L model, was given as a gift from the Sultan of Brunei to King Abdullah II upon his accession to the throne. He became the King of Jordan when his father King Hussein passed away on 7 February, 1999. Both father and son were accomplished Black

Fig. 240   Other then the paint scheme, the Jordanian Black Hawks are similar in configuration to the U.S. Army UH-60A and L models. The aircraft pictured is the earlier A model. The two-rung steps on either side of the cabin indicate that this aircraft is for executive transport. It has a finished VIP-style interior with eight passenger seats. (©Igor I. Sikorsky Historical Archives, Inc.)

Hawk pilots and often flew their own transport missions. Prior to transitioning to this larger helicopter, King Hussein also piloted the Jordanian fleet of S-76 helicopters, having been taught to fly that model by Sikorsky pilot Nick Lappos during the 1980s. King Abdullah II also was a certified AH-1 Cobra pilot when he was commander of the Jordanian Special Forces. The King's brother, Prince Feisal who served as Commander of the Royal Jordanian Air Force, is also a qualified Black Hawk pilot.

Shortly after receiving the gift of the UH-60L from the Sultan of Brunei, the Jordanian Air Force purchased two of the later L model Black Hawks. These aircraft were bought in order to provide King Abdullah II with additional security while flying throughout the kingdom. They also provide the Jordanian Royal Squadron with backup aircraft for intracountry transportation requirements including the movement of its National Command Authority.

The Royal Jordanian Air Force (RJAF) in July 2004 ordered eight more UH-60L helicopters, bringing to 14 the number of Black Hawks in Jordan. These aircraft, which began entering service in 2006, are intended to support the RJAF in providing rotorcraft assistance to all services of the Jordanian Armed Forces.

MEXICAN BLACK HAWKS

Models and missions in Mexico

Service	Base model	Aircraft delivered	Missions
Air Force	UH-60L Black Hawk (S-70A-24)	6	VIP transport Special forces Disaster relief

The Mexican Air Force made its first purchase of Black Hawks in 1991 when it bought two Sikorsky S-70A-24 models. These helicopters were similar to the U.S. Army UH-60L but were configured to the Mexican specification. One was equipped for use as an executive transport, whereas the second was to be used as the main helicopter for the Mexican Air Force's new Special Forces group.

In December 1994, another four Black Hawks were purchased directly from Sikorsky. These aircraft were brought into the 216th Special Operations Squadron equipped with the external stores support system and with the hover infrared suppression system that can be seen in Fig. 241.

The Mexican government created the Disaster Relief Rapid Reaction Force in early 2000, drawing aircraft from several units. This force is headquartered in Santa Lucía and is made up of S-70A-24 aircraft and various other

Fig. 241   Black Hawks for Mexico were basic U.S. Army UH-60L models equipped with the hover infrared suppression system and the external stores support system. (Mexican Air Force photo)

helicopters and fixed-wing aircraft. The Black Hawks are the first aircraft to be deployed in a disaster situation for transport of engineers and special forces personnel, using their global positioning systems and night-vision goggles to assist in reaching the disaster location.

PEOPLE'S REPUBLIC OF CHINA BLACK HAWKS

Models and missions in the People's Republic of China

Service	Base model	Aircraft delivered	Missions
Air Force	UH-60A Black Hawk (S-70C-2)	24	Utility transport Search and rescue

Improved relationships between China and the West during the late 1970s gave the Chinese military an opportunity to modernize its helicopter fleet. That expansion included licensed production of certain European helicopters as well as direct procurement of large transport models from Europe. In 1978, the Chinese helicopter industry began a series of cooperative projects with Western partners to meet the PRC helicopter operational needs.

However, for its next-generation utility transport, the PRC elected to conduct what at the time was the largest helicopter competition ever sponsored by the Chinese government. This was designed to be a competitive evaluation conducted under extreme altitude conditions in China. The helicopter manufacturers invited to participate were Bell Helicopter Corporation, the Aerospatiale Corporation, and Sikorsky Aircraft. Bell offered its 214-ST while Aerospatiale offered its model 365 Super Puma. Sikorsky offered a commercial version of the UH-60A Black Hawk. This competition was for an initial lot of 24 aircraft with the prospect of many more to follow.

The PRC conducted the evaluation in the mountains of Lhasa, Tibet, over a two-week span in late 1983. Living and maintenance conditions for the crews during this test period were primitive by western standards. These demonstrations included takeoff and landings at altitudes to 17,000 ft (5181 m) and enroute operations to 24,000 ft (7315 m). Sikorsky pilots, maintenance personnel, and flight-test engineers assisted the PRC team in conducting flight operations and in acquiring and reducing test data to understandable terms. This latter task was one of the more difficult aspects of these flight demonstrations because of problems with technical communications caused by language and some cultural differences. Some of these differences were moderated by good fellowship during the flight-test period in a very remote area. Figures 242 to 244 provide a glimpse into the Lhasa test camp in December 1983.

Several months after the flight demonstrations had concluded, the PRC selected the Black Hawk for the utility helicopter to be operated by the Air Force branch of the People's Liberation Army. The sale to China was a direct sale from Sikorsky Aircraft rather than a foreign military sale administered by the U.S. Army. In October 1984, three months after contract execution, the first S-70C-2, shown in Fig. 245, was delivered to China. The last of the 24 was delivered in 1985.

Fig. 242   Black Hawk was kept in good flying condition by Bob Barressi and Walter Lee, kneeling; Frank Pacileo; Paul Swanson, crew chief center; and Mark Tucker. (©Igor I. Sikorsky Historical Archives, Inc.)

Fig. 243   Part of the Sikorsky team is waiting for their steaks to broil over an abandoned bed spring serving as a charcoal grill near their unheated sleeping barracks. They were to serve the steaks in a banquet with the Chinese team at the end of testing, but lack of refrigeration forced the banquet to be moved forward. From L to R, the Sikorsky team members are Bob Barressi; Jim Kay, pilot; Thorne Taylor; Frank Pacileo; and Bob Kefford. (©Igor I. Sikorsky Historical Archives, Inc.)

The major difference between the U.S. Army UH-70A, which had been demonstrated during the fly-off at Lhasa, and the S-70C-2 was the installation of the T700-GE-701A engines that produced approximately 10% more

Fig. 244   Even though the banquet was held indoors, outdoor clothes were needed. Added warmth and fellowship were provided by more than sufficient Chinese liquor, Mao-tai, with frequent Ganbei (bottoms up) toasts offered by the Chinese crew. Bob Kefford is in the center surrounded by the PRC test evaluators. (©Igor I. Sikorsky Historical Archives, Inc.)

Fig. 245 S-70C-2 delivered to the People's Republic of China in 1984 was a basic UH-60A with more powerful engines. The PRC helicopter pictured is preparing to land at Lhasa, Tibet, with the Himalayan Massif in the background. (©Igor I. Sikorsky Historical Archives, Inc.)

power. In addition the S-70C-2 was equipped with a rotor brake from the Seahawk program plus special avionic equipment requested by the PLA.

By January 1985, nine aircraft had been delivered to China, and all were operating out of Sha He Air Base near the Ming Tombs north of Beijing. All flights were training flights using the eight Chinese pilots who were earlier trained to become instructor pilots at Sikorsky's West Palm Beach facility. Sikorsky had positioned a company pilot, Jim Kay, in China to help train the new pilots. Overall coordination of Sikorsky's support to the PLA was by Ernie Brace, who was the company's PRC program manager stationed in China for several years.

At the time of their first deployment to Tibet, the Black Hawks were being operated by the PLA Air Force. In early 1988 all of the utility helicopters in the Air Force were transferred to the newly created PLA Army Air Corps. They used these aircraft for personnel rescue and disaster relief operations especially in mountainous regions.

One of PLA'S earliest rescue mission took place in October 1985. Two Black Hawks, on a training mission west of Beijing, were dispatched to Golmud in the Qing Hai Provence to try to rescue tribesmen trapped by an early snowfall on the north slope of the Tibetan Plateau. The PLA flight crews successfully rescued many tribesmen, but they did it with a makeshift oxygen system. They had to fly at altitudes of over 15,000 ft, but the oxygen systems intended for the crews had not yet been installed in the aircraft. Instead they used rubber bladders inflated with oxygen that had snap clamps on the output tube. By manually opening and closing the clamps, the flight crews were able to breathe enough oxygen while flying over the mountain peaks.

A week later in the same area the PLA Black Hawks made numerous rescue flights into remote areas bringing food and animal fodder into the site and carrying the sick and elderly out to safety. Fueling was done from trucks parked at wide spots on the mountain road. For this sustained rescue operation, the pilots and crews were widely praised by the Chinese government. It was the first publicity that the Black Hawks received since their arrival in country a year earlier. The crews were also awarded the Sikorsky Winged-S rescue awards in recognition of their bravery, skill, and dedication.

As a result of many long-distance training flights, a series of successful humanitarian missions, together with a growing familiarity with their new helicopter, the PLA flight and maintenance crews became proficient Black Hawk operators. They began to understand and use the aircraft manuals; they asked more questions as time went on, as their confidence in the local American support people increased. They even overcame a hesitancy to use external lift to transport cargo, and they eventually became proficient in the operation seen in Fig. 246. It took a while for them to become convinced that many cargo transport missions could be completed more quickly using external lift even though some types of cargo could be stuffed into the cabin.

Limited rescue missions continue to be flown by PRC Black Hawks, especially those where the aircraft's altitude performance is essential for success. Such a mission took place in December of 1996 when hundreds of people were trapped in mountains without food and supplies [39].

Heavy snowstorms in the Altay and Tacheng areas of China isolated nearly 1000 geology workers and miners who had set up camps around the mountain. All ground-based rescue attempts had failed to the extent that on

Fig. 246   PLA Army Air Corps using the Black Hawk's external cargo hook to transport a small truck. (PLA Army photo)

Fig. 247   Stranded mine workers wave greeting to a PLA Black Hawk bringing much needed food and supplies. (PLA Army photo)

2 January, 1997 a government request for helicopter search and rescue operations was sent to the PLA in the Xinjiang Military Region.

On January 6, with clearing weather, one Black Hawk was en route to Altay bringing food, medicine, and communication equipment. The sound of the helicopter's arrival brought the stranded workers out from their underground shelters. Figure 247 shows one of the many welcoming celebrations to be repeated often during three days of virtually nonstop flying.

Waist-deep snow prevented a full landing, and so sacks of food and supplies were pushed out of the cabin to the crowd, which speeded up the turnaround to again load up with lifesaving supplies. Captain Wang Daobin of the Peoples Liberation Army was the pilot in command. He and his crew flew four sorties in six hours that first day. Seventeen people were airlifted, and more than 25,000 kg of food and relief supplies were delivered.

After trampling down the snow, the miners created a hard pad that permitted the Black Hawk, without a ski kit attached to its landing gear, to land and begin the evacuation. That process was also enthusiastically endorsed by the trapped people, as noted in Fig. 248.

Less than a week after the January relief and evacuation missions were completed, snowstorms continued to ravage the Altray area. The supply routes for another group of 300 gold miners became impassable. Their situation reached a critical stage when several people suffered injuries from frost bite and sudden avalanches. On January 13, Captain Wang and his Black Hawk crew again were directed to provide help. They flew 36 sorties in three days of virtually nonstop flying and were able to evacuate the entire group to safety.

The PLA helicopter-based relief and rescue missions in January 1997 were significant accomplishments and a tribute to crew training and dedication as well as to the capabilities of their helicopter. These missions were especially significant because of the limited supply of Black Hawk spare parts in China. The operational status of the PRC S-70C-2 fleet had suffered a setback

Fig. 248   As has been the case in many Black Hawk humanitarian missions, if the rescuees can fit in the cabin, they will be carried to safety. The number of people that this flight brought home was not recorded. (PLA Army photo)

following the Tiananmen Square demonstrations in 1989. The resulting embargo of defense-related goods imposed in that year significantly reduced flight operations. Efforts continue on both sides to permit Black Hawk spare parts to be exported to China to permit more of its fleet to be operational for rescue and humanitarian missions.

REPUBLIC OF CHINA HAWKS

Models and missions in the Republic of China

Service	Base model	Aircraft delivered	Missions
Air Force	UH-60A Black Hawk (S-70C-1/1A)	21	VIP transport Search and rescue
Navy	SH-60 Seahawk (S-70C M-1/2)	21	Antisubmarine Antiship

ROC AIR FORCE BLUE HAWKS

The Republic of China (ROC), Taiwan, made an early selection of both the Black Hawk and Seahawk for upgrading its helicopter fleet. In June 1986, the ROC Air Force received 14 Black Hawks. Four were designated as S-70C-1 models and assigned to VIP transport services. They were powered by the CT7-2D commercial version of the T700-GE-700 engine.

Ten of these aircraft, designated as S-70C-1A models, were outfitted for search and rescue missions and named Blue Hawks by the ROCAF. Special features of the Blue Hawks included installation of a new external fuel tank support structure called the Sikorsky stores support system (SSSS), in place

Fig. 249 Initial ROCAF search and rescue variants of the Black Hawk, designated as S-70C-1A models, are equipped with the external stores support system carrying range extension fuel tanks. (©Igor I. Sikorsky Historical Archives, Inc.)

of the ESSS developed for the U.S. Army. In addition, the Blue Hawks incorporated the hover infrared suppression system in place of the conventional engine exhaust used on the four S-70C-1 models. They each were equipped with rescue hoists installed on their right sides. The SAR units were assigned to the Rescue Squad at Chia-Yi Air Base. Figure 249 shows their distinctive colors of blue, white, and yellow.

In April 1998, the ROC Air Force took delivery of four new S-70C-6 aircraft, which they named Super Blue Hawks. These models were upgraded versions of the S-70C-1A SAR helicopters. They were equipped with an AN/AAQ-20 FLIR system, weather radar, a night sun search light in the nose, and high-power loud hailers on both sides of the tailcone. They also were equipped with the higher-powered T700-GE-701 engines as well as hover infra-red suppressor systems and hydraulic-powered rescue hoists similar to the earlier S-70C-1A.

Their introduction greatly enhanced the all-weather and night search and rescue capabilities of ROCAF. One of the most dramatic rescues performed by these dedicated SAR machines is illustrated in Figs. 250 and 251, during the sinking of a freighter, the Golden Tiger.

On 2 August, 1997 as Typhoon Victor was sweeping across Taiwan, the ROCAF'S Seagull Rescue Squadron received a distress call from a ship that ran aground 150 yd offshore in southern Taiwan [40]. The 7800-ton vessel was attempting to reach a safe harbor when it was blown off course by 55 miles per hour winds and 20-ft waves. Two Super Blue Hawks were sent to try to help the 10 Taiwanese and seven Burmese crew members. All 17 made their way to the ship's bridge to stay above breaking waves as the ship listed 70 deg. Fighting the high winds and trying to avoid the ship's masts and superstructure, the pilots brought their helicopters in position to lower their crewmen and rescue slings. With the ship threatening to overturn at any moment, all 17 crewmen were hoisted safely and flown to local hospitals. Figure 251 shows the anxiety on the faces of both the rescuer and rescued.

Fig. 250 ROC Air Force Black Hawk lowering a helicopter crewman to haul up the boat crewmen from the Golden Tiger that is about to capsize during a typhoon. (China Post photo)

Fig. 251 One of 17 crewmen lifted to safety by the Super Blue Hawk rescue hoist with the helicopter crewman holding him from falling. (China Post photo)

The Air Rescue Group Super Blue Hawk crews have been the "Guardian Angels" of Taiwan and its surrounding waters since their introduction in service. One disaster in particular etched the image of Super Blue Hawks in the minds of well over a thousand people. That was on 1 August, 2001 when Typhoon Toraji ripped through the central portions of Taiwan with winds gusting well over 100 miles per hour [41]. The storm hovered over the island for hours, causing widespread damage. The most damaging aspect of this storm was not the wind but the torrential rain that deluged the mountainsides for an entire day and triggered massive mudslides. It left a death toll of record proportions.

Even before the storm had completely subsided, the Super Blue Hawk helicopter crews of the ROCAF Air Rescue Group were mobilized for search and rescue and humanitarian missions. When all disaster relief missions were completed on August 8, the Air Rescue Group had amassed record numbers. Its crews flew 453 missions and conducted 72 rescues during the emergency. The Super Blue Hawk crews evacuated 1343 stranded persons, transported 435 medical personnel and hauled over 88,000 lb of food, fresh water, and medicine. Figure 252 shows the urgency of that relief effort as the helicopter was unloaded with its wheels not yet on the ground. When the typhoon finally passed, the damage was almost overwhelming. More than 150 lives had been lost, hundreds of people were injured, and thousands were left homeless by the devastating storm. If not for the Super Blue Hawks, the toll would have been far worse.

On 9 June, 2002, four ROC Super Blue Hawks responded to the distress calls of a fishing vessel that erupted in flames during a tropical storm off the coast of China [42]. The blaze forced most of the 133 mainland Chinese fishermen to the boat's bow, Fig. 253, while the rest of the vessel was engulfed in flames. Hovering over a burning ship, the rescue helicopters hoisted 36 fishermen to safety. They helped many more by dropping flotation devices.

Fig. 252 Rescue workers wasting no time in unloading food and medicine from a Republic of China Air Force Super Blue Hawk while it is in a hover. (China Post photo)

Fig. 253 Approaching the burning fishing ship with a helicopter crewman lowered to assist fishermen into the rescue basket. (Wide World photo)

The Super Blue Hawks at times recovered two rescuees on a single hoist cable in wind-swept seas. Rescue vessels pulled survivors from the water adding to the total of 133 mainland Chinese fishermen saved. The boat's cook was missing and was the only reported fatality.

The ROCAF rescue crews were recognized for their heroic performance by Sikorsky Aircraft several weeks following their successful mission. The crews were awarded the traditional Sikorsky Winged-S rescue awards at a ceremony at their air base in Taiwan, Fig. 254.

These crews were also recognized by the American Helicopter Society when it selected them to receive the Frederick L. Feinberg Award. That award is given to the helicopter pilot or pilots who have made the most outstanding

Fig. 254 Each member of the Super Blue Hawk crews who helped rescue the Chinese fishermen from their burning vessel were presented with the Sikorsky Winged-S rescue award at the Chia-Yi Air Base. (©Igor I. Sikorsky Historical Archives, Inc.)

achievement in the previous year. It is given in memory of Frederick L. Feinberg, who was an exceptional helicopter test pilot. The honors were presented 2003 May 7 at the American Helicopter Society (AHS) International 59th Annual Forum and Technology Display in Phoenix, Arizona.

REPUBLIC OF CHINA NAVY THUNDERHAWKS

The Fleet Helicopter Squadron of the ROC Navy was formed in September 1977 at the Tsoying Naval Base. Its first-generation helicopters dedicated to antisubmarine warfare were 12 Hughes 500 MD/ASW models. Their primary sensors were search radar housed in a nose-mounted radome and a towed magnetic anomaly detector. They were able to carry two Mk 44 or Mk 46 torpedoes but normally carried only one to maximize range and endurance.

The 500 MD/ASW helicopters were relatively small machines able to operate from destroyers. As a result of their small size, their useful load capability was limited relative to that of the Sea King and of the Seahawk helicopters in widespread operation. More ASW capability in terms of surface and subsurface sensors, weapons, data processing, and on-station endurance was found to be needed. That led the ROCN, in the 1980s, to initiate a program for modernization of its naval forces that included procurement of frigates similar to the U.S. Oliver Hazard Perry class and of the U.S. Navy's SH-60 Seahawk helicopters. The Seahawks were to become the backbone of their antisubmarine and antisurface ship warfare capability.

The first Seahawk in a lot of 10 aircraft purchased direct from Sikorsky was delivered to the ROCN in July 1990. These first 10 aircraft were identified as the S-70C (M)-1 model by Sikorsky and named Thunderhawks by the ROCN. They were powered by commercial General Electric CT7-2D-1 engines and equipped with a full suite of sensors, data processing, communication, and navigation systems.

After spending six months at Sikorsky's West Palm Beach, Florida, facility engaged in training the ROCN pilot and maintenance crews, the first Thunderhawk arrived in Taiwan in June 1991. It was assigned to the newly commissioned 701st Squadron within the Fleet Helicopter Group. Following extensive training, this squadron achieved initial operational status in March 1994.

In mid-1999, the ROCN ordered a second lot of 11 Thunderhawks in order to form a second antisubmarine aviation group. These aircraft, powered by the higher power General Electric T700-GE-401C engines, were identified as S-70C (M)-2 models. The 702nd Squadron was commissioned in March 2000 to accept the new Thunderhawks and to begin operational training leading to operational status and inauguration in July 2001.

The configuration of the ROCN Thunderhawk, Fig. 255, is similar to the U.S. Navy Seahawk.

Fig. 255   ROCN Thunderhawk hovering with its sonar transducer being lowered. One torpedo is carried on the port inboard stores station. (©Igor I. Sikorsky Historical Archives, Inc.)

It has three external stations for weapons and/or auxiliary fuel tanks. Mark 46 torpedoes can be carried on all stations, but fuel tanks can be carried on only the two inboard stations. The search radar system installed under the cockpit detects and tracks surface and air targets over a wide sea surface area up to a range of 200 n miles. It also can be used for weather detection.

The Thunderhawk's sonar systems can detect, track, and classify underwater targets. It can be operated as either dipping passive/active sonar or as an acoustic processor for real-time display of data from passive/active sonobouy sensors. It also can provide underwater voice communications and bathythermograph recordings. Other onboard systems include a tactical navigation system, defensive electronic equipment, and sonobouy receivers.

REPUBLIC OF KOREA BLACK HAWKS

Models and missions in the Republic of Korea

Service	Base model	Aircraft delivered	Missions
Army	UH-60P Black Hawk (S-70A-18/22)	130	Utility transport Medivac VIP Transport
Air Force	HH-60H/P Black Hawk	10 planned	Search and rescue
Navy	UH-60P Black Hawk	10	Special operations

Fig. 256   This ROK Army UH-60P is outfitted with the ESSS with fuel tanks attached to the outboard stations and rocket launchers on the inboard stations. (ROK Army photo)

The Republic of Korea Army began to modernize its helicopter fleet in 1990 when it selected the Black Hawk for utility transport missions. The UH-60P, its Korean designation, was equipped with uprated engines and transmission, an external stores support system, and rotor brake, Fig. 256. The first aircraft was delivered in 1990, and by 1995 the ROK Army had 80 UH-60P aircraft in service. This ramp-up reached approximately 130 aircraft by 1999 as the army replaced nearly all earlier-generation UH-1B and H models. Primary UH-60P missions include troop and cargo transport as well as medical evacuation, command-and-control, search-and-rescue, armed escort, and transportation of the president of South Korea.

The Aerospace Division of Korean Air Lines built nearly all of the UH-60P helicopters under license from Sikorsky. The first UH-60P was the only one delivered by the company as a completed aircraft in December 1990. The next 19 units were assembled by KAL from kits supplied by Sikorsky, whereas the remaining 110 airframes were built by KAL. By 1999, KAL had essentially completed high-rate production of the UH-60P for the Korean Armed Forces. KAL estimates that 52% of the aircraft's parts were produced in country. Additional production of special-purpose UH-60P versions at low rate is expected for both the needs of new special missions and for attrition replacement of in-service aircraft.

The Republic of Korea Air Force began using specially equipped UH-60P models for combat search and rescue operations starting in the early 1990s. These were transferred from the ROK Army and equipped as pictured in Fig. 257. They are planned to be upgraded to the configuration developed for the U.S. Air Force HH-60P Pave Hawk search and rescue helicopter. Ten HH-60H/P models are planned for the ROKAF.

Fig. 257   ROK Air Force HH-60P model uses a different external stores support system than the ESSS used by the army. The ROKAF system, identified as the SSSS, is angled upward and has only a single stores station on each side. This configuration permits easier cabin access and visibility during search and rescue missions especially when lifting litter patients. (ROKAF photo)

The ROK Navy employs the UH-60P as a multi-purpose helicopter used for Navy Seal special operations, medical evacuation, executive transport, and general utility tasks. Ten were received by 1993 and formed the 623rd squadron at Pohang, South Korea, in the configuration pictured in Fig. 258.

Fig. 258   ROK Navy Black Hawk makes use of the same stores support system preferred by the ROKAF for range extension while retaining excellent cabin access. This navy configuration is similar in landing-gear arrangement to the U.S. Navy's new MH-60S, and both share the basic Black Hawk cabin size. (ROK Navy photo)

SAUDI ARABIA BLACK HAWKS

Models and missions in Saudi Arabia

Service	Base model	Aircraft delivered	Missions
Royal Saudi	UH-60A/L	12	Utility transport
Land Forces	Black Hawk	(24 more	
	(S-70A-1)	planned)	
Same	(S-70A-1L)	8	Medivac
Same	(S-70A-1V)	1	VIP transport

Saudi Arabia purchased 21 Black Hawks through the foreign military sales program. Of these "Desert Hawks," 12 are configured for utility transport, 8 for medical evacuation aircraft, and 1 for VIP transport. Saudi Arabia is planning to purchase an additional 24 UH-60L helicopters.

The Saudi utility transports can be fitted with a French GIAT 20-mm cannon on pintle mounts, while the medivac Desert Hawks have an external hoist, provision for six litters, and a searchlight. The medivac litter system shown in Fig. 259 was developed by the U.S. Army and Sikorsky early in the UH-60A development program for medivac configured models.

Fig. 259   Saudi medivac Black Hawks are equipped with a litter system that can accommodate up to six patients. The unit shown is configured to carry four people. This litter assembly pivots to face outwards as shown for ease of loading. It then pivots 90 deg for ease of attending to the patients from either side. (©Igor I. Sikorsky Historical Archives, Inc.)

Fig. 260   Saudi Air Force training flight. (©Igor I. Sikorsky Historical Archives, Inc.)

Figure 260 pictures a flight of Saudi Air Force Desert Hawks in desert camouflage.

The interior seating of the Saudi Black Hawk configured for VIP transport is shown in Fig. 261.

Fig. 261   This executive VIP interior with comfortable seating, carpeting, consoles, and other amenities has been installed in one of the S-70A-1 Black Hawks for use by the royal family. (©Igor I. Sikorsky Historical Archives, Inc.)

SPANISH SEAHAWKS

Models and missions in Spain

Service	Base model	Aircraft delivered	Missions
Hellenic Navy	SH-60B/F Seahawk (S-70B-1)	12	Antisubmarine Antiship

The Spanish Navy has been operating Sikorsky SH-3D Sea King helicopters for anti submarine and anti surface ship missions since 1966. Its current inventory of approximately 12 Sea Kings is down from a peak of 18. The Spanish Navy's plan is to gradually replace these aging Sea Kings with the U.S. Navy SH-60B LAMPS MK III Weapons System. "LAMPS" is the acronym for light multi-purpose system. Spain began to implement this modernization plan in 1988 when it received the first of six S-70B-1 Seahawks to operate from FFG-7 frigates at Rota Naval Base in Cadiz Spain.

Those Seahawks were purchased through the U.S. Navy as a foreign military sale and were essentially the same configuration as the U.S. Navy's SH-60B, but they were equipped with a Honeywell dipping sonar system in place of the sonobouy system. Figure 262 is one of the first Spanish Seahawks with its main rotor blades folded.

In October 2000 the Spanish Navy ordered six more SH-60B aircraft to be equipped with an integrated suite of dipping sonar, search radar, night-vision system, electronic support measures, and antiship missiles. At the same time, similar new equipment was ordered to upgrade the initial group of six

Fig. 262   In addition to automatic folding of the main rotor blades, the tail pylon, horizontal stabilator, and tail rotor blades also fold to minimize the space required for each helicopter when stowed in the below-deck hangar. (©Igor I. Sikorsky Historical Archives, Inc.)

Fig. 263   Some of the new equipment can be seen such as the nose-mounted FLIR for night vision and missile warning antennae on the fuselage. (Spanish Navy photo)

Seahawks in service to the same standard as the second group. This included armament kits compatible with the AGM-114 Hellfire laser-guided and AGM-119 Penguin air-to-surface ship missile. Also included were a FLIR system for night vision, a Spanish-built acoustic processor for the dipping sonar, and a missile targeting system.

Lockheed Martin performed much of the installation work at its Systems Integration Facility in Owego, New York. That facility, formerly operated by IBM, has been a prime contractor to the U.S. government for installation of the mission equipment package for all U.S. Navy Seahawks as well as for special Black Hawk models. Figure 263 is one aircraft of the new group of six Seahawks delivered to Spain beginning in 2001.

Upgrade of the initial group of six Seahawks was a four-year effort completed in 2004 by Lockheed Martin, Sikorsky Aircraft, a Spanish contractor, TECNOBIT, and the Spanish Navy.

THAILAND HAWKS

Models and missions in Thailand

Service	Base model	Aircraft delivered	Missions
Royal Thai Army	UH-60L Black Hawk (S-70A-43)	7	Utility transport
Royal Thai Navy	SH-60B/F Seahawk (S-70B-7)	6	Antisubmarine Search and rescue Surveillance

Fig. 264   Multimission Royal Thai Navy Seahawk incorporates dipping sonar, search radar, stores pylons, and external rescue hoist typical of the Seahawk family. The aircraft pictured is serial number 3202 during pilot training in West Palm Beach, Florida. (©Igor I. Sikorsky Historical Archives, Inc.)

Thailand selected variants of both the Black Hawk and Seahawk during the 1990s to begin modernizing their helicopter inventory. The Royal Thai Army (RTA) had a substantial fleet of Bell UH-1 models for troop transport missions, plus it operated several CH-47 Chinooks. The Royal Thai Air Force (RTAF) as well operated several squadrons of Bell Hueys in addition to an obsolete fleet of Sikorsky CH-34 piston-powered helicopters. During the 1980s, the Royal Thai Navy (RTN) operated Bell UH-1N models equipped for anti submarine warfare missions.

In 2001, the RTA ordered its first lot of three Black Hawks through the foreign military sales process. Later in 2003 two more UH-60L models were ordered. They were accepted in November 2004 by Kasit Piromya, Royal Thai Ambassador to the United States, who accepted the aircraft logbooks as part of the ceremonial transfer of title. In 2005 an additional two S-70A-43 aircraft were ordered for the RTA and delivered the same year, increasing the Thai Black Hawk inventory to a total of seven to that time. The configuration of these aircraft closely matched that of the U.S. Army UH-60L model.

The Royal Thai Navy began the process of upgrading its ASW capabilities during the 1990s by selecting the U.S. Navy Seahawk. Six were ordered with the Sikorsky designation S-70B-7. Deliveries began in 1997 with the first aircraft pictured in Fig. 264 flown to Sikorsky's West Palm Beach, Florida, facility for pilot and maintenance training.

The RTN Seahawks are equipped with dipping sonar and full electronics for their basic ASW mission as well as for search and rescue, maritime patrol, and coastal surveillance missions.

Six S-70B-7 Seahawks operate from a relatively new vertical/short-take-off-and-landing carrier, the Chakri Naruebet. That aircraft carrier was a major addition to the Royal Thai Fleet built in Spain and delivered to the RTN in 1997. The carrier's main role is surveillance, protection, search and rescue, and secondary roles including command and control, air support for the Thai surface fleet, and disaster relief.

In 2006, the government of Thailand requested procurement of up to six of the U.S. Navy's new MH-60S helicopters, citing its need to enhance maritime defense and disaster relief capabilities. This latter need was highlighted by the tsunami search and rescue operations conducted in December 2004 and January 2005. Among other improvements, the MH-60S, described in Chapter 10, has an integrated cockpit, upgraded engines and transmission, forward-looking-infrared and terrain-following radar, additional internal and external fuel tanks, and an external rescue hoist.

TURKISH HAWKS

Models and missions in Turkey

Service	Base model	Aircraft delivered	Missions
Jandarma	UH-60A/L Black Hawk (S-70A-17)	6	Border control
National police	Same	6	Urban area control
Land forces	UH-60L (S-70A-28)	95	Utility transport
Navy	SH-60B/F (S-70B)	8 (17 more planned)	Antisubmarine Antiship

TURKISH BLACK HAWKS

Turkey was among the first countries to buy Black Hawks, and it is now one of the largest operators. Its selection of the UH-60A was finalized in 1988 after the Jandarma forces evaluated its performance capability in the mountainous regions. The Jandarma is the Turkish Armed Forces branch responsible for maintaining public order in rural areas. Its duties include ensuring internal security and general border control. The Black Hawk was found to be especially well suited to that mission because of its performance at high altitude. Its survivability features were an added bonus given the hostile character of certain regions.

The aircraft was demonstrated in unplanned but convincing ways. In March 1988, Sikorsky leased a U.S. Army UH-60A for demonstration in the Turkish mountain regions. It was flown by Sikorsky pilots in support of the Jandarma, National Police, and Turkish Land Forces. This leased UH-60A was based at the Jandarma post in Diyarbakir along with the other helicopters in the competition including a Puma from Aerospatiale and a BO-105 from MBB. During a day in May 1988, while the Kurdish PKK rebellion was at its peak, Sikorsky pilots, Gary Kohler and Andy Evans, were called to pick up a group of soldiers just completing a mission north of Diyarbikir. On arrival, the pilots found the soldiers very anxious to leave but there were 43 of them in all. They carried rifles and day packs as well as some equipment including mortar base plates. The Sikorsky crewmen, Derek Sharp and Rick Thurlow, devised a packaging arrangement where they stuffed the soldiers in rows with succeeding men sitting on the knees of those behind. All 43 soldiers were loaded in the UH-60A cabin along with Sharp and Thurlow, and the aircraft took off for a 20-min flight back to base. When the aircraft touched down, the Turkish troop commander could not believe his eyes when all of his 43 men tumbled out of

Fig. 265   Jandarma S-70A-17 part way out of a split-S maneuver. (©Igor I. Sikorsky Historical Archives Inc.)

Fig. 266   S-70A cabin generally accommodates what needs to be carried while the aircraft's performance margins encourage maximum utilization. (©Igor I. Sikorsky Historical Archives, Inc.)

the Black Hawk. The Black Hawk won that competition and became the Jandarma's primary utility helicopter. Figure 265 shows the Jandarma Black Hawk in spirited flight and Fig. 266 illustrates typical people and cargo loading that redefines cabin capacity.

The Jandarma's experience operating their Black Hawks in hostile areas has confirmed the aircraft's combat survivability. Several Jandarma S-70A-17s hit by rocket-powered grenades (RPG) and projectiles from other hand-held weapons were able to continue flight and return safely to base.

Fig. 267   This RPG strike did not cause catastrophic structural damage nor were the adjacent fuel cells punctured. The aircraft was flown back to base after local repair and inspection by its flight crew. (©Igor I. Sikorsky Historical Archives Inc.)

The most noteworthy was the RPG strike in a Black Hawk's fuselage transition section that remained flightworthy in spite of severe damage. Figure 267, copied from Fig. 95 in Chapter 5, illustrates the damage sustained by that aircraft.

Another RPG strike to the bottom of the Black Hawk cabin resulted in the death of one soldier and serious injuries to several others. This aircraft was able to fly back to base in spite of the damage to the cabin floor and substructure shown in Fig. 268.

In a separate incident, the survivability of the Black Hawk's flight control system was demonstrated during hostile ground fire in which a projectile found its mark against great odds. During a troop extraction mission, the Jandarma reported that an S-70A-17 had one of its tail-rotor control cables severed by ground fire. The tail-rotor control quadrant, whose survivability function is explained in Chapter 5, operated as designed. Severance of the cable was highlighted to the pilots through the caution/advisory panel, and the remaining cable was automatically tensioned to a magnitude wherein the pilots retained full control of tail-rotor pitch with only a single cable. This was the first in-flight confirmation that this survivability feature functioned as intended and with no loss of pilot control authority.

Whereas the Jandarma paramilitary forces carry out the security function in the countryside along the borders, the Turkish National Police (TNP) has primary responsibility for security in urban areas. The successful adoption of the Black Hawk to the Jandarma's missions encouraged the TNP to also

Fig. 268   **Although the RPG blew a gaping hole in the cabin floor, the fuselage's main structural beams had sufficient residual strength to carry normal flight loads and permit continued safe flight. (©Igor I. Sikorsky Historical Archives, Inc.)**

Fig. 269   Flight of two Turkish National Police S-70A-17 Black Hawks on patrol. (©Igor I. Sikorsky Historical Archives, Inc.)

gradually upgrade its helicopter fleet as well. Two of its newly acquired S-70A-17 aircraft are shown in Fig. 269.

Procurement of S-70A-28 models for the Turkish Land Forces, pictured in Fig. 270, began in 1992 when Sikorsky won an order for 45 Black Hawks in competition with Eurocopter. In 1999 Turkey ordered an additional 50 Black Hawks directly from Sikorsky, which significantly expanded the capabilities of the land forces.

Fig. 270   Turkish Land Forces S-70A-28 Black Hawk in camouflage paint scheme. (©Igor I. Sikorsky Historical Archives, Inc.)

Although not dedicated to search and rescue missions, the Turkish Black Hawks are very capable of performing rescue missions because of the aircraft's performance capability. In November of 2002, that capability was put to the test during an attempt to rescue three professional mountain climbers from the dangerous slopes of Mount Ararat, between Turkey and Armenia [43]. After reaching an altitude of approximately 15,000 ft, the mountaineers had radioed an emergency message after a loose rope caused a fourth member of the party to plummet out of sight. By then, the party was lost in darkness and zero visibility.

Responding to the call for help, a Turkish Land Forces Black Hawk tried to reach their position but was unable to because of severe weather conditions. On the next day, another Black Hawk flew over the summit looking for the lost climbers and finally spotted them. But it took several approaches before the aircraft could find a suitable place to set down between rock outcroppings and slopes to pick up the survivors. One of the stranded climbers and several rock outcroppings can be seen in Fig. 271. A search with seven persons aboard the Black Hawk revealed the fourth climber's body wedged in an ice crack 11,000 ft above sea level.

Shortly after this dramatic rescue, Sikorsky presented Winged-S rescue awards to the crew of the Turkish Land Forces Black Hawk that conducted the highest rescue mission in Turkish aviation history.

Upgraded plans for Turkish Black Hawks include conversion of cockpit instrumentation to an integrated digital "glass" installation shown in Fig. 272. The new Turkish Army cockpit will be common in many respects to the Turkish Navy cockpit mentioned next.

Fig. 271   Turkish Black Hawk crew braves the heights of Mount Ararat searching for a clear landing area to pick up stranded climbers at 15,000 feet elevation. Turkish Land Forces photo.

Fig. 272   Rockwell Collins has developed this integrated flat panel cockpit display system planned for retrofit in the Turkish Land Forces Black Hawks. (©Igor I. Sikorsky Historical Archives, Inc.)

TURKISH SEAHAWKS

The Turkish Navy selected the U.S. Navy Seahawk in 2000 as the platform to create a ship-based helicopter to perform antisubmarine and antisurface ship warfare missions. Eight Seahawks, designated as S-70B models, were ordered, and deliveries were completed in 2002.

Fig. 273   Turkish Navy Seahawk firing a Penguin antisurface ship missile. This missile, made by Kongsberg of Norway, uses a passive infrared seeker rather than active radar for guidance. The Penguin is propelled by a solid rocket motor and can perform weaving maneuvers as it approaches the target ship. (Turkish Navy photo)

The S-70B helicopter is an international derivative of the U.S. Navy SH-60B Seahawk, but includes a fully integrated glass (digital) cockpit and a mission management system supplied by Rockwell Collins. Its flexible mission package includes dipping sonar, electronic surveillance measures, forward-looking-infrared sensor, multimode radar and aircraft survivability equipment. It is equipped to fire Penguin and Hellfire missiles as well as to launch torpedoes. Figure 273 shows a penguin missile launched during a training flight. Equipped as it is, the S-70B is closer in configuration to the U.S. Navy's MH-60R rather than its earlier SH-60B.

The S-70B can perform search and rescue, medical evacuation, surveillance, vertical replenishment and utility missions in addition to its antiship and antisubmarine fighting capabilities. The Turkish Navy deploys the Seahawks on Perry-class frigates, which it earlier had acquired from the United States. Since becoming operational, the Turkish Navy has lost one of its Seahawks.

In 2006, Turkey finalized an order for 17 additional S-70B models to be delivered beginning in 2009.

VIP BLACK HAWKS

Many countries operate VIP helicopters as part of a larger Black Hawk multimission fleet, whereas several countries have purchased Black Hawks configured for executive transport. These specialized missions tend to be served by very small fleets dedicated for use by the heads of state. They

Fig. 274 Argentina purchased one Black Hawk with an executive eight-passenger interior in 1990 identified as an S-70A-30. This aircraft, a UH-60L model, is operated by the Presidential Air Group. It is the usual means for transport between the president's residence, the Quinta located in the Olivos Province and the Casa Rosada, which is the seat of government in Buenos Aires. (Sikorsky photo)

Fig. 275   Royal Malaysian Air Force operates two VIP UH-60L Black Hawks identified as S-70A-34 variants. They were delivered in 1998 equipped for VIP service including the navigation and weather radar system mounted in the nose. (©Igor I. Sikorsky Historical Archives, Inc.)

include Argentina, Malaysia, Morocco, and the Philippines, whose VIP models are pictured in Figs. 274–277.

Several countries operating Black Hawk variants are selecting the new Sikorsky S-92 to meet their VIP transportation missions because of its spacious cabin together with its advancements in aerodynamics,

Fig. 276   Royal Moroccan Police Air Squadron operates two VIP variants of the UH-60L that entered service in 1993. One is an eight-passenger version identified as an S-70A-25, and the second is a 12-passenger version identified as an S-70A-26 model. Both aircraft have been flown by King Hassan, who is a Black Hawk pilot. (©Igor I. Sikorsky Historical Archives, Inc.)

Fig. 277   Philippine Air Force purchased two UH-60A Black Hawks in 1984 configured for VIP transport and identified as S70A-5 models. (©Igor I. Sikorsky Historical Archives, Inc.)

vibration control, and fail-safe design innovations. Both the S-70 and S-92 models are expected to increase their international presence as new variants of each are introduced. The UH-60M model in particular will likely become the international Black Hawk of choice for a wide variety of missions.

REFERENCES

[1] "Man, Moment, Machine," The History Channel, Catalog Number AAE-74640, Dec. 2005.

[2] Gormont, Ronald E., and Wolfe, Robert A., "The US Army UTTAS and AAH Programs," NASA Paper 78 N 19131, May 1977.

[3] Chuen, Maj. Chin Pak, "Air Mobility and Its Impact on Military Operations," POINTER, *Journal of Singapore Armed Forces*, Sept. 1999.

[4] Army Aviation Hall of Fame Induction of General Howze, Fort Rucker, AL, June 6, 1974.

[5] DeMaria, Anthony J., *Memorial Tributes: National Academy of Engineering*, Vol. 4, 1991, pp. 183–187.

[6] U.S. Army Request for Proposal, DAAJ01-72-R-0254 (P-40), Jan. 1, 1972.

[7] U.S. Army Contract DAAJ01-73-C-0006 (P40), awarded to United Aircraft Corp., Sikorsky Aircraft Div., effective Aug. 30, 1972.

[8] Arcidiacono, Peter, and Zincone, Robert, "Titanium UTTAS Main Rotor Blade," *Journal of the American Helicopter Society*, p.12, May 1975.

[9] Zincone, Robert, Bettino, John, and Tracy, Robert, "Development of the CH-53D High Performance Titanium Main Rotor Blade," American Helicopter Society, 29th Annual Forum, Paper Number 78346, May 1973.

[10] Burroughs, Lester R., and Vitolo, Sylvester A., "Titanium Spar Manufacturing Development," American Helicopter Society, 33rd Annual Forum, Paper Number 77.33-51, May 1977.

[11] Silverstein, Stanley M., "Processing of Titanium Tubes—An Approach to Helicopter Blade Spar Manufacturing," American Helicopter Society, 30th Annual Forum, Paper Number 853, May 1974.

[12] Rybicki, Robert, "The Sikorsky Elastomeric Rotor," American Helicopter Society, 35th Annual Forum, Paper Number 79-48, Jan. 1981.

[13] Cheney, M. C., "Results of Preliminary Studies of a Bearingless Helicopter Rotor Concept," American Helicopter Society, 28th Annual Forum, Paper Number 600, p. 16, May 1972.

[14] Fenaughty, Ronald R., and Noehren, William L., "Composite Bearingless Tail Rotor for UTTAS," *Journal of the American Helicopter Society*, 32nd Annual Forum, July 1977.

[15] "Crash Survival Design Guide," USAAMRDL Technical Report 71-22, U.S. Army, 1967.

[16] Carnell, Brian L., "Crash Survivability of the UH-60A Helicopter," AGARD CP 255, Fort Rucker, AL, May 1978.

[17] Waldock, William D., "A Brief History of Crashworthiness," *SAFE Association Journal*, 1997.

[18] Shanahan, MD, LTC Dennis F., "Crash Experience of the US Army Black Hawk Helicopter," *AGARD Journal*, 1992.

[19] Bowden, Mark, *Black Hawk Down,* Atlantic Monthly Press, 1999.

[20] "Night Stalker," documentary, The History Channel, Catalog Number AAE-72456, Nov. 1992.

[21] Foulk, James B., "Survivability of the Army/Sikorsky YUH-60A Helicopter." Proceedings of the American Helicopter Society, 32nd Annual Forum, pp. 1011-1–1011-21, May 1976.

[22] Landgrebe, Anton, Moffitt, Robert C., and Clark, David R., "Aerodynamic Technology for Advanced Rotorcraft," Part 1: *Journal of the American Helicopter Society,* p. 21, Apr. 1977; Part 2: *Journal of the American Helicopter Society,* p. 2, July 1978.

[23] Cooper, Dean E., "YUH-60A Stability and Control," *Journal of the American Helicopter Society,* Vol. 23, p. 2, July 1978.

[24] Ellis, C.W., Diamond, J., and Fay, C.B. "Design, Development and Testing of the Boeing Vertol/Army YUH-61A," Boeing Vertol, American Helicopter Society, 32nd Annual Forum, Paper Number 1010, May 1976.

[25] U.S. Army Contract DAAJ01-77-C-0001(P6a), awarded to United Technologies Corp., Sikorsky Aircraft Div., 23 Dec. 1976.

[26] Miller, Edward A., Press Release, 1150 hrs, Assistant Secretary of the Army (R&D), Pentagon, Washington, DC, 23 Dec. 1976.

[27] Sikorsky Lifeline—Helicopter Humanitarian Missions, Fall 1999–Winter 2001.

[28] Sikorsky Lifeline—Helicopter Humanitarian Missions, Fall 1999–Winter 2001.

[29] Sikorsky Lifeline—Helicopter Humanitarian Missions, Spring/Summer 1998.

[30] Sikorsky Lifeline—Helicopter Humanitarian Missions, Fall/Winter 1998/1999.

[31] Sikorsky Lifeline—Helicopter Humanitarian Missions, Spring/Summer 1999.

[32] Sikorsky New, Fourth Quarter 1997.

[33] "Brazilian Army Rescues Seven After Bridge Collapse," Sikorsky Lifeline—Helicopter Humanitarian Missions, Spring/Summer 1999.

[34] U.S. Dept. of Defense, News Release No. 298–99, 17 June 1999.

[35] "Brunei Black Hawks Join Firefighting Efforts," Sikorsky News, First Quarter 1999.

[36] Sikorsky Lifeline—Helicopter Humanitarian Missions, 2002.

[37] "Colombian Air Force Black Hawk Pilots Honored with Sikorsky Rescue Awards," Sikorsky Lifeline—Helicopter Humanitarian Missions, Fall 1999/Winter 2001.

[38] "Hellenic Navy Seahawk Mission Lifts 20 from Stricken Migrant Ship," Sikorsky Lifeline—Helicopter Humanitarian Missions, Spring/Summer 1997.

[39] "PLA Black Hawk Crew Rescues Hundreds from Snow-Besieged Mountains in China," Sikorsky Lifeline—Helicopter Humanitarian Missions, Fall/Winter 1997.

[40] "Republic of China Black Hawks Rescue 17 During Typhoon," Sikorsky Lifeline—Helicopter Humanitarian Missions, 2003.

[41] "Taiwan Super Blue Hawks Rescue 72 after Typhoon," Sikorsky Lifeline—Helicopter Humanitarian Missions, Fall 1999–Winter 2001.

[42] "Taiwan Blue Hawks Swarm to Rescue Stricken Fishermen," Sikorsky Lifeline—Helicopter Humanitarian Missions, 2002.

[43] "Turkish Black Hawk Crew Honored for Record Rescue," Sikorsky Lifeline—Helicopter Humanitarian Missions, 2003.

THE BLACK HAWK STORY
CREATING A WORLD CLASS HELICOPTER

Ray Leoni's professional career has been with Sikorsky Aircraft from college graduation until his retirement in 1992 after 41 years of service followed by three years of advance design consulting work. He started as a design engineer of helicopter transmission and rotor systems and later became a designer participating in new V/STOL concepts and helicopter designs. He conducted concept formulation studies for the Army UTTAS program and led the team whose design was selected to be proposed to the Army for what later became the Black Hawk helicopter. After contract award to Sikorsky in 1972 for the Black Hawk prototype program, Mr. Leoni was appointed Program Engineering Manager responsible for all Black Hawk engineering design and test activities. He was awarded the design patent for Black Hawk as well as nine other patents. He also served as Program Manager through the later stages of development until Sikorsky won the Black Hawk production contract in 1976.

Mr. Leoni was appointed Vice President for Research and Engineering shortly after his Black Hawk assignments and later became Senior Vice President, Engineering and Advanced Programs. Included in his responsibilities were the Manufacturing Engineering and Industrial Engineering departments and for several years he also was responsible for all factory major and final assembly operations as well as the Product Integrity and Industrial Engineering Departments.

Mr. Leoni received his Bachelor of Science degree in engineering from Brown University in 1951 and Master of Engineering degree from Yale University in 1962. He has been a member of the American Helicopter Society since 1952 and received an AHS Fellow Award in 1990. He is also a member of the American Institute of Aeronautics and Astronautics and serves as a trustee of the Igor I. Sikorsky Historical Archives, Inc.

INDEX

SUPPORTING MATERIALS

A complete list of AIAA publications is available at http://www.aiaa.org.